The Arc of Story: Writing Realistic Fi

Lucy Calkins and M. Colleen Cruz

Photography by Peter Cunningham

HEINEMANN ◆ PORTSMOUTH, NH

This book is dedicated to Sam, for reminding me of the wonder of story every day. —Colleen

This book is dedicated to Miles, who helps me appreciate that stories are in our DNA. —Lucy

firsthand
An imprint of Heinemann
361 Hanover Street
Portsmouth, NH 03801–3912
www.heinemann.com

Offices and agents throughout the world

The authors and publisher wish to thank those who have generously given permission to reprint borrowed material:

Reprinted with the permission of Simon & Schuster Books for Young Readers, an imprint of Simon & Schuster Children's Division from *Fireflies!* by Julie Brinckloe. Copyright © 1985 Julie Brinckloe.

From *Pecan Pie Baby* by Jacqueline Woodson, copyright © 2010 by Jacqueline Woodson, text. Used by permission of G.P. Putnam's Sons, a division of Penguin Group (USA) Inc.

Cataloging-in-Publication data is on file with the Library of Congress.

ISBN-13: 978-0-325-04736-2
ISBN-10: 0-325-04736-7

Production: Elizabeth Valway, David Stirling, and Abigail Heim
Cover and interior designs: Jenny Jensen Greenleaf
Series includes photographs by Peter Cunningham, Nadine Baldasare, and Elizabeth Dunford
Composition: Publishers' Design and Production Services, Inc.
Manufacturing: Steve Bernier

Printed in the United States of America on acid-free paper
17 16 15 14 13 VP   2 3 4 5

Acknowledgments

THIS IS THE SECOND INCARNATION OF THIS BOOK. It was a great joy to work together on the original version, passing a manuscript from one person to the other. This newest incarnation wasn't as equally shared as that first process; Lucy's hands were very full of all the many books in the series, and this one book, out of all the books in the original series, seemed like it required a bit less of a total make-over. So Colleen took the lead this time around and brought Lucy in as needed. Questions still arose that required us to think in altogether new ways. How, in the CCSS world of today, could we bring more close reading and more analytic thinking into this unit? How could we lift the DOK level of our teaching? How could we rally youngsters to produce more writing, to spend less time in the fine-tuning of a single draft and more time on major revisions? It has been a great joy to reach these hard parts together and to use them as invitations to talk, think, laugh, research, and invent. We both believe the book is better off because we outgrew our own best ideas many times over in the process of writing and rewriting.

Many of the same people who lent a hand the first time played important roles the second time. We thank Liz Phillips and the students and faculty of PS 321 for being a lab for some of the earliest thinking about ways we can best teach students to write fiction. We are also appreciative of Dr. Peter McFarlane and the PS 180 community for their generous support and their willingness to pilot this work in its early stages. We thank especially Anisha Burke, Carolyn Montalto, Rachel Nall, Amanda Pagan, and Jhimy Rodriguez. Kathy Doyle, Shannon Rigney, and Julia Mooney all contributed to this project, and we thank them.

Our newest thinking around fiction writing and fourth grade was drafted, revised, and refined in the company of teachers and children. We are grateful to Darlene Despeignes and the staff and students at PS 63, particularly fourth-grade teachers Alison Mack and Megan Fallon. We also are appreciative of Ruth Rivera and Lauren Catania's work and their generous contributions to this project during their time working at PS 376. Additionally, we thank the upper-grade teachers at Hope Street Elementary in Huntington Park, California, for their tireless cheerleading and willingness to share their classrooms with us. We also thank Sandy Pensak and her hard-working team of teachers at Hewlett Elementary School.

There have been colleagues who helped along the way—some as editors, some as producers, some as cheerleaders. We especially thank Kate Montgomery, Abby Heim, Julia Mooney, Beth Neville, and Zoe White.

The class described in this unit is a composite class, with children and partnerships of children gleaned from classrooms in very different contexts, then put together here. We wrote the units this way to bring you both a wide array of wonderful, quirky, various children and also to illustrate for you the predictable (and unpredictable) situations and responses this unit has created in classrooms across the nation and world.

From Colleen: As has been the case for many people, Lucy Calkins has been a huge influence on my development as a teacher of literacy. Lucy taught me so much about what it means to streamline one's thinking in some spots and flesh it out in others. She taught me the importance of how, just as good fiction builds in an arc, so too should a unit of study. I was consistently amazed at her ability to challenge my beliefs of how fiction "should" be taught, often leading me to explore unmapped terrain. I am even more appreciative of the way she consistently (and sometimes doggedly) pushed me to challenge her own latest thinking in order for us to come to a consensus. The seamlessness of that process is completely Lucy's doing.

Contents

Acknowledgments • iii

Welcome to the Unit • vi

BEND I   Creating and Developing Stories and Characters that Feel Real

1. Imagining Stories from Ordinary Moments • 2

In this session, you'll teach students that fiction writers get ideas for stories from small moments in their lives. You'll help them get started doing that.

2. Imagining Stories We Wish Existed in the World • 12

In this session, you'll teach students that writers get ideas for stories by imagining the books they wish existed in the world and by thinking about issues in their lives.

3. Developing Believable Characters • 19

In this session, you'll teach students that, like all writers, fiction writers need to choose a seed idea (a story idea) and then begin to develop characters by creating their external and internal traits.

4. Giving Characters Struggles and Motivations • 31

In this session, you'll teach children that writers can develop characters by telling about their characters' motivations and struggles and also by creating scenes that show these things.

5. Plotting with a Story Arc • 41

In this session, you'll teach children that writers sketch out possible plotlines for stories, often in story arcs that represent traditional story structure.

BEND II   Drafting and Revising with an Eye toward Believability

6. Show, Don't Tell: Planning and Writing Scenes • 54

In this session, you'll teach children that writing scenes is, in a sense, the same as writing Small Moment stories. Writers often begin by putting the character into action or by laying out the character's exact words and then unfolding the moment step by step.

7. Feeling and Drafting the Heart of Your Story • 65

In this session, you'll teach children that fiction writers create their best drafts when they experience the world through their character's skin, letting the story unfold as it happens to them.

8. Studying Published Texts to Write Leads • 74

In this session, you'll remind writers of various strategies for writing effective leads. You will also remind children that writers reread literature, letting it teach techniques for writing.

9. Orienting Readers with Setting • 86

In this session, you'll remind students that writers "stay in scene," making sure the action and dialogue are grounded in the setting.

10. **Writing Powerful Endings** • 100

In this session, you'll teach children that writers of fiction do their best to craft the endings that their stories deserve. In particular, they make sure their endings mesh with and serve the purposes of their stories.

BEND III   Preparing for Publication with an Audience in Mind

11. **Revision: Rereading with a Lens** • 110

In this session, you'll teach children that when revising, writers don't simply reread; they reread with a lens. Writers vary their lenses according to what they value for their work.

12. **Making a Space for Writing** • 117

In this session, you'll teach students that writers create their own intimate work spaces inside their writing notebooks and their homes.

13. **Using Mentor Texts to Flesh Out Characters** • 125

In this session, you'll remind students that writers study mentor authors to notice what other writers do that really works. One thing writers do is use actions and revealing details to show rather than tell about or explain the character.

14. **Editing with Various Lenses** • 134

In this session, you'll teach students that just as fiction writers revise with "lenses," they edit with them as well, rereading their writing several times for several reasons, making edits as they go.

15. **Publishing Anthologies: A Celebration** • 143

In this session, you could give writers an opportunity to see their work "published" in book form and to experience the thrill of receiving "reviews" on their contribution to the class short story anthology.

BEND IV   Embarking on Independent Fiction Projects

16. **Launching Independent Fiction Projects** • 150

In this session, you could teach students that writers take all they've learned about writing fiction stories to new projects.

17. **Planning and Drafting Stories with Agency** • 153

In this session, you'll teach students how writers quickly apply their planning and drafting skills to new projects.

18. **Mining the Connections between Reading and Writing Fiction** • 162

In this session, you'll teach students that writers study the work they do as readers of fiction and graft those skills into their revisions.

19. **Focusing the Reader's Gaze** • 170

In this session, you'll teach students how writers can learn from visual artists and help readers visualize from different angles to make a variety of points.

20. **Choosing Punctuation for Effect** • 177

In this session, you'll remind students that writers use punctuation to make sentences easier to understand, as well as to have an effect on how their readers engage with the text.

21. **Surveying Your Work and Planning for the Future** • 186

In this session, you could teach students that writers reflect an the work they have done, celebrating their accomplishments and making new goals for future project.

Welcome to the Unit

FOR ELEMENTARY SCHOOL CLASSROOMS, some things have not changed at all since the first Units of Study for Teaching Writing, Grades 3–5 series was written almost a decade ago; other things have changed dramatically. The fiction book, in the same way, is both the same and different.

Our students still love to read and write fiction. We've often described fiction as the genre students "want worst to write." The lure of fiction is as strong as ever. This is no surprise because, really, the desire to spin stories has been around since the beginning of time. Long, long ago, cavemen used berries and charcoal to put the stories of their hunts and travels on stony cave walls. They told stories around the fire, spinning all that they saw and did and thought into stories that helped them make sense of the world. Patricia MacLachlan has pointed out, "Other creatures have travels far grander than ours. The arctic tern criss-crosses the Atlantic many times, the Monarch butterfly summers in Maine and winters in Mexico. Other creatures have journeys far greater than ours," she says, and adds, "But we are the creature that live to tell the tale."

This unit, then, will continue to be an all-time favorite. Tell your children that they'll launch the year with a unit on fiction, and you'll see them look startled: really? And then they'll smile.

The other thing that won't have changed is that if your teaching is not decisive and strong, your children's fiction stories will be pretty weak. Yes, this is the genre children want worst to write, but it is also the genre they write the worst. Because we have taught tens of thousands of classrooms full of children to write fiction, we know the predictable problems, detours, side tracks, and dead ends, and we'll help you direct youngsters on a path that will work, but more on that later. For now, it is enough to say that children's energy for this genre is both a gift and a curse, because yes, if you can channel students in a productive direction, they'll be willing to work themselves to the bone to make their writing work. But on the other hand, if your teaching is not decisive and strong, students will carry on, undeterred by your teaching. Your teaching can be very minor—like a housefly, brushed away. So you will see that this book sets you up to teach in ways that make a difference and that save students from some of the problems they're otherwise apt to encounter.

The Common Core State Standards say essentially that to make all students "college-ready," the work students do in college needs to have more influence on the work they do in elementary schools. Narrative writing should now become 50% of the writing they do (that's a lot!), and expectations for narrative writing are nothing to sneeze at. A fourth-grade fiction story has been included in Appendix C of the Common Core, and again, it sets the bar high. You can read it for yourself online.

But the other important thing to note about the Common Core State Standards is that the reading as well as the writing standards require that students are able to bring a writerly consciousness to literary texts. Readers are expected to note the choices that an author has made, to reflect on the reasons an author may have had for his or her craft moves. Common Core State Standards 4, 5, and 6 for reading literature all expect that students can read literature like an insider, like a participant.

If a person has wrestled with whether to write his story in first or third person, it is easier to reflect on why an author may have made that decision. If a person has worked to tuck a necessary backstory into her own story, she can see when an author has done the same move. The ability to do this kind of thinking comes from being a participant in the work of making fiction. Although teachers of literature want students to notice the carefully placed image, the ending that ties back to the lead, the truth is that when a reader is trying to make sense of the substance of a text, the reader focuses on content, and those sorts of concerns aren't foremost. As Randy Bomer has said, "Most of the time when we are focused on teaching reading, we want students to let language be a window they look through to the world on the other side . . . But when we look at writing like writers, we ask them at attend to the glass of the windowpane itself: the text structures, sentences, phrasing, words, choices in arrangement and style."

We chose to begin this year's fourth-grade curriculum with fiction, one of students' most beloved units, knowing that for many of them, this is will be a dream come true. For most of their years in school, they have begun with personal narratives. We will lean heavily on those years of experience as we launch into this unit and explain to students that we expect them to carry all those years of experience into this brand-new year. Indeed, you might find it useful to enlist the input of your third-grade colleagues when planning for this unit to more seamlessly connect your realistic fiction plans with their narrative work from the past.

OVERVIEW OF THE UNIT

The first part of this unit, the first bend, begins with learning ways to live like writers, seeing ideas for fiction stories everywhere. At the start of this unit, we let students know that fiction writers get their ideas by paying attention to the moments and issues in their lives. Children collect story ideas in their writer's notebooks, learning to flesh the ideas out a bit so that they contain some of the elements of an effective story. They will likely want to collect a few true Small Moment stories, or at least pieces of those stories, to help launch into fictionalizing those moments. A child who has recently moved could make up a story about a girl who moved, only this time giving the character the companion (A dog? A sister?) the writer wishes she'd had. In these entries, children will not actually write their possible stories; instead, they will write plans for how their stories might go.

After a few days of collecting entries that could possibly become fiction stories, students will profit from trying a few of these ideas out. A great way for them to do this is by story-telling their ideas to a partner. We teach children some storytelling techniques. For example, the beginning of their stories might sound like the beginning of a famous book or a fairy tale, of the sort they studied in third-grade: "Once, not long ago, a boy named Liam . . ." Elevating storytelling helps each youngster bring a storyteller's voice—and an aura of literary language—to his or her own story plans.

Once children have each chosen a story idea, it is important for them to develop their ideas. One way fiction writers do this is to develop their main characters, perhaps in notebook entries that never appear in the final story. A fiction writer once said, "Before you can begin writing your story, you need to know your characters so well that you know exactly how much change each one has in her pocket." When children are asked to develop ideas about their characters' traits, most children will list external traits, such as "She has red hair." We encourage children to also think of a character's internal traits. What is she afraid of? What does she want? This helps students delve deeper into developing three-dimensional characters than the lighter character work they undertook while writing fairy tales in third-grade. The trick to getting beyond sketches of characters into ones that feel as if they breathe upon the page is to help students create coherent characters with characteristics that fit together in ways that seem believable. When children use broad generalizations, for example, suggesting that a character is a good friend, we ask them to open these terms up, to be more specific. What are the unique ways that this character is a good friend? After the writer gathers entries developing his character, he may dramatize the character, having him perform action in a scene, a fiction writer's term for a Small Moment story.

Finally, it is important to be sure that your fourth-grade fiction writers think especially about a character's wants and needs. Usually a storyline emerges out of the intersection of a character's motivation and the obstacles that get in the way.

In the second bend in the unit, we remind children that what they learned once through revision and editing now needs to move forward in the writing process. In the earlier version of this unit, we used the story mountain as a crucial tool for planning, drafting, and revision. In this unit, we decided to streamline things a bit and revert to the time-honored tool that fiction writers frequently refer to: the story arc. This decision was made partly because we saw many ambitious children, perhaps inspired by the term *mountain*, create plans for stories that had far too many scenes to reasonably be culled into a short story. However, we still felt it was important for students to use a planning strategy that made clear the rising and falling action of a good story. In this version of the unit we focus on the story arc, showing students how stories with two to three strong scenes can successfully show a character, plot, and even setting change over the course of the story. The arc we create in the planning stages becomes a touchstone that students will refer to again and again throughout the unit.

When students begin to draft, they rely on their story arcs as road maps. Each moment on the story arc is usually designated its own page in a story booklet, and this, plus an emphasis on using skills developed in earlier years and on storytelling rather than summarizing, makes it more likely that children's stories will sound and feel like stories.

The third bend in the unit moves into preparing these pieces for audiences through more focused drafting, deep revision work, and editing. Since the stories will be long, even with the streamlined planning structure, revision will need to begin early; we will begin to teach revision even as many students are still drafting, so that they can include these moves in their drafts from the earliest stages. We help children see that these story arcs are a way to ensure that their characters struggle, deal directly with their problems, and then come to some sort of resolution.

Although the unit focuses on writing fiction, it is also a unit on rehearsal and revision. Capitalizing on students' beginning-of-the-year energy and their zeal for fiction, this unit encourages them to do more than they have done in years past. Although we emphasize the efficiency of revising as they write, once a draft is completed we then emphasize that writers look back on the trail of a story to consider making substantial revisions. Above all, we teach writers to consider the importance of setting in a story. Earlier, when our students were younger, they were taught to intersperse dialogue with action. Now we highlight the need to ground the entire story (not just the introduction) in a sense of place.

Then, too, children are led to rethink the evolution of their stories. Oftentimes, they approach a fiction story planning for the character to magically receive his or her fondest dream in the form of a solution that flies in out of nowhere like Superman. With help, we show children that in fiction, as in life, the solutions we find are generally those that we make, and if there are magic answers to be found, they usually have been before our eyes all along. This is something that aligns with the Common Core Standards' emphasis on narrative endings.

In the final bend, we take a dramatic turn from the previous edition of the unit. We switch from teaching our fourth-graders how to write fiction, taking them step by step through the content and the craft of the genre, and instead teach them how to conceive, develop, plan, and carry through their own independent fiction projects. While it is true that this immediate transference of skills reaches for the highest levels of Webb's Depths of Knowledge, it is also true that independence in writing is one of the goals we hold nearest

and dearest to our hearts. This has never been more so than when narrative and fiction begin to take a backseat to persuasive and informational writing in fourth grade. There is no doubt that those two types of writing are crucial to students' future academic success. In this series, the unit on realistic fiction is the only narrative unit in the fourth-grade curriculum to reflect those needs. However, it is also true that many students would like, perhaps even need, to keep their narrative muscles strong throughout the year. By teaching students how to take the reins of independent fiction writing projects, we give them the skills they need to feel confident that they can continue their fiction writing even alongside the whole-class units that are most assuredly not narrative.

ASSESSMENT

Prior to teaching this unit, we suggest you take a little time to establish a baseline understanding of your students' skills as narrative writers by setting them up to do a narrative writing task. In *Writing Pathways: Performance Assessments and Learning Progressions, K–5* we describe the instruments—learning progressions, rubrics, checklists, and a set of child-authored exemplar texts—that will help you to see where, in the trajectory of writing development, each of your students lies. This initial assessment will help you and your students track their progress over the course of this unit, and this year, and can also serve as a valuable source of information to inform your own teaching.

You may be tempted to assess your students by giving them a fiction on-demand writing task rather than a personal narrative one. But pause for a moment and consider this: most children are much more apt to produce writing that accurately reflects their narrative writing skills when the onus of coming up with a fictional character, a bit of challenge or trouble that character faces, and how he or she handles that trouble, is lifted. That is, it's far easier to recall a true life story on the spot and then to use the allotted forty-five minutes to write a Small Moment story that is focused, includes detail, introduces a setting, weaves together action and dialogue, and so forth. If you want a measure of your students' skills in and understanding of the narrative genre, then we suggest you use the Narrative Writing Learning Progression that you'll find in *Writing Pathways: Performance Assessments and Learning Progressions, K–5*. After all, the basic qualities of writing that make a strong narrative are the same ones that make a strong piece of fiction.

For this initial assessment to provide accurate baseline data on your writers' narrative skills, be careful not to scaffold your students' work. After all, the more poorly they perform now, the more dramatic their progress may be later! You'll want to simply remind students of the basic qualities you'd expect in a piece of narrative writing, then step back and leave them to their own devices. We recommend that you give students this prompt to start them off:

> "I'm really eager to understand what you can do as writers of narratives, of stories, so today, will you please write the best personal narrative, the best Small Moment story, that you can write? Make this be the story of one time in your life. You might focus on just a scene or two. You'll have only forty-five minutes to write this true story, so you'll need to plan, draft, revise, and edit in one sitting. Write in a way that allows you to show off all you know about narrative writing. In your writing, make sure you:
> - "Write a beginning for your story
> - Use transition words to tell what happened in order
> - Elaborate to help readers picture your story
> - Show what your story is really about
> - Write an ending for your story"

Some of you may worry that welcoming children to the start of a new year by evaluating them may seem uninviting. If so, be a little creative; tell children you're eager to get their work up right away, for all to see. Or let them know that this bit of writing will help you be the best teacher you can be—*and* it will help them track their growth as writers across the year.

Whatever you decide, you will want to administer the actual assessment task—and then respond to it—in a way that is consistent across your grade. We recommend that you and your colleagues meet as a team to decide on the conditions so that these are the same, and you can then compare children's results across not only a single class but an entire grade.

We suggest that when you read the prompt and additional suggestions, students are sitting in their writing seats with enough paper on hand. The paper should be familiar to them, and there should be additional pages available for any kids who are keen to write a lot.

We also suggest that you make copies of the writing children produce for them to paste onto the first page of their writer's notebooks. This writing will serve as a reminder of what each child's starting point was in narrative writing. As the year progresses, students can periodically review that piece, making sure that they are doing work that is increasingly more developed and stronger than this start-of-the-year writing. Certainly, as students collect narrative

entries in the days ahead, you'll suggest that they look back frequently at their on-demand piece.

Of course, the immediate goal of this initial assessment in narrative writing is to understand where the bulk of your class falls in regard to the Narrative Writing Learning Progression, letting that information inform the upcoming unit of study. Read each student's draft, comparing it to the exemplar texts (bear in mind that no one piece will perfectly match the learning progression), and then read the specific descriptors to determine your students' strengths and needs. The descriptors will be particularly useful as you suggest specific steps each writer can take to improve his or her writing. If a writer's on-demand narrative is level 4, you and that writer can look at the descriptors of, say, character development for level 4 and note whether the writing adheres to those. If so, tell that child—or your whole class, if this is broadly applicable—"You used to develop the people in your stories by . . . ," and read the descriptors from the prior level, "but now you develop them this way," and read the level 4 descriptor. Then offer a pointer from the level 5 descriptor for how to improve. You can even say, "Let me show you an example," and then cite a section of the level 5 exemplar text.

One final word. This baseline assessment is not assessing you. It is assessing the background your children have when they enter your classroom. But when this unit ends, you'll repeat this assessment exactly, and when you collect the student writing and look between the first on-demand and the second, the progress that you see will allow for an assessment not only of your students but also of your teaching, and of this curriculum, too. Remember, always, that the goal of any writing instruction is not to produce strong *writing*. It is to produce strong *writers*. It is essential that we teach in ways that lift the level not only of today's piece of writing, but of any piece of writing that a writer does on any given day. We're confident that if you view this baseline data through the lens of wanting to improve your writers and your teaching, you'll be able to say, as the year progresses, "Look at your progress!" And this will describe both the student's progress *and* yours.

GETTING READY

Because this is the first unit of the year, the chances are pretty good that you are inundated with scores of things that need to get done right away. Getting ready for this unit is just one more thing on your list of to-dos. You will want to scan this section quickly for the must-dos and move on from there, knowing that you will have another stab at this unit next year. If, however, you are ahead of the game, maybe reading this unit a few weeks before the school year starts, we encourage you to take a more leisurely route to getting ready, not just simply reading through the unit, but also immersing yourself in the genre. Take some time to head to your local library and read through a small stack of realistic fiction stories. The best ones for your purposes (and for your fourth-graders) tend to be picture books and short story anthologies, although many teachers we've worked with over the years swear by some children's magazines, such as *Highlights*, as well. Look for clear, realistic plot lines, a few central characters, and good writing. Study them to see what they have in common, what you admire, and what you think you might want to teach.

Next, you will want to dig through that stack to find your favorite text to use as a class mentor. It is important to choose a text that you will enjoy reading again and again, as will your students. We chose Julie Brinckloe's classic *Fireflies!* After much searching for a newer, perhaps more cutting-edge, text we found ourselves returning to this book for it's beautiful simplicity, understandable character struggle, and finely crafted language. A longer list of possible mentor texts can be found on the CD-ROM.

Finally, you and your students will be well served if you decide to carve out some time to work on using your own writing to create a demonstration text. This will give you an opportunity not only to practice your own fiction writing skills, but also to create a powerful teaching tool you and your students will return to and rely on throughout the unit. Try to make some time to try out a few of the first teaching points in this book. Better still, invite some colleagues to join you when you do. Not only will you be more likely to try it, but it will be more fun too. You might even decide to co-write your demonstration text. When writing, you might find it easier to choose a plot line and character that you know your students can relate to and will likely be interested by—the best ones being characters who are fourth-graders like themselves whose struggles mirror their own. Take a small bit of time now to write, knowing that you can easily follow up this work during stolen moments every few days throughout the unit.

Creating and Developing Stories and Characters that Feel Real

BEND I

Imagining Stories from Ordinary Moments

IN THIS SESSION, you'll teach students that fiction writers get ideas for stories from small moments in their lives. You'll help them get started doing that.

COMMON CORE STATE STANDARDS: W.4.3, W.4.4, W.4.5, W.4.8, RL.4.1, SL.4.1, L.4.1, L.4.2, L.4.3

GETTING READY

✔ A celebratory song, such as "Olympic Fanfare and Theme" by John Williams (see Connection)

✔ Students' writer's notebooks to pass out during the Connection

✔ Anecdote you can tell to describe how fiction writers get their ideas from real life (see Teaching)

✔ Entries from your own writer's notebook that you can use to demonstrate thinking about potential stories

✔ Several published stories for each child

✔ A premade chart, preferably from a third-grade classroom, or with strategies you know your students learned in third grade titled "Ways to Get Ideas for Personal Narratives" (see Active Engagement)

✔ Copies of the Narrative Writing Checklist, Grade 3 📀

IN THIS SESSION, you'll teach children that writers collect ideas for realistic fiction stories by mining the details of their lives and writing small moments that they can then build fiction ideas from.

Of course, you will first want to create some momentum and energy around today's work because it will be the launch of the first unit of the fourth-grade year. You'll want to make a big deal about the fact that students will be launching a new year of writing workshop—and with that launching a whole new body of work that is beyond anything they have ever done before. You will want to acknowledge that they learned so much about writing last year in third grade, even ending their year writing fairy tales (another type of fiction), skills that they will be building off of this year. You will want to talk about how much they have grown over the summer too, both inside and out, and how you expect them to bring those new experiences and maturity into their writing.

If you know that your students kept writer's notebooks going over the summer and wrote in them rather religiously, you'll want to carve out a bit of time to celebrate that—even if only for a quick round of applause. If, on the other hand, you find out that your students didn't write much over the summer, you'll want to acknowledge that as well, putting a positive and energizing spin on it. Richard Ford, the acclaimed novelist, writes about the advantages for a writer to take long breaks every so often. He writes, "Stopping and then starting up again is of course what all writers do. It's what any of us does: Finish this, pause, turn to that" (from "Writers on Writing: Collected Essays" in *The New York Times*, 2001, 66). New energy is built up during the pauses.

In your first writing unit of the year, you will be channeling that energy to realistic fiction. This is the genre that most children especially want to write, yet it is one of the more deceptively challenging genres.

Children are born fiction writers. From leaning against the knees of grown-ups, listening to their stories and absorbing the rhythms of fairy tales, picture books, and novels, they have already learned about pacing and punch lines, about the humor and tragedy of story. They have soaked up the phrasing and structures of story, from the opening invocation

"Once upon a time" to the classic signals that something is going to happen—"Suddenly . . . " or "One day . . . " If your students' third-grade teachers followed the *Units of Study*, they will have wrapped up the year with a deep study of fairy tales, and will bring that knowledge and expertise with them to your classroom.

"In today's minilesson, you'll invite children into the world of fiction writers, showing one way to collect ideas for fictional stories."

In school, children beg to write stories. Sometimes, perhaps out of fear of the runaway stories that go on and on or out of discomfort over the retold comic book story lines, we've steered them away from this genre. How much wiser to take their energy and passion for fiction and to channel it with crystal clear teaching, right from the start of the school year!

In today's minilesson, after distributing their writer's notebooks with fanfare, you'll invite children into the world of fiction writers, showing one way to collect ideas for fictional stories. Students will start by first collecting Small Moment stories from their lives, then looking at those moments for possible fictional information. They'll learn that not only are there great story possibilities in everyday moments, but also that the best realistic fiction stories are the ones grounded in reality. In the process, you'll help children fall in love with stories all over again.

Imagining Stories from Ordinary Moments

CONNECTION

Orchestrate a short opening ceremony, passing out the students' new writer's notebooks.

I asked the students to come as quickly to the rug as possible, making it clear that I was very excited to begin and also a little impatient. Once the students had all found a seat on the rug, I said, "I am so thrilled that today marks our first day in writing workshop together! We are about to embark on a thrilling year of creating, learning, and sharing writing. Of course, to get started, we need to do something to mark this momentous occasion. You know how often for big sports tournaments, like the World Series, the Super Bowl, or the Olympics, they have an opening ceremony? Well, I thought it was only fitting that for the start of your fourth-grade writing workshop we would do just that. I am going to call each of you by name to come up and receive your new writer's notebook."

I played "Olympic Fanfare and Theme" by John Williams as I called each of the students up to the front, shaking hands with each student as I passed them their notebooks.

Remind them of what they learned in third grade.

"Last year you became very strong writers. Your wrote personal narratives, taught with expert books, made a real-world difference with persuasive writing and learned to craft fairy tales, just to name a few. Wow! You are quite the accomplished group."

Explain that they will begin their fourth-grade year by writing realistic fiction.

"Now that you all have your new fourth-grade notebooks, I know you are dying to dive right in and start writing. And don't worry, you will do that today." I paused to let the students simmer down a bit before continuing. "In fact, because you are fourth-graders, and you already know so much about writing and have matured so much over the summer, you will be starting the year in a way that closely matches the new more grown-up version of you. Our first unit this year will be realistic fiction!"

❖ **Name the teaching point.**

"Today is an important day because you're going to begin collecting ideas for fictional stories in your new writer's notebooks, and I want to teach you where writers look to find those ideas. And the most important thing I can teach

We chose to use music from the Olympics because there was already a timely buzz about this event in the classroom. For your opening ceremony, you may want to think about music that will particularly resonate for your students.

you is this: writers get ideas for fiction, just as they get ideas for almost all kinds of writing, by paying attention to the small moments in their own lives!"

TEACHING

With an anecdote, tell children that you've come to realize fiction writers get their ideas from real life.

"When I was a little girl, I thought all fiction writers looked up into the clouds and *imagined* make-believe stories about castles and puppy dogs.

"But when I grew up, I learned how real fiction writers truly get their ideas. Did you know that E. B. White got the idea for *Charlotte's Web* by lying on a bale of hay in his barn, watching a spider spin her web? The barn animals, the pigs, and the geese were all around, and on the rafters above them all, this little spider delicately wove her tapestry. He probably wrote an entry about that moment in his writer's notebook, and then later, sitting at his desk, he reread his notebook, remembered that moment, and thought, 'I could write a story about that!'

"Of course, when I say that writers get ideas for writing by paying attention to their own lives, I do not mean that writers just record exactly what happened and call the text fiction. When E. B. White lay on that bale of hay and watched a spider, he did not watch her spell out the words, *some pig*, and he did not watch her save a runt pig from the butcher."

Suggest that the imagination that matters is one that allows a writer to see story ideas in the grit of everyday life.

"Fiction writers do, however, pay attention to their lives. They cup their hands around tiny true particles of their lives, and they wait. Sometimes, while they wait, the idea for a story grows. And here is my biggest lesson of all. The imagination that *really* matters to fiction writers is this. You—like E. B. White—can find significant stories in something as ordinary as an entry you've written about a spider in the rafters of your barn. You can write a Small Moment story from your lives or remember that spider—or anything else you have seen or done—and you say, 'Wait a minute. This is giving me an idea for a fiction story. Maybe I could write a story about . . . '"

Tell children what to watch for as you demonstrate writing Small Moment stories from your life that could be seeds for a fiction story.

"Let me show you what I mean. I am going to think about a small moment from my life, remembering some of the strategies I learned in the past for getting Small Moment stories. Like, one of my favorite strategies is to write about times when I was feeling strong emotions. And I think that's a particularly good strategy here because I know that strong emotions can make for great fiction stories too." I uncapped my pen and prepared to write, clearly indicating that I was thinking through what I was going to write, that it wasn't coming to me "magically." "One time I remember that I had a really strong emotion was when I fell down the stairs in fourth grade. I was so embarrassed. I'm going to try to write that story now, as a Small Moment story, telling it bit by bit but also remembering, at the back of my mind, that I'm on the lookout for any ideas for possible fiction stories."

Usually when we tell "I used to but now I realize" stories, we are trying to persuade kids who identify with the first way of thinking to be brought along to the new thinking.

Notice that there are lots of ways to create cohesion or unity within a minilesson. In this one, I thread references to imagination, clouds and puppy dogs, E. B. White, and Charlotte's Web throughout the minilesson. That, plus repetition of the teaching point, helps to make the minilesson clear to the students.

Even though Charlotte's Web *is not realistic fiction, I use it as an example because it is a story I'm certain my children know (and I suspect your children know this story too!). If you worry that your students could get confused by the aspects of* Charlotte's Web *that don't fit into the unit's emphasis on realistic fiction, then select another book. You don't want this minilesson to seem as if it is an invitation to write unrealistic stories. You could refer instead to more realistic fiction books such as* Cassie Binegar, Fig Pudding, *or* June Bug—*or to a picture book. Be sure to refer to a story that all your students know well.*

"Hold onto the railing," I heard Miss Schmidt say as our class headed down the stairs. We had just practiced square dancing in the gym and I was feeling a little wild after all that dancing. I turned to my best friend Rachel and started joking around. "Want to do-si-do?" I asked. Just then I felt my feet start to slip out from under me.

"Oh! Writers, I'm going to stop right there! As I was writing down that story, I realized I don't even need to finish writing it down in my notebook, because I started to get some possible fiction story ideas from my real-life story. I started thinking, gosh, I could write a whole fiction story just about square dancing for gym class! Or maybe I could write a story about a kid showing off for her friends. Or maybe—I'm just going to draw a line under my first entry here and jot down a couple of little story blurbs, just my thoughts for possible story ideas."

- I could write a story about a girl dreading going to gym because she knows that square dancing is that day, and she hates square dancing. So she pretends to hurt her ankle on the way to the gym. But, her gym teacher doesn't let her just go back to the classroom. Her teacher makes her be the DJ.
- Maybe there's a story about a kid who has to do something that he needs to pay attention as he goes down the stairs. Maybe he is carrying a sculpture for art class and he starts to get cocky, so he lets go of the railing and falls.

I put my pen down and indicated that I was moving out of writer mode into teacher mode. "Writers, did you notice how first, I thought back to all my personal narrative work from third grade, and I remembered one of my favorite strategies so that I could begin collecting small moments in my notebook? Did you see how I started writing a Small Moment story, and then, as I got some ideas for possible fiction stories, I jotted those down?"

ACTIVE ENGAGEMENT

Set children up to practice with their partners writing Small Moment entries verbally that could lead to possible fiction ideas.

"Let's think of a small moment we've had together as a class since the first day of school. Luckily it hasn't been so long, so it should be really easy for us to think of a moment. If you're having a hard time thinking of one, look back at the chart for ways to get personal narrative ideas to help." Some of the students assumed a thinking pose, some referred to the chart, and some whispered to each other. "Thumbs up when you've thought of a small moment."

Notice how I showed a personal story to draw ideas from. You'll want to use your own. You may want to share two examples that are very different, for example—an observation and a narrative—to open up possibilities for your students.

Ways to Get Ideas for Personal Narratives

- Think of a person who matters to you, list small moments, choose one, and write the whole story.

Once the majority of the class was holding up their thumbs, I continued. "Now, can you share your Small Moment story with your partner, making sure to tell it like a small moment with dialogue, action, and thinking? If, as you're telling your partner your story, you get an idea for a possible fiction story, go ahead and share that new idea with your partner."

Help one child demonstrate how she used a Small Moment story idea to come up with fiction story ideas.

After two minutes, I convened the group. "Marissa, I'm excited by the story you imagined. You took a story from the first day of school and grew it into a possible story idea. Will you share how you did that, and what your story idea is?"

Marissa said, "I was thinking about the first day of school, and how while we were all lined up on the blacktop, we saw this little kindergartner walk by, crying, and we could tell she was lost. None of us knew what to do. Whether we should wait in line or try to help. Eventually a couple of fifth-graders walked over and helped her find her teacher. But that made me think that maybe a good story could be about helping a lost little kid find her family. It wouldn't be at school, though. It could be at a park. And the kids, in my story, they'd be fourth-graders. They wouldn't wait around for bigger kids to help. They'd jump right in."

"Wow! I love that your story is reversing the feeling of helplessness that it sounds like so many of you were feeling on the first day of school when you saw that lost kindergartner and didn't know what to do. That's the way that we, as writers, take the true stuff of our lives, even if it's hard or embarrassing, and *imagine* that things could go differently."

LINK

Repeat the teaching point, celebrating that fiction writers find story ideas in the moments of their lives. Send children off to do this.

"Writers, I have always known that fiction writers need imagination to write. But I used to think that most fiction writers found ideas by looking up into the clouds and imagining stories about castles or puppy dogs. What you have shown me today is that fiction writers *do* have imaginations. They look into everyday moments of their lives—into moments as ordinary as watching a spider make a web or a girl falling down the stairs—and they see possibilities.

"Today and for the rest of your lives, whenever you want to write fiction, try to either gather small, true moments from your lives or read your notebook once it's tattered and filled with them. Look at these real moments from your lives with a fiction writer's eyes. It's easy to just flick away the idea of a story about a spider, thinking, 'That's not important.' Don't do that. Have the imagination to say, 'Wait. There might be a story here.' And when you get a story idea, mark it with a sticky note, and then write a new entry based on your original entry, putting the idea it sparks onto your page."

When children talk to their partners and I listen in, I get a chance to decide which child's suggestion will be especially helpful to the class. It's not an accident that Marissa has imagined a very realistic story, one that features a child who is her age and that revolves around an everyday life issue.

When we are teaching anything, we are teaching values. Be conscious of the messages that are tucked into your teaching and make sure you are empowering your children to imagine alternatives.

In the link, I generally revisit the teaching point. Here I also repeat a few tiny details from the very start of my minilesson. Writers of all sorts often find that one powerful way to end a text is to return to some of the details with which they began the text.

Because this is the first minilesson of the year, I want children to be inspired. I want them to believe, as I do, that there is something majestic about finding significance in the small moments of our lives and writing these as stories. I also want to spell out very concrete, doable strategies they can use today.

Using Your Imagination to See Promise and Power in Children's Work

IN TODAY'S MINILESSON, I have told children that writers need the imagination to look into everyday moments and see possibilities. I have urged young writers to resist flicking away the little bits of life—observations of a spider making her web—and to instead get used to saying, "Wait. There may be a story here."

Of course, this advice is even more important for *teachers* than for writers. Our students will bring us entries and story ideas. We need the imagination to look at what they bring us and to see that these entries could become something grand. Even if we can't quite see what the writer values in his or her entry, it is important to remember that almost any topic can become a spectacular piece of writing. E. B. White, after all, wrote an essay on warts! The secret to finding something of value in all writing is to slow down, to listen to what the writer is saying, and to be moved by the details of the subject. Teachers, therefore, would be wise to be pushovers. "What a topic!" we say. "This is going to be some story! You definitely need to write the details, because this is amazing stuff."

Beccah, for example, wrote an entry describing her observations during recess. She noticed the faded yellow paint lines that marked the playground boundaries, two third-grade boys who tempted nearby pigeons with cracker crumbs, the way one recess monitor clasped her hands firmly behind her whenever she walked around the playground, and the way one fifth-grade girl rolled her eyes once the girl she had been talking to turned away. At first, Beccah couldn't figure out why she was drawn to this entry; she thought she had just collected a series of random observations.

"Hi, Beccah," I said. "I noticed you keep staring at this entry. There must be something rich there that you can write about."

"I don't know," she mumbled, shrugging and sighing. "I like the way I wrote these descriptions, but I don't know if there's a story idea here."

MID-WORKSHOP TEACHING
Using Notebooks to Plan Possible Stories

"Writers, can I stop you? I love the energy in this room. It feels like a fiction factory here! Marco just asked a really important question. He asked, 'How do fiction writers put ideas for stories on the page? Is it a list?' He wasn't sure which words you actually write, what it should look like. He felt really comfortable with how a small moment would look, how it would sound—like a story! But once you get your fiction ideas, they're only ideas, so they must be a bit different. So I thought it might help if I shared what I wrote in my notebook when I thought about turning my entry about moving to a new place into a story." Opening my notebook, I read:

> Maybe I could write a story about trying to fit in with other kids by trying to be funny. And maybe my character will be around 10. Yes! 'Cause friends really matter to kids of that age. This girl (boy?) wants to have lots of friends but he (or she) is a little odd, and not at all cool. So my character thinks that acting silly will make people laugh, and tries to do something crazy one time (what?), but it gets messed up and she (or he) realizes that's not what makes people want to be your friend.

"Do you see how I began with some of the 'true stuff' from my entry about being embarrassed as a kid, but then I started to imagine layers that would turn it into a juicy fiction story? And do you see how I am not actually writing *the story* in my notebook now, how instead I'm thinking, planning, on the page? I even asked myself questions in the entry, questions like whether the character should be a boy or a girl.

"When you are working on your fiction story ideas, make your entry sound as if you are thinking on the page. Write with phrases such as 'I'm thinking I might' or 'later I could tell about.' And write five or six sentences about that one story idea. Then, of course, skip a line and do similar work for another story idea. You'll probably do this for about five story ideas today."

"Hmm," I said, crouching beside her to read her entry along with her. "Well you certainly did write vivid descriptions! Your observations come to life right off the page. And remember that one way we can find ideas in stories is to think about what moves us. Something here, other than your descriptions, must have moved you enough to make you keep from moving on. Maybe that's where the story idea lies."

Beccah reread her entry, twisting her lips in thought. After a few seconds, she sat straight up, pointed to a line in her entry, and announced, "Well, I thought the way that girl rolled her eyes was funny."

"I wonder why she did that?" I mused.

"I know! I thought they were friends. So maybe I could write about some girls who pretend to be friends, but really don't like each other."

"Why don't they like each other?"

I could tell Beccah had latched on to something because she began rattling off a list of possibilities: "Maybe they used to be friends, but one copied the other's homework and got her in trouble. Or maybe one of them didn't invite the other to her birthday party. Or, I know! Maybe someone else was making fun of the first one and the other one thought it was funny, so now they're not friends anymore."

"This would make a great story, Beccah. I can't wait to find out how it develops," I replied. Before I could finish that sentence, though, Beccah had already taken up her pen again. She turned to a fresh page in her notebook and started writing out her story idea.

If, on the other hand, you find as you move around your classroom, or from your initial on-demand assessment, you discover that there are students who are struggling to come up with Small Moment story ideas or are simply struggling with the focus and control of a Small Moment story, you will likely want to gather those students together into small groups and perhaps, using the third-grade Narrative Writing Checklist as a guide, teach these students a few strategies that will help move them.

There is also a possibility that some of your students will be leaning heavily on their fairy tale work from third grade. Since that unit was predominantly a deep study of narrative in sheep's clothing, this should be mostly a good thing. However some students might need to be reminded that this is a study in *realistic* fiction, and not all the strategies or characteristics of the genre will be applicable here.

Elexa

Elexa is a 11 year old girl that,
wants to be the head cheer
leader, but her best Fexie also
wants to,so will she do it
in the cost of her friendship.
She has noticed that the boy
that was following her around
[Max] is now following Lexie, what
will happen next

FIG. 1–1   Deveonna's story idea

Story: Harrison's parents
are getting divorced, his mom
is dating a construction worker
who only talks about jack hammer.
his dad is in England. In the
midst of all this, Harrison
is starring in a play that is
the schools biggest event.
Can Harrison juggle it all?

FIG. 1–2   Ari's story idea

Revisiting the Third-Grade Narrative Writing Checklist

Congratulate the students on their work filling up their notebooks with Small Moment stories that lead to fiction ideas.

Once the students had all gathered back in the meeting area, I began. "I am so in awe of you today, writers! I knew our plans for today were ambitious—to remember what you learned about narrative writing before you came to fourth grade and to come up with possible ideas for fiction stories to boot. But look at you! Your notebooks are already overflowing with Small Moment stories and fiction ideas. I see that some of you have three, four, five pages filled already. Can you all just give yourself a round of applause for having such a productive first writing workshop of the year?"

Tell the students that they are going to revisit the work they did in third grade and see how they have changed (or not changed) and use that knowledge to help their writing become better than ever.

"I thought because you have really shown that you remember quite a bit from years past, that it might make some sense to look back at what the expectations were for narrative writing in third grade, to see how much of that work you remembered to do in your notebook entries today."

I projected a copy of the third-grade Narrative Writing Checklist. "Some of you might remember using this, or something like this last year. You'll notice right away that it has three main categories to think about: structure, elaboration, and language conventions. Underneath each of those categories you'll see different things strong writers do when writing

The Narrative Writing Checklist, Grade 3 can be found on the CD-ROM.

Narrative Writing Checklist

	Grade 3	NOT YET	STARTING TO	YES!
Structure				
Overall	I told the story bit by bit.	☐	☐	☐
Lead	I wrote a beginning in which I helped readers know who the characters were and what the setting was in my story.	☐	☐	☐
Transitions	I told my story in order by using phrases such as *a little later* and *after that*.	☐	☐	☐
Ending	I chose the action, talk, or feeling that would make a good ending and worked to write it well.	☐	☐	☐
Organization	I used paragraphs and skipped lines to separate what happened first from what happened later (and finally) in my story.	☐	☐	☐
Development				
Elaboration	I worked to show what happened to (and in) my characters.	☐	☐	☐
Craft	I not only told my story, but also wrote it in ways that got readers to picture what was happening and that brought my story to life.	☐	☐	☐
Language Conventions				
Spelling	I used what I knew about spelling patterns to help me spell and edit before I wrote my final draft.	☐	☐	☐
	I got help from others to check my spelling and punctuation before I wrote my final draft.			
Punctuation	I punctuated dialogue correctly with commas and quotation marks.	☐	☐	☐
	While writing, I used punctuation at the end of every sentence.			
	I wrote in ways that helped readers read with expression, reading some parts quickly, some slowly, some parts in one sort of voice and others in another.			

a narrative. You'll also notice that it has three different ways for you to describe how you're doing with those things: 'Yes!' (I definitely am doing this), 'Starting To' (I do this sometimes), and 'Not Yet' (I haven't done this in my writing).

"I'm going to pass out a copy of this sheet to each of you. Can you pick a small moment that you wrote? It doesn't have to be completely finished, but you should have a sense of how it would go if it were finished. And can you look at it through the lens of this checklist?"

As the students looked over their pieces alongside the checklist, I circulated, giving thumbs up to writers who were being particularly honest and gently nudging students who were perhaps being less so. I also encouraged students to chat with their partners if there were any particular things they weren't sure about. Then I brought them back together. "Writers, I can hear so many of you becoming more and more proud as you look through this checklist. There are so many things you have already done or are planning to do. And maybe just a few things you needed to refresh your memories about. Sometime in the next week or so I'll introduce the fourth-grade Narrative Writing Checklist. Until that time, you'll want to work toward making sure most of your writing is matching up with what you learned in third grade."

Imagining Stories We Wish Existed in the World

IN THIS SESSION, you'll teach students that writers get ideas for stories by imagining the books they wish existed in the world and by thinking about issues in their lives.

GETTING READY

✔ Example of a student who found a story idea from her own life (see Connection)

✔ Your own story idea for a book you wish existed (see Teaching)

✔ Chart paper with the start of a list: "How to Find Ideas for Fiction" (see Link and Mid-Workshop Teaching)

✔ Your own writer's notebook or other demonstration text to use during conferring

✔ *The Three Billy Goats Gruff* or other fairy tale students know well (see Share)

TODAY'S SESSION WILL HELP YOUR STUDENTS take the risk of writing stories that are deeply significant and personal. This can be a challenge. When we first invite children to write fictional stories, it can be as if we've opened Pandora's box. Suddenly, from all corners of the room, one finds children planning to write stories about people who win the lottery, fly into outer space, escape from kidnappers, and star on Broadway.

You'll try to bring children back to earth by emphasizing that they are writing realistic fiction and by spotlighting stories that revolve around everyday life events. But your goal is not only to encourage children to write stories about the hopes and heartbreaks of everyday life. Your goal is also to show children that fiction can be a way to explore and to write about the truest and deepest parts of ourselves. Although you do not address this directly, there is no question that today's session helps children to write stories that are often more personal and more real than those they wrote last year during the personal narrative unit of study. Fiction can give children a cloak of invisibility, allowing them to travel fearlessly into areas of vulnerability.

Specifically, you will teach children that fiction writers sometimes get ideas for stories by thinking about the stories they wish existed in the world. You can tuck in tips about how writers go from an image to a story idea, imbue ordinary details with significance, and live with notebooks always open, ready to record everything that catches their attention.

Additionally, to wrap up the unit, you will tap into your students' knowledge of story by having them practice storytelling a classic fairy tale with their partner. This work will early and gently encourage students to develop a storytelling rhythm and if your students studied fairy tales in their third-grade writing workshop, will feel very familiar. It aligns nicely with the Common Core Standards, particularly the Speaking and Listening Standards (SL. 4.1).

COMMON CORE STATE STANDARDS: W.4.3, W.4.5, W.4.8, RL.4.3, SL.4.1, SL.4.4, L.4.1, L.4.2, L.4.3

Imagining Stories We Wish Existed in the World

CONNECTION

◆ COACHING

Tell a story about a child who grasped that writers often find story ideas in the details of our lives.

"During the previous share session, I heard you all telling each other story ideas that sounded like they could be written into real library books, sitting on our shelves. And this morning, as you came in, many of you told me that when you read a short story last night, the text gave you ideas for stories that *you* could write.

"At home last night, Rashann wrote a story idea that was sparked by an entry in which she'd written about just sitting on her porch, watching a squirrel crack and eat a nut. The squirrel was sitting inside a place where two branches formed a *V;* it sat right in the bottom of the *V,* all cozy and safe. Rashann watched the squirrel travel all over the tree until it found just that special, protected spot, and when she reread the story idea, she realized she could write a story about a kid watching that squirrel, a kid who doesn't have a home and is also trying to find a cozy spot, a safe spot, like the space at the bottom of a *V.* Rashann thought maybe the story would start with the girl watching that squirrel search for a nook. Inspired, the girl decides to find *herself* a similarly safe spot.

"Do you notice that Rashann's story idea began with her looking at something so tiny and ordinary? Her work reminds me of the lesson we learned yesterday when we saw that E. B. White got the idea for *Charlotte's Web* from something as ordinary as a spider at work on her web."

❧ **Name the teaching point.**

"Today I want to teach you that writers collect ideas for stories not only by finding bits of life or entries that could grow into whole stories, but also by paying attention to the stories *they wish existed* in the world. Sometimes they get ideas for stories by thinking, 'How can I write a story for people like me, so we can see ourselves in books?'"

This minilesson lays out the great work one child has done. The child's work illustrates the previous session's teaching, but describing what Rashann did also makes this one child famous to others, and this is terribly important. Many people go through life feeling invisible; by telling just this tiny story about Rashann's writing, this gives Rashann a voice and shares a model of good work with the class. By likening her to E. B. White, Rashann is elevated as a writer.

Over and over, you'll see that when I tell children about a story idea, the idea is fleshed out. In this example, the story idea encompasses several scenes, and it conveys the main character's desires and struggles. Notice that the plotline in the story idea we share is not a long one. The children will write short stories, not novels!

For many children, today's minilesson, about finding stories they wish they could read, involves revealing some of those injustices—revealing, perhaps, that there are too few stories of females acting powerfully in the world, or too few stories with immigrant children as main characters.

TEACHING

Point out that we each hope to find ourselves in the pages of books.

"Many times when any one of us looks through the library shelves for a book, we are looking to find ourselves in a story. I may find myself wanting a book about a kid like me who is afraid of the dark, or a book about a kid who is usually the last one picked for sports because she's not any good at them, or a kid whose mother said, 'Every night before bed, you have to tip your head down and brush your hair one hundred strokes.'

"Maybe one of you searches library shelves for a kid who lives with his grandma or a kid who likes to draw cartoon cats and dreams of having a cartoon strip in the Sunday paper. If you want to find yourself in a book on the library shelves and no book seems to tell the story that you want told, then you might decide it is important to put your truth onto the page in your own story."

Demonstrate by creating a story idea out of your longing to see books you'd like to read—in this case, books that contain people like you.

"Let me show you how I use this strategy to come up with a story idea," I said. "First of all, I'm thinking about the books I want to read. For one thing, I wish there were more books about people like me who are half Mexican, kids whose fathers are Mexican and whose mothers aren't. *And* who are afraid of the dark. So in my notebook I'll write down my story idea. I don't just write the big outline of my story—girl with Mexican dad and American mom. I want to put the stuff about a Mexican father together with true little details, like the part about being afraid of the dark and wanting a night-light. Those had been separate items on my list—the girl who is half Mexican, the girl who is afraid of the night—but in a story plan, I often combine things that were once separate. Watch."

Then I wrote:

> A girl who is half Mexican lives with both her parents but she thinks her father works too much.
> She wishes her father were around more because when he's home she isn't so afraid of the
> dark. But his job keeps him far away so the girl usually sleeps with the light on to make her feel
> less alone in the night.

Debrief. Point out that you also invented a character who has desires and difficulties.

"Do you see, writers, that when writing my story idea, I didn't just say, 'I wish there were books on kids who are half Mexican'? I actually jotted a few sentences about how such a story might go. And specifically, I thought about what the character might want and what she might struggle for. Characters in all stories have big longings.

"What I want to tell you is this: when you are collecting ideas for stories in your writer's notebook, you get ideas not only from rereading old entries, but you also get ideas for stories from thinking about books *you wish existed* in the world. Today you can use either of these ways to grow story ideas."

Notice the contribution that details make to this minilesson. The details act like pictures, and a picture is worth a thousand words. Notice, too, that when we want to speak or write with specifics, this generally means that we use more words. Children are apt to describe characters with generic terms, saying, for example, "the girl who loves soccer." How much more effective it is to use more words.

It is worth noticing that this is a unit on fiction, and the message is that we can develop ideas for fictional stories if we try to put the truth on the page. Donald Murray once helped me to write fiction by suggesting I write the Truth with a capital T, but not necessarily the exactly true story. "Change things around so that you convey the Truth of your experience," he said to me.

In any unit of study, it is important to decide on the qualities of good writing that you want to highlight, and then you need to be sure that you refer to those qualities a many junctions in the unit.

ACTIVE ENGAGEMENT

Set children up to try turning a wish for a certain kind of book into a story idea.

"So let's try it. Pretend that you think to yourself, 'I wish there were books about kids like me who aren't that good at sports.' Remember that to make that wish into a story idea, you need to invent some details. You can do so by asking questions of your story idea. Why isn't the kid in the story good at sports? Which sports? What has happened lately that shows these struggles?"

Ask children to turn and talk about the character traits and the struggles the character in the exemplar story might encounter.

"Tell your partner how you could turn this into a story idea. Remember, think about the character, his or her character traits, the character's very particular struggle, about what he or she wants, and about what the character does." After children talked, I recruited Ramon to share. "I'd write, 'A kid comes to school at the start of fourth grade and everyone else has gotten taller. He is a shrimp, so he is no good at basketball anymore. He doesn't get called on to play.'"

"I love the way you gave your character certain characteristics: he's a fourth-grader who isn't as tall as the others, he used to be a great basketball player but now that height gets in the way, kids call him a shrimp. Those details really make your story start to grab me!"

LINK

Send writers off after reminding them of their growing repertoire of strategies for finding fiction ideas.

"So, writers, we pretended we wished there were more stories about kids who aren't good at sports and then imagined a character in such a book. When you are living your life as a fiction writer, you won't write about the character *I* lay out. You'll invent your own characters. You can use any of the strategies we've learned, or others that you invent, to do this. Let's start listing these strategies in a chart," I said, gesturing to the list I had started on chart paper.

How to Find Ideas for Fiction

- Observe the world or reread entries. Mine your notebook for story ideas.
- Ask, "What books do I wish existed in the world?" Let this question lead you to invent a character with traits, struggles, actions.

"The blue table can get started. Now the red table."

The main point here is to help children come up with story ideas by thinking, "What stories do I wish existed in the world?" But I also devote some teaching to a subordinate tip I tuck into the main idea. I tell children that writers embellish their ideas with details. I then go further and show children a sequence of questions that will help them do this. These questions are carefully chosen—notice the sequence, because the questions, asked in this order, scaffold children to do some good work. First the questions channel a writer to think about the character's traits and related struggles, then the questions move writers to consider how these struggles play out in an event.

In example after example throughout this book, you'll see that story ideas contain some tension; they contain a predicament. When I was a kid and wrote fiction, my stories had magic carpets—but no tension. Hopefully, your children will sense that "a boy becomes a billionaire" is not yet the stuff out of which one makes stories.

Because you gave a hypothetical starting point, this is just an exercise. You don't expect children to write about the character from the day's minilesson, but instead to invent their own characters. There will probably be a few children, however, who decide that the story idea you have given to them could become their very own idea, and that's okay.

By now you are anticipating that in the early sessions of any unit, we'll offer children a repertoire of strategies for gathering entries that pertain to the work, and genre, of that unit.

Using an Exemplar Text to Respond to Predictable Problems

WHEN YOU CONFER AND LEAD SMALL GROUPS, you will probably notice that many students have long lists of undeveloped story ideas. Children won't be sure whether they are expected to write actual stories in their notebooks or whether you are asking for lists of story ideas—and actually, you are hoping for something in between. You'll want to teach kids to stay a little longer with each idea, fleshing it out a bit. You might carry with you the first story idea you wrote in your notebook. For example, I had started with this.

> Girl is afraid of the dark

Then I revised my initial cryptic note to say a bit more.

> The girl is afraid of the dark. She knows she is being silly but sometimes she thinks she sees things, like monsters, in bed. She gets scared enough that she has started sleeping with the light on. Sometimes in the middle of the night, she crawls into bed with Mom. Her birthday is coming up. She wants to have a sleepover party but she is worried the other girls will make fun of her because she is afraid of the dark.

I will probably want to carry both versions with her me. Similarly, I could carry my story idea around with me—the idea about the girl who moved.

When conferring, it helps to carry your own exemplar text around with you so that if you decide to use the teaching method of demonstration or the "explain and show an example" method, you'll have the materials to do so. But don't let the fact that you have materials under your arm propel you into using them. As always, begin your conferences by asking, "What are you working on as a writer?" and by trying to understand what the writer has already done and is trying to do.

MID-WORKSHOP TEACHING
Sharing Struggles with Characters

"Writers, can I have your eyes? I want to teach you one more strategy for collecting ideas for fictional stories: you can write stories in which the character wrestles with issues that are important to you. I once knew a young writer named Donald who had a big issue with 'fitting in.' In his school, cool kids all had a certain haircut. Donald wanted to be popular, but he didn't have the money to go to the 'cool' barbershop. So he tried to cut his own hair, but it looked ridiculous and kids made fun of him. He didn't just ignore that this was happening to him; Donald wrote a story about a kid who struggled with and overcame a similar issue. The kids in his story didn't have haircut troubles, but they had similar struggles.

"This was Donald's story plan."

> I'm going to write a story about a kid who tries really hard to fit in, but the more he tries, the worse it gets. Maybe he will do something bad like he steals sneakers to be like everyone else. Then he gets caught by a secret camera. Now he's in trouble with the manager, with his mom, with his principal. Maybe he gets really sick and all the people who were mad at him feel bad about it. Nah—that's dumb. Maybe he DOES something that everyone thinks is cool and makes people look at him differently. Not sure.

"Do you see how Donald took the same issue that *he* was dealing with—trying to fit in with kids at school—and he started thinking about a story where the character wrestles in a different way with the exact same issue? Donald was incredibly brave to write about an issue that is hard in his own life." I said this because, in a subtle way, I hoped to encourage children to write from the heart. "When Donald read the story idea to his class, they got really quiet; I realized that the issue wasn't important just in Donald's life. It was important to most kids in the class. It really helped them when Donald had the courage to name the issue.

"I am telling you this because I know some of you will want to think about the issues that are big in your lives or in the world. You might write an issue on the top of the page and then see if you can spin some story ideas that could possibly allow you to address the issue. We can add this strategy to our list."

How to Find Ideas for Fiction

- Observe the world or reread entries. Mine your note-book for story ideas.
- Ask, "What books do I wish existed in the world?" Let this question lead you to invent a character with traits, struggles, actions.
- Think about an issue that is important to you and create a character who struggles with that issue.

It will help if, before this unit begins, you and your colleagues try to predict the conferences you'll probably need to conduct early in this unit. As I mentioned earlier, you can expect that you'll often need to help children say more when they write about their story ideas. You may also:

- ◆ Help students postpone closure and entertain the prospect of a wider range of story ideas. Some students will generate a story idea and immediately start writing that story from start to finish. Teach them that writers force themselves to imagine more possibilities before making a commitment to one story idea. And once a child does settle on a particular story idea, the child needs to spend a lot of time rehearsing before she begins a draft. I think of this unit on fiction as a unit also on rehearsal and revision.

- ◆ Remind students that they know a lot about how stories generally "go," and specifically, remind them that story ideas usually originate from a character who has motivations and faces a predicament. If a child imagines a story in which an unnamed guy lives through ten daredevil activities, you'll want to explicitly teach the importance of developing a very particular character. You'll also want to show children that a character's traits and motivations lead that character to encounter struggles, and in this way a story hangs together.

- ◆ Steer children to grow story ideas from the particulars of their own lives. It is inevitable that some will want to write adult stories, and you'll want to channel them toward dramas they know from the inside.

- ◆ Anticipate that children will imagine their stories as containing a necklace-full of events. Teach them that they are writing short stories, and this generally means they'll be writing two or perhaps three Small Moment stories.

Although it is helpful to plan for and anticipate conferences, if you find yourself giving mostly preplanned, almost canned conferences, then you probably need to listen more intently and to expect children to surprise you, to take you to new places. That is, it's helpful to expect that when you confer with children, they will stir up new ideas in you. As you draw a chair alongside a child and ask, "What are you working on as a writer?" expect that the child's response will be instructive to you.

Practicing Storytelling through a Return to Fairy Tales

Glory in children's stories and suggest they deserve to hear each other's stories. Demonstrate storytelling by retelling a familiar tale, extrapolating pointers.

"Writers, I am so lucky because I have been able to move among you, listening in on your story ideas. So many of your stories are giving me goose bumps! You all deserve the chance I have to hear each other's stories. Right now, before you share, I'm going to give you a quick lesson in being storytellers. Then before you tell your stories to each other, we'll practice storytelling by telling just the beginning of *The Three Billy Goats Gruff*. Many of you might remember that story from third grade, when you studied fairy tales.

"After that I am going to ask some of you to tell the story of one of *your* story ideas. Are you ready for some hints on being a storyteller? First, begin the story by sweeping the listeners with your eyes, as if saying, 'Welcome, draw close, for I have a story to tell.' Second, tell the start of the story in such a way that it sounds like a famous book or a fairy tale; start it with a phrase like, 'Once, long ago' or 'One day, a little girl . . . ' or something else that sounds like a real story. Third, as you tell the story, be sure your mind is picturing whatever you are telling. If your mind isn't painting pictures, how will you choose the words that can help your listeners paint pictures as they hear the story? I'll try storytelling first, using *The Three Billy Goats Gruff*. I'll try to follow all those tips. Then Partner 1, I am going to ask *you* to story-tell the same story (but in your own way) to your partner. Here goes."

Once, long ago, there were three billy goats Gruff. They lived on one side of a stream, and every day they would look across the stream to a lush field of grass. There was a bridge across the stream, but the three billy goats Gruff knew they were never to cross that bridge, for a mighty troll lived there.

One day, however, the three goats were so hungry they decided to cross the bridge so they could eat the sweet lush grass on the far side. First the littlest goat started across the bridge. Trip, trap . . .

Set children up to retell with a partner the story you modeled, and then to story-tell one of their own ideas.

"Okay, Partner 1, try telling the same Billy Goats Gruff story to Partner 2. It doesn't matter if you remember the details of the story. You can change it as you go. But tell this story like you are a professional storyteller and this is the most amazing story in the world. Go nice and slow, creating a storytelling aura."

After a few minutes I interrupted. "Now using the same storyteller voice, Partner 1, take one of your own story ideas, and tell your partner that story. Start it in a way that signals, 'I'm telling a story!,' perhaps with a phrase like 'Once, long ago' . . . '"

It may seem abrupt to suddenly channel students to go from generating lots of story ideas to storytelling one. I've brought storytelling into this very early session because I want the magic of literary language and the storyteller's persona and voice to help children generate and select between story ideas. But it is true that children are still generating lots of story ideas.

The hints here are ones I learned more than a decade ago when I studied with Mem Fox, author of Koala Lou. I teach these tips to children now because I think that by following these bits of advice, children will take the opportunity to story-tell more seriously. I hope these tips elevate the storytelling and allow it to make a bigger contribution to children's work.

Practice telling the fairy tale you select so that you can tell it very well. As you tell the story, alter the pace of your voice and remember the power of a pause. Appreciate crescendo—the hurrying of time and intensity. When you reach a section of the story that is especially significant, slow down and tell these events in smaller steps. And when you reach the ending, slow your voice almost to a halt. Your timing will have terrific implications for the emotional power of the story.

Developing Believable Characters

TODAY'S LESSON IS A CRITICAL ONE. You'll teach children that once writers get some ideas for how a story might go, they resist the temptation to begin drafting the story and instead they rehearse for it. When writing fiction, we need more than just the topic: we need to create the story world; we need to know our characters with intensity—well enough that we can live inside their skin and see through their eyes.

Children often think that the central element of a story is plot, and they enter a fiction unit expecting that the story of a father and a son hiking will revolve around all that happens to them (perhaps they meet a grizzly bear, get caught in a rock slide, fall into a cavern, are bitten by a rattlesnake). However, the truth is that the better story will revolve not around what happens to the father and son, but rather, what happens between the father and the son or within them.

You'll begin with the fairly easy work of teaching children that fiction writers rehearse by fleshing out their characters—detailing their external features. You'll soon up the ante, pointing out that these external features need to reflect and describe the internal features.

Throughout this work, you will teach children that fiction writers write not only drafts of a story, but also plans. They mull over possible directions, to gather and sort information. More specifically, children will learn that rehearsal is also a time for revision! By thinking through a story idea in some detail, writers progress through a whole sequence of possible ideas—even before they actually begin their first drafts. We want to make sure students have as much agency as possible in both designing their plans and carrying those plans out. This is work that would be considered a Level 4 task in Webb's Depths of Knowledge, as well as distinguished teaching in the domain of instruction while engaging students in learning according to Charlotte Danielson's Framework for Teaching.

In this session, youngsters choose their story idea and begin developing that idea by developing their characters. This will involve thinking about their internal attributes, as well as their external attributes.

IN THIS SESSION, you'll teach students that, like all writers, fiction writers need to choose a seed idea (a story idea) and then begin to develop characters by creating their external and internal traits.

GETTING READY

✔ "How to Find Ideas for Fiction" chart from previous session

✔ Your own character and story line that you will use to model throughout the unit (see Teaching)

✔ Start of a "Developing My Character" T-chart on chart paper, with two columns: Outside (external features) and Inside (internal features)

✔ "Advice for Developing a Character" chart on chart paper

✔ "How to Write a Fiction Story" anchor chart (see LInk)

COMMON CORE STATE STANDARDS: W.4.3, W.4.4, W.4.5, W.4.9.a, RL.4.3, SL.4.1, L.4.1, L.4.2, L.4.3.a

Developing Believable Characters

CONNECTION

Chronicle the learning journey the class has been on in this unit to date. Emphasize that children have learned the ingredients of a good story.

"For the past few days, you've been living like fiction writers, seeing ideas for stories everywhere. You've been writing entries in which you think on the page about your story ideas. I read through your notebooks during gym yesterday, and what I saw blew me away.

"Listen carefully to what I noticed, because it is important. Although our minilessons have been about the strategies fiction writers often use to come up with story ideas (and the chart 'How to Find Ideas for Fiction' lists those ideas), you guys are so alert as learners that on your own you have gleaned a whole lot about the ingredients that go into a good story idea.

"Looking over your notebooks, I could tell that when we started this unit, you thought a good story idea might be one like this."

A girl climbs a mountain by herself and she's proud.

"And I could tell that now many of you realize that a story idea needs to include some more specifics about the character and the story, so it might go like this."

A 9-year-old girl has had a knee injury and will never be able to bend her knee. At first she gives up on life but then something happens to change this and she decides to not give up anymore. To prove herself she sets out to climb the mountain that overlooks her house. She doesn't get to the top but she proves herself in a different way and learns something, I am not sure of the specifics.

◆ COACHING

Children are choosing their seed ideas very early in this unit, because once they've chosen their story ideas they still need to devote lots of time to rehearsal. I have a few options right now. One option is to summarize the previous session's work, aiming to either consolidate what students have learned so that it becomes more memorable for them or aiming to put a new slant on their prior learning. Then, too, another option is to simply share observations about students' work.

Tell writers that today they'll select a story idea.

"Today each of you will reread all your entries and select one seed idea to develop into a publishable story (in this unit, we'll call it your *story idea*)."

❖ **Name the teaching point.**

"I am going to teach you that fiction writers don't just go from choosing a story idea to writing a draft. Instead a fiction writer *lives with* a story idea for a time. Specifically, I will teach you the thinking-on-the-page strategies that fiction writers use to live with their characters and to rehearse for their drafts.

"You will see that these strategies focus less on planning what will happen in your stories and more on bringing to life the people who will make things happen. A fiction writer once said, 'Before you can begin writing your story, you need to know your characters so well that you know exactly how much change each one has in his or her pocket.'"

TEACHING

Set the children up for your teaching by quickly summarizing your process of selecting a story idea.

"I mentioned earlier that we'll need to reread all our story ideas and select one to develop into a publishable story. Honestly, I think the truth is that usually there is one idea that chooses *us*. Usually I find that, in the end, one idea stays with me and haunts me enough that it feels inevitable that I must write about it.

"This morning on my way to school, I realized that I had already decided to write about that girl who is afraid of the dark and wants to buy a night-light. So I put sticky notes on the pages related to that entry, and now I am going to begin developing that seed idea, that story idea.

"Notice that I don't start by thinking about what will *happen* in the story. I rein myself in, I hold myself back from doing that and try instead to get to know my character."

Demonstrate that you develop your story idea by listing external and internal features of your main character.

"I already know she's part Mexican, so I add that to the external side of my chart. I need to give her a name that goes with the fact that she's Mexican. I'm thinking whether there's anything else about my character that could help me find a good name. I definitely know she's afraid of the dark." I added that to the internal side of the chart. "Oh! I'll name her *Luz* 'cause that means 'light.'"

Developing My Character

OUTSIDE (EXTERNAL FEATURES)	INSIDE (INTERNAL FEATURES)
Part Mexican	Afraid of the dark
Luz	

Notice that this sentence—today you will reread your entries and select a story idea—is not a teaching point. This is an assignment, not a lesson! Sometimes, as in this instance, we will want to tell writers to do something, and of course we can tell them so within a minilesson. But it's important to keep in mind that telling writers to do something can't substitute for teaching them a strategy or a skill.

It is often tempting to keep the teaching point vague, saying something like, "Today I'll teach you a strategy for writing good leads." Then, in the teaching component of a minilesson, we can name the strategy. However, I've found that when we force ourselves to be more explicit in the teaching point, then we are less likely to fool ourselves in the teaching component into thinking that simply naming the strategy amounts to teaching it. Notice today's teaching point is specific and contains several sentences.

I try to weave little facts, quotes, stories, and tips into minilessons. I want children to feel as if the moments when they gather close for a minilesson are heady times. We want them to come to a minilesson expecting to learn, learn, learn.

I will soon introduce a story that weaves through this entire book, becoming the class's story. You'll want to substitute your own class's story, but the story that weaves through this book is one that can belong to many of us.

There are lots of reasons to rein children in so that they don't bolt ahead into writing a draft before they develop their characters. One reason for postponing the draft is that the work on character development will enrich the eventual draft. But another reason to ask children to work on developing their characters before they launch into a draft is that this gives us a bit more time to confer, making it more likely that children get off to as strong a start as possible.

Shifting from the role of author to that of teacher, I addressed the children directly. "Did you see that I don't just come up with any ol' random characteristics for my character? I try to put together a person in such a way that the parts of who she is fit together, they cohere, into a person who begins to come to life."

Returning to the role of author, I looked at my chart and mused, "What else? I want Luz to be a bit like me. If this chart were about me, not Luz, I think that in the internal column I'd write that I'm sensitive. I think I want Luz to be sensitive too, and sort of artistic." I added this to my chart.

Think aloud to highlight the fact that the external and internal traits need to cohere.

I reread all of what I had written. "Let's see, does being sensitive and being artistic fit with everything I know about Luz? When her father is gone, she is afraid of the dark. She's sensitive. Sensitivity often goes hand in hand with imagination and creativity. I can imagine Luz conjuring up all sorts of inventive, frightening thoughts about the dark. I can also picture her creating interesting artwork. So yes. Those go together."

Debrief. Highlight that you first decide on the main goals for your character and let these guide what the character develops into.

Shifting again to the role of teacher, I said, "Do you see that when I am creating a character, I begin with whatever I know? I knew I wanted my character to be a bit like me. You may know that you want your character to resemble someone else in your life or that you want your character to go from being tough to being gentle. Start with whatever you know you want for your character.

"I hope you also noticed that I often pause to reread everything I have created, asking, 'Do these different things make sense within one person? Do they fit together in a believable way? Are the traits here for a reason?' I reread to test whether the character I've created thus far stands up to the test of believability."

Show children a chart of advice for developing characters and model how you might use it.

"I'm going to do one last thing that I want you to notice. I am going to look at that word *sensitive* and say exactly what it means. Lots of people can be sensitive, but what exactly does it mean for Luz? Um, let's see. I think for Luz this means she really cares about people. She is really kind.

"But as I write this, I am still keeping in mind that question, 'Does the character seem believable?' I'm worried that I just made Luz too good to be true. If she is human, she can't be all-caring, all-kind. She needs to be more complicated."

Watch the way in which I weave between demonstrating and debriefing, embedding writing tips or pointers into my debriefing. Notice also that although I give a lot of pointers, my written work is lean. Within a minilesson that aims to be just ten minutes long, I can't rattle on and on about my character. Everything I say here is chosen because it helps illustrate a larger principle I want to teach.

Notice the way I emphasize that the traits I give to my character need to fit together in a logical fashion. This is an emphasis we added after seeing children throw random traits together with abandon ("my character likes peach ice cream, her favorite color is purple, she walks funny," and so on). The fact that I model the process of developing a coherent character does not ensure that students will follow this example!

When you debrief, you have another chance to incorporate tips into your demonstration. So be sure that when you retell what you have just demonstrated, you do so in a manner that highlights whatever it is you want children to take from your demonstration.

Alternatively, you could ask children to extrapolate their own tips for creating a character from what they saw you do, perhaps listing across their fingers the steps they saw you take that they could also take. If you do this, however, avoid trying to extract your points from them through a series of leading questions!

Children are often apt to throw around trite words like mean *and* happy *without giving too much thought to what those words mean. By teaching them to think about the words they choose, we're encouraging them to be as precise as possible about who their characters are—to challenge clichés and to get at the truth.*

Advice for Developing a Character

- Start with whatever you've decided matters to you about your character. Is he or she like you? Like someone you know?
- Put together a character so that all the parts fit together into a coherent person.
- Reread often, asking, "Do these different things make sense within one person? Do they fit together in a believable way? Are these traits here for a reason?"
- Open up any broad, general descriptors—words like sensitive—and ask, "What exactly does this word, this trait, mean for this particular character?"
- If a character seems too good to be true, make the character more complex and more human by asking, "What is the downside of this trait? How does this characteristic help and hurt the character?"

"I am going to think some more about Luz being sensitive and about her caring about people. I am thinking about why she cares for people and about how there needs to be a downside to this.

"Okay. I think Luz is really thin-skinned. Things get to her easily. Like the dark gets to her, and her father being away gets to her. People's judgments get to her too. Her feelings get hurt easily. This is why she is careful of other people. She assumes other people are thin-skinned like she is. I'll add these things to the internal side of my 'Developing My Character' chart."

ACTIVE ENGAGEMENT

Set children up to join you in creating the main character in your story.

"So now it's your turn to try. Let's think about this character, Luz. For now, will you and your partner try to add some things to the other side of the chart—the external side? (By the way, I often develop the internal side first and then make sure the external reflects the internal.) As you work, remember these things we've learned so far about developing characters," I said, and pointed to the "Advice for Developing a Character" chart.

"Also, as you talk through things you might add about the external side of Luz—her hobbies, her looks, her ways of acting in the world, her friends or family, her experiences at school—remember that you are going to talk about external features that *fit with the internal ones*. So begin by rereading what we've already written, and then turn and tell your partner how the things we've already written affect your ideas about the external side of Luz." The room erupted into talk.

I steer students toward the often shortchanged aspect of a character's internal nature. Young people can easily list external, physical features, and love doing it: tall, baggy clothes, dark brown hair, and so on. But we fall in love with characters not for what they look like, but for who they are—how they feel about things, their particular perspectives on the world— so the more time spent learning how to flesh out the character's interior life the better. Still, there may be some children who begin creating their characters by elaborating on the external features. When you confer with these children, ask questions that will help them link physical and external qualities to internal states. For instance, if a character is tall for her age, ask the child how the character feels about this.

Intervene to lift the level of what children are saying by reminding them to use pointers from the chart.

After three minutes, I interrupted. "Writers, can I have your eyes? Please pause to reread the chart of 'Advice for Developing a Character' and then use that advice to revise what you are saying about Luz's external features." Again, the room erupted into talk.

Elicit suggestions for character development from a few partnerships, and add these to the list of external and internal features.

I soon requested the children's attention, asking Paige to report back on what she and her partner had said. "We thought about how Luz is part Mexican, so we said she has light brown skin, and then we thought she has a ponytail with long brown hair. We thought casual clothes would go with that and with her being sort of artistic. This is probably stupid, but we made a sketch of some dangly earrings we thought she wore; she made them herself." I added Paige and Francesca's suggestions to the chart.

Developing My Character: Luz

OUTSIDE (EXTERNAL FEATURES)	INSIDE (INTERNAL FEATURES)
Part Mexican	Afraid of the dark
Luz	Artistic
Light brown skin	Cares for people
Long brown hair in ponytail	Thin-skinned
Casual clothes	
Self-made dangly earrings	

"Sketching her earrings is not in the least stupid. In fact, it is really smart to know your character well enough that you can sketch her dangly earrings. Do you know what color beads she used in the earrings? I bet you could tell me why that is her favorite color. Remember, you need to know your characters well enough to know how much change they have in their pockets!" Then I added, "I'm beginning to think that Luz needs to become shared property and that this story is being cowritten by all of us!"

If we want a particular pointer (or a particular chart) to influence how children go about their work, we need to thread it through our conversations.

Keep in mind that just because a writer knows the color of a character's earrings and knows even why this color is special to the character, this information will probably not show up in the actual story! And bear in mind, too, that your children learn as much from the writing that does not end up in their publications as from the writing that does. You are, after all, hoping to develop great writers, not simply great writing. So nothing is wasted!

LINK

Rally members of the class to choose their story idea and begin charting external and internal characteristics of a character. Remind children that fiction writers do this often.

"You've got some big work to do during the writing workshop today. You'll begin by thinking whether one of your seed ideas, one of your *story* ideas, has chosen you. If nothing seems inevitable, if nothing feels like it can't be ignored, you may want to spend a bit more time collecting story ideas, going back to generating ideas. Either way, you need to end today feeling committed to one story idea. And once you have your story idea, you can begin getting to know your character.

"To think about what your character is like on the inside and the outside, you may want to use a two-column chart like the one we made together. I've got forms in the writing center. When you go to your writing spot, you can tape one of these forms into your notebook. Or you may prefer to just divide a page of your notebook into two columns. Or you can alternate paragraphs, with some paragraphs telling the internal side of your characters and others the external. You are in charge, of course.

"From this day on, I hope that whenever you write fiction, you remember that instead of launching right into a draft or focusing only on planning the plotline of a story, you always rein yourself in, taking the time to develop your character. I've started an anchor chart for our unit to help you remember."

> ### How to Write a Fiction Story
>
> - Develop a strong story idea, character(s), and setting.

Listening to this, you may think, "Geez, I bet none of my kids feel as if a story idea has chosen them!" I encourage you to act as if your kids are zealously committed to their stories. Act as if they love writing. You'll surprise yourself by finding the drama becomes real life. As you've heard me say before, the literacy researcher, Jerry Harste, once said, "I see teaching as creating, in the classroom, the kind of world we believe in and then inviting our children to role-play their way into becoming the readers and writers we hope they'll become."

The truth is that this minilesson channels children in a very direct way. So it helps to highlight that, within the constraints of this directive, children still have some choices.

Anticipating the Help Children Will Need Developing Their Characters

AS YOU CONFER WITH INDIVIDUALS OR, more likely, with small groups, you'll no doubt see that many children begin by simply listing phrases to describe the character. Ariana, for example, began with the list in Figure 3–1.

Don't be surprised that children are making lists. This should be what you expect. But when conferring, help these youngsters realize that their lists can be more specific and more elaborated. Pay attention to places where the child provides a bit more detail and celebrate these. For example, with coaching, Ariana progressed from developing her character with a mere list of words toward doing this with phrases (see Figure 3–2).

As you confer, you will probably notice that many of the characters seem like stereotypes. This is natural. Luz, even, begins as a half-Mexican artist with dangly earrings and loose, swinging clothes. It would be tempting to teach students to think critically about the work they've done developing characters by putting their characters on trial: "Is your character a stereotype? Is your character simplistic?" I don't recommend this. For now, it is very important for youngsters to bond with their characters, and therefore we are wise to avoid treating the character or the character development work harshly. If a character seems generic, stereotypical, or underdeveloped, instead of saying so, simply help the writer outgrow this surface-level character development.

For example, when a character's internal characteristics are generic, I find I can help the child open up those generic terms if I ask the right questions. If the character is "good at soccer," then I can point out that people can be good at soccer in different ways. "What is your character's *specific* way of being good at soccer?" I can even press further and ask, "What is going on inside the character that makes her so good at soccer?" Once the child has answered by creating some revealing details about this one dimension of the character's life, I might ask, "How does that connect to other things the character does?" It also helps to ask, "What's the downside of this?" The character who is always pushing during the soccer game may not know when to relax. In a conference, I'll ask these questions of a child, but I will also pull back and talk

FIG. 3–1 At first Ariana simply listed phrases as she developed her character.

FIG. 3–2 With coaching, Ariana's descriptors become more detailed.

"Writers, I just must stop you! I've been thinking that as we work on creating the insides of our characters, we don't want to forget one really important thing. We need to think about how our characters feel about themselves. We know, as real people, that how we feel about ourselves is really important. It only makes sense that our characters would think something about themselves too. Does your character like himself or herself? Does the character think he or she is funny? If your character is strange, does she know she's strange? Is the character humble? Or does the character think she or he is the best thing since sliced bread?

"Ariana has wisely set up two columns in her notebook. One is labeled 'attitude toward self' and the other is 'attitude of others toward her' (see Figure 3–3). Some of the rest of you may want to follow Ariana's example. Before we go on, look back and see if you have included what your character thinks of himself or herself."

Attitude toward self

- she thinks she's dumb, grumpy, rude, and obnoxious
- she hates her lips
- she knows all of what she thinks isn't true but she still thinks that

Attitude of others toward her

- Mrs. Jorach her teacher thinks she's great in writing
- Mr. Megrache her math teacher thinks she's good in word problems

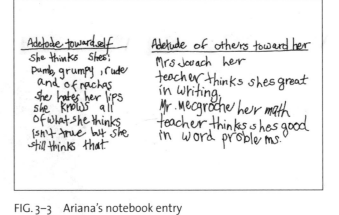

FIG. 3–3   Ariana's notebook entry

about the importance of asking (as well as answering) questions such as these. That is, I will pause in a conference and say, "Will you notice, for a moment, the questions I've asked you about your character, because these are questions you, as a writer, need to be able to ask yourself and each other." It helps to chart these questions. My goal, of course, is for the young writer to learn that another time, he or she can ask these same questions while writing. Children can also ask these questions of each other's characters.

If a character seems wooden, I often find the youngster has been trying to make up the character out of thin air. When this is the case, I find it helps if the child learns to lend his or her own life experience to the character. A child can do this even if the character is in many ways very different from himself. For example, a child might be writing a story about an old man who has outlived all his family members. The child

doesn't know much about being old, but he can think, "When I feel lonely, what do I do?" Perhaps, when no one is home and the place echoes, the child sometimes looks through sports trophies, remembering the games. Why couldn't the old man do something similar? Perhaps the youngster finds that when the house is especially empty, he finds that he waits for phone calls and sometimes even picks up the receiver to check that there's a dial tone so that calls can come through. Why couldn't the old man do this as well? Details grounded in real life have power.

Sometimes when I confer with a child, I find that the child feels as if he or she has hit a dead end with a character. I sometimes let the child know that problems with a character's development can be early warning signals that the story idea itself doesn't fit the writer or that the story idea has problems that need to be addressed. As a result, then, I may encourage the writer to rethink the entire story idea.

You might also want to use this as an early opportunity to make a connection to the student's reading work, especially if you have been studying characters in reading workshop. Guide the student to open up her independent reading book and point to some of the places where she learned about her character. What did the author include? What did the author leave out? Why do we think the author made those decisions? By guiding the student to look back at her reading, you are not only including the student in the company of authors, but you are also making clear and explicit connections between what the student is learning as a reader and applying it to writing. This is something the Common Core State Standards explicitly call students to do (W.4.9.a).

Finally, I always keep in mind that secondary characters need to be developed too! Everything that the writer has done with the main character needs to be done with the secondary characters.

Creating Complex Characters

Spotlight one student who decided his character was one-sided and asked, "What's the flip side of this trait?"

"Writers, you've done some wise work today. I especially want to celebrate the wise decision Henry made when he realized that his character, Max, was too good to be true. So Henry went back to alter his early work with the character, Max. Henry had already said Max had a rich imagination. He'd already said that the character's lively imagination meant he had big, imaginative dreams, and plans and schemes, too. Henry worried, though, that Max sounded *too* perfect. He could have just added some other, less ideal qualities, but instead he did something really smart. He thought, 'If my character has a lively imagination, this is probably bad as well as good for him.' Then Henry wrote that his character imagines everything that could go wrong and consequently has lots of big worries and always seems nervous.

"I hope all of you learn from what Henry has done. He realized his character was too good to be true, but he didn't just jump into a list of bad as well as good things about him. Instead, Henry took one thing—that his character imagines a lot—and thought carefully about the ways this would help *and hurt* his character."

Extrapolate the larger principle. Writers develop complex characters by thinking of the bad as well as good aspects of a trait.

"Writers call characters like the one that Henry has created *complex*. With your partner today, would you look at your characters and think whether they have bad as well as good sides, and whether you've really worked through the ups and downs of your characters' personalities?" As I listened in on partnerships, Ariana read her entries aloud and Jesse signaled with her thumb to indicate whether Ariana was showing the good side, the bad side, or a neutral side of a trait. This is what Ariana read aloud (Figure 3–4).

Seamus

INTERNAL INSIDE	EXTERNAL OUTSIDE
is afraid of everything	brown hair
doesn't like his father	really active
he likes to go on high roller coasters	doesn't watch TV
doesn't obey his father	2nd grade
has a girlfriend	hates ice cream

Although the share session gives children one opportunity to talk about their characters, you needn't shoehorn all this thinking and talking into the writing workshop. If you want to stoke the fires of excitement that came when launching this unit, whenever you have an extra five minutes before the end of the day or before gym, assume children will be dying to talk and think about their characters and "let" them do so.

Seamus

internal inside — external outside

is afraid of everything
  doesn't like his father
he likes to go on high roller coasters
  doesn't obay his father
has a girl friend
a girl likes him but he only likes her as a friend
loves chocolate
loves pupys
loves his babysiter more then anything
hates school but doesn't tell anybody

brown hair
really active
doesn't wach tv.
2nd grade
hates icecream
has 1 friend
people don't like him even though he doesn't do anything wrong
good at math
good with plants

FIG. 3–4 Ariana read this aloud to her partner, noticing whether she'd included negative as well as positive traits.

INTERNAL INSIDE	EXTERNAL OUTSIDE
a girl likes him but he only likes her as a friend	has 1 friend
loves chocolate	people don't like him even though he doesn't do anything wrong
loves puppies	good at math
loves his babysitter more than anything	good with plants
hates school but doesn't tell anybody	

Deveonna, meanwhile, showed Ari that she'd developed her characters by first revising her original story idea. Whereas earlier, she'd imagined that Elexa would be struggling to be chosen as a cheerleader, now Elexa struggles instead to shake off the fawning attention of Max. Beautiful, popular Elexa (the would-be cheerleader) isn't sure if geeky Max is after her or after her best friend, Lexie. This is what Deveonna wrote (Figure 3–5).

> Today I was walking around the schoolyard, and I saw that Max kid, but he wasn't chasing after me, in fact he was after Lexie, and she let him catch her. Showoff! She wants to be the one, so she can get the part. I wonder if I should call him over and talk, or end my longest friendship over him.

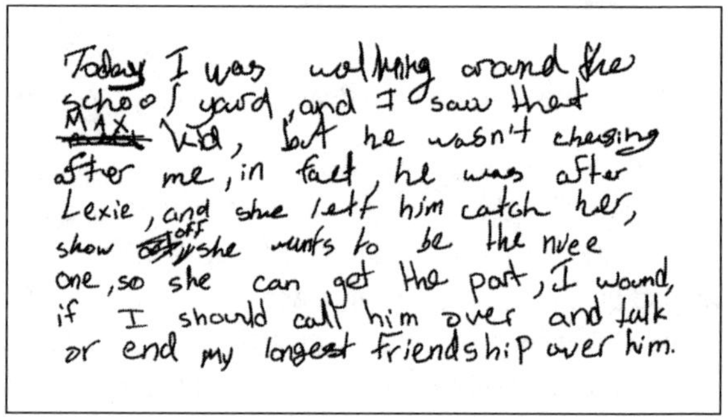
Today I was walking around the school yard, and I saw that ~~MAX~~ kid, but he wasn't chasing after me, in fact, he was after Lexie, and she left him catch her, show off she wants to be the nice one, so she can get the part, I wound, if I should call him over and talk or end my longest friendship over him.

FIG. 3–5 Deveonna's revised story ideas

SESSION 3 HOMEWORK

FLESHING OUT SECONDARY CHARACTERS

We've spent the last few days getting to know our main characters. Yet we all know that there are other characters in our stories: secondary characters. They are important characters and deserve our attention because they really help to make our stories believable. It's not enough for us to have a great main character if all the other characters in our story seem like we rushed through them.

Tonight for homework, take a look at the secondary characters in your story idea. Try some of the same work with a secondary character that you did with your main character. You can make an internal/external T-chart or explore different things about them that we have on our lists. Whichever you try, the most important thing to keep in mind is that writers know all the characters in their stories well, not just the main characters.

Session 4

Giving Characters Struggles and Motivations

I N TODAY'S SESSION you will guide students into what many fiction writers consider the heart of fiction: character struggle and motivation. You will teach your students that readers will root for a character when they know what the character wants and they see the character struggle toward these goals. As Gerald Brace writes in *The Stuff of Fiction* (1972), "The first essential is the creation of believable persons who wait for something or want something or hope for something—they themselves hardly know why or what. Suspense is created by the waiting and wanting."

We know this from our reading lives. Charlotte wants to help Wilbur, and this longing leads Charlotte to weave her web. Readers, too, want to save Wilbur. We want this so much that we flinch when Charlotte is almost discovered, and we root for a rat to bring back the much-needed newspaper clippings. Students, like E. B. White, can rope readers in by creating characters who have desires that are intrinsic to their personalities. A shy person might dream of one day overcoming her fear of performing on stage. Encourage students to think not only about what their characters desire, but why these motivations matter so, so much. This will help children create richer, more complex characters.

In life, of course, the path is never smooth. This is true in stories, too. This is something our students spent a good deal of time studying in third grade. We want to live inside a character's shoes, facing his dragons, reaching for her gold medal. And we want to do so slowly so that we can savor the final outcome after the long buildup. The Common Core State Standards call for students to "organize an event sequence that unfolds naturally" (W.4.3.a). One of the most accessible aspects of fiction that allows students to reach toward that standard is in the familiar work of character.

Even though students are still sorting out how they want their stories to go, this session sets them up to create the right combination of motivation and obstacles. In preparing for this session, make sure that you have read aloud at least one mentor text you plan to refer to throughout this unit. We will refer to Julie Brinckloe's *Fireflies!* Today's session builds on the work students have done with familiarizing themselves with the text prior to today.

IN THIS SESSION, you'll teach children that writers can develop characters by telling about their characters' motivations and struggles and also by creating scenes that show these things.

GETTING READY

✔ Chart of all the different character ideas students have developed (see Connection)

✔ Passage from a text students know well that illustrates a character's yearning, such as *Fireflies* by Julie Brinckloe

✔ Idea for an ordinary scene with your character that you and your students can quickly compose together on chart paper (see Active Engagement)

✔ Class story in mind that children can use for practice text in "Advice for Developing a Character" chart

✔ "Qualities of Good Personal Narrative Writing" chart (made by you or borrowed from third-grade teacher)

COMMON CORE STATE STANDARDS: W.4.3.a,b,d; W.4.5, RL.4.1, RL.4.3, RL.4.10, SL.4.1, L.4.1, L.4.2, L.4.3.a

Giving Characters Struggles and Motivations

CONNECTION

Celebrate the character development work children have already done in a way that honors it.

"Writers, I feel as if a whole crowd of people came into the classroom with you this morning. You brought with you Griffen, who dreams of impressing Julie and of having a pet of his own; and Mario, who is hoping to get a chance to play jazz at his church's coffeehouse; Mrs. Randoff, who has nasty teeth like an old rusty pole and who tells the black kids to get off her block; and Alex, with her horse bracelets and horse T-shirts and horse-sized hole in her life. I jotted down the sorts of details you have been inventing for your characters. Look at the list of what you have done!"

Instead of beginning this minilesson by telling specific ways that I hope children have learned to flesh out their characters, I try to simply applaud their enthusiasm and show a list that records what writers have done so far. My fondest hope for the class right now is that they are absorbed in their characters, carrying these "people" with them all the time. I therefore act as if this is already happening.

Develop Characters by Thinking about Their:

collections

favorite clothes

special places on earth

treasures

worries

quirks

secrets

relatives

ways of walking, talking, and gesturing

rituals for waking up, going to sleep

meals and mealtimes

best friends

phone calls

This session is very full, and of course it could have been broken into separate sessions: we need to know our characters' wants; we need to know our characters' struggles (or what gets in the way of achieving their wants); and we need to show, not tell, these details. I decided to consolidate all three of these tips into one teaching point because otherwise, I felt the children's work would be odd. I didn't think it'd be valuable for children to spend an entire writing workshop listing only characters' wants, for example. Also, I'm aware that sometimes separating items that belong together can actually make them more, not less, complicated. Notice that in an instance like this, I don't hesitate to devote a few sentences to making my teaching point as clear as possible.

❖ **Name the teaching point.**

"Today I want to teach you this: every fiction writer needs to know what his or her characters want and what keeps these characters from getting what they want. I also want to teach you that when you know what your characters yearn for, you don't just come right out and say what this is. You *show* what your characters want by putting examples of this into little small moments, into what fiction writers call *scenes*."

TEACHING

Show students an example of a published text in which the character wants something and encounters difficulties. Show that the author conveys this through showing action in a scene.

"I learned to do this by studying how published authors—writers like Julie Brinckloe and the authors of the short stories you've been reading—write little scenes (which could be called vignettes or Small Moment stories) that show what a character yearns for and what gets in the way for that character.

"In the book *Fireflies!*, at the very beginning of the story, the narrator sees the fireflies out the window while he's eating dinner. When we read the story, we come to know that he *yearns* to go out and catch fireflies so he can keep them as pets—but the author doesn't come right out and say that. Instead Julie Brinckloe shows this by putting examples of that yearning into scenes. Watch how Julie Brinckloe tells a Small Moment story (or a scene) that reveals what the narrator wants."

> *I ran from the table, down to the cellar to find a jar. I knew where to look, behind the stairs. The jars were dusty, and I polished one clean on my shirt. Then I ran back up, two steps at a time. "Holes," I remembered, "so they can breathe." And as quietly as I could, so she wouldn't catch me dulling them, I poked holes in the top of the jar with Momma's scissors. The screen door banged behind me, as I ran from the house. If someone said, "Don't slam it," I wasn't listening. I called to my friends in the street, "Fireflies!" But they had come before me with polished jars, and others were coming behind.*

Debrief. Mention that writers create little scenes and then piece them together like bricks. Point out that the scenes show characters in action in ways that reveal their desires and struggles.

"Some people say that fiction is like a brick wall, and the bricks that go together to make the story are scenes, or vignettes. This scene shows how much the narrator wanted to collect fireflies, how excited he was. When he races down the steps to the place where he knows the jars are we see how he's been thinking about catching fireflies for a while, and that he's done it before. When he remembers to poke holes in the jar, he knows it's important, but he also knows his mom wouldn't want him to dull her scissors, so he does it super quietly—the better to get outside quickly to the fireflies. We also see how excited this kid is when he mentions that if someone told him not to slam the door, he didn't hear it. He's seemed like a fairly polite kid and a good listener, so that fact that he couldn't hear anything the adults would have said to him tells us how focused he is on his task.

"When we are developing characters, then, we need to think not only about what our characters want and what gets in the way for them. We also need to think about how we can create little scenes that show all this."

Notice that I am referring to texts the whole class already knows. It would be very rare to read aloud a new text within a minilesson. There is nothing that makes Fireflies! *uniquely suited to this minilesson—any story would work. Use one that your class knows well.*

Also notice that usually there are two texts in any one minilesson. One of these is a text that threads through the teaching component of many minilessons, and the other is a text that threads through the active engagement of many minilessons.

Of course, you can decide to simplify this mini-lesson by letting some points fall aside. You may well want to end the minilesson by simply repeating that there are many things writers can show about characters, but there are just one or two things that writers must show: a character's wants and struggles.

ACTIVE ENGAGEMENT

Rename the longings and difficulties experienced by the character in the class's story, and then have children talk with their partners to bring these motivations and struggles to life in a scene.

"Let's try this with Luz. I'll get us started by thinking a little bit about what she wants." I assumed the posture I usually take when demonstrating that I am thinking.

"Let's see. Luz is afraid of the dark. We've already decided she's going to have a slumber party but she doesn't want everyone to know she's scared of the dark. That's the story, but what does she really *want*? I think she wants her friends to think she is cool. She feels different because her father is Mexican, and she wants them to accept her.

"So will you guys imagine a scene that could show some of this? Let's put Luz somewhere—packing for a slumber party, climbing into her sleeping bag at the party—and she is doing *something* (see if you and your partner can come up with an idea) that shows that she is afraid of the dark but doesn't want to use her night-light when her friends come because she wants to be accepted by them. Turn and talk. See if you have any suggestions for how we could write this into a scene." The room burst into conversation.

Convene the class and ask a child or two to share a suggestion. Help the child to turn an explanation into a scene. Debrief to point out the process needed to make a scene.

After a bit, I interrupted. "Writers, can I stop you? What ideas did you have for a little scene we could write that might show all this?"

Sirah's hand shot up. "You could show the slumber party and she says, 'Good night' and turns off the light and then lies there in the dark, listening to the noises and worrying."

Ramon added, "Or you could have her lying in her own bed, a couple days before the slumber party, with the lights off, practicing sleeping in the dark. She could get scared and get up and leave the closet light on."

"Those are both exciting ideas," I said. "Ramon, help me actually write what you envision. Class, you'll notice that Ramon and I can't actually write a scene until we can picture exactly what happens in a step-by-step way, with all the tiny, tiny actions. So Ramon, let's picture the whole thing like a movie in our minds. Luz is lying in bed, trying not to be afraid of the dark. What *exactly* is she doing? More specifically, what is Luz doing or saying to herself that shows the reader that she is scared of the dark and shows the reader that she is practicing sleeping with the lights off?"

"She is just looking up. She looks where the lamp usually shines. She doesn't want to lie in the dark but she tells herself, 'I gotta practice.'"

"I can picture it," I made it clear I was writing in-the-air: "'Luz stared through the darkness to where the light usually shone. "I've got to practice," she said to herself. She . . . ' What? What does she do next?"

Notice that although this is the active engagement section of the minilesson (when it's the kids' turn to do the work), I review the facts and begin the work I've proposed. In this way I give the children a running start, passing the baton to them only once momentum has been well established. This makes it much more likely that children can be active and productive even within a three-minute active engagement section.

Novice fiction writers are apt to explain what's going on rather than to show it. Notice that I help Ramon take his explanation of what's going on and imagine the actions that a character might take that would convey this. I do this not because I want to teach Ramon (I could do that later in a conference) but because I know that by helping him I can help most of the class.

You'll recall that this is the portion of the active engagement when the teacher calls on one member of the class to share what he or she just said or did. Usually we select carefully so that we call on children who help us make the point we hope to highlight. But sometimes we call on a child whose contribution is not exactly what we're after. This revision of one child's "writing-in-the-air" is a helpful way to demonstrate complex, sophisticated writing work.

"She closes her eyes so she won't see that it is dark. Then she gets out of bed and she opens the closet door and she pulls the light string on and she leaves the door open just a crack."

"So let me try that," I said. "Class, pay attention to the power of Ramon's tiny, tiny details. I'll even add some more," I said, and quickly wrote this scene on chart paper.

> I stared through the darkness to where my lamp usually shone brightly. "I've got to practice," I said to myself. I turned onto my stomach and squeezed my eyes shut. But even through my closed eyes, I could tell that the comforting glow from my bedside lamp was gone.
>
> Climbing out of bed, I opened the door to my closet, pulled the light string on, and then closed the door partway, careful to leave a crack of light shining into the bedroom.

Debrief. Reiterate that writers put their characters into situations—small scenes—that reveal their desires and their struggles.

"Ramon and I have put Luz in a situation where we can show what she wants and what she struggles with, and we have tried to write a little scene, a small moment, that shows all of this. Notice the words we chose that really brought the scene to life: *squeezed, shut, comforting glow, crack of light*. Do you see how these words highlight Luz's struggle to overcome her fear of the dark? All of you will write lots of scenes like this for your own character today, tomorrow, and whenever you want to write fiction."

LINK

Put today's teaching point into context by reminding writers of all they now know how to do. Stress that deciding what their character wants is not an option but is essential, and add this to the chart.

"So, writers, whenever you write fiction, remember there are oodles of things you *can* think about when you want to develop characters: a character's special places on earth, best friends, quirks, collections, and ways of waking up. There are oodles of things you *can* think about, but just one or two that you *must* think about: as fiction writers you must know what it is that your characters yearn for and what gets in their way.

"You usually build the story line out of your character's motivations and struggles—so once you know what your character yearns for and struggles to have, then it's wise to create little scenes that show this. Remember how we just put Luz somewhere—in bed—and came up with something she could be doing—practicing sleeping without a light on to get ready for the slumber party—to show what she longs for? You'll want to do this same work with your story idea, not once but many times today, and you'll want to remember to do this whenever you write fiction. The scenes you end up writing today may not end up in your stories. Writing them, like making the two-column chart, is a way to bring characters to life, and that's our greatest job right now." I added the latest point to the chart of advice.

Notice that I pick up exact phrases I used earlier in the minilesson. There are "oodles of things you can think about . . . and just one or two things you must think about." Notice, also, the parallel structure.

Donald Graves has said, "Fiction is really about character. It is about showing characters wanting things, having aspirations they hope will be fulfilled, or wanting a different life from the one they are living at the moment. Of course, it isn't long before all this 'wanting' produces tough choices, and negative and positive reactions from others. Usually the main character learns something about life itself" (Inside Writing: How to Teach the Details of Craft, 2005, 36).

Advice for Developing a Character

- Start with whatever you've decided matters to you about your character. Is he or she like you? Like someone you know?

- Put together a character so that all the parts fit together into a coherent person.

- Reread often, asking, "Do these different things make sense within one person? Do they fit together in a believable way? Are these traits here for a reason?"

- Open up any broad, general descriptors—words like <u>sensitive</u>—and ask, "What <u>exactly</u> does this word, this trait, mean for this particular character?"

- If a character seems too good to be true, make the character more complex and more human by asking, "What is the downside of this trait? How does this characteristic help and hurt the character?"

- Know your character's motivations (longings) and struggles.

Showing Characters by Writing Scenes

YOU MAY FIND THAT MANY OF YOUR WRITERS could benefit from a conference like the one I had with Francesca. I pulled my chair alongside her and saw she'd written the entry shown in Figure 4–1.

> Griffen likes to act like he is 13. He likes to act really cool.
> Sometimes he embarrasses himself in front of Julie Colings.
> Griffen really loves Julie. He is always trying to impress her but
> this boy Mikey the Bully always takes her away.

"Francesca," I said. "You've got a great idea for your story, and you've sketched out some notes on Griffen. Your next step will be to try writing some scenes that show Griffen and Julie in action. They probably won't be scenes you actually include in your final story, but writing them will help you know these characters better. Remember in the minilesson how we remembered what Luz wants, which is for kids to think she's cool and to not realize she's afraid to sleep without a night-light. So all of us imagined a scene that might show Luz doing something around those fears and wants. Ramon started off just summarizing by saying, 'Luz is lying in her bed, practicing sleeping in the dark. She could get scared,' but then he ended up making a movie in his mind that *showed* this. He had to picture it in a step-by-step way, and he started by thinking, 'What exactly is she doing?' That scene turned out this way."

I stared through the darkness to where my lamp usually shone brightly. "I've got to practice," I said to myself. I turned onto my stomach and squeezed my eyes shut . . .

"Francesca, you'll get to know Griffen so much better if you make him come to life in a scene in your notebook. I guess you already know he wants to impress Julie. Can you think of one particular time when Griffen acted cool, trying to impress Julie?" I waited until she nodded. "Now you need to ask yourself the same question: 'What *exactly* is Griffen doing? How does it start?'"

MID-WORKSHOP TEACHING
Sharing a Scene that Shows a Character's Traits

"Writers, I want to show you the important work Ariana is doing. Yesterday she wrote entries about her character. In one of them, she'd written this."

> Sally is different in front of her friends than her mom. She tries
> to talk really cool. Sally hates tomatoes, but her mom keeps making
> stuff she has to eat with tomatoes in it. That makes her mad.

"So today Ariana decided to try her hand at writing a scene that showed this, just like we did with Luz's fear of the night. You'll remember that to get started, we began by thinking, 'Where could Luz be? What could she be doing?' And so Ariana asked herself these same questions. She knew she wanted to show that her character, Sally, sometimes gets mad at her mother for making her eat things with tomatoes, and also Sally acts differently when she's talking to her friends. Pretty soon she'd written this scene." (See Figure 4–2.)

> Griffen likes to act like he is 13.
> He likes to act really cool sometimes
> he ImBarases his self in front of
> Julie Colings. Griffen really loves
> Julie. He is always trying to
> Impress her but this Boy Mikey
> the Bully always takes her away.

FIG. 4–1 Francesca's first draft of a scene

(continues)

I thump, thump, thump down the stairs into the kitchen.

"Hurry, we are having tomato soup tonight."

"Mom, I HATE tomato soup!" I yelled

"You have to."

"I don't got ah" I said in a strong voice. "Go upstairs right now, young lady," she said. I thumped back up the stairs and yelled, "I hate you." That's when my mom got really mad. I picked up the phone and dialed Sarah's number.

"Hello" she said.

"What-up?" I said.

"Nothing up, I got punished."

"I love that Ariana brought her character to life, writing a Small Moment story that *showed* the kind of person she is! So when you sit with your notebook in front of you today, before you start an entry, make a choice. Will you add to your chart, listing internal and external characteristics? Will you write *about* your story idea, thinking on the paper so that your entry sounds like, 'In my story, I might show . . . '? Or will you try the new work you learned about today and write a scene?"

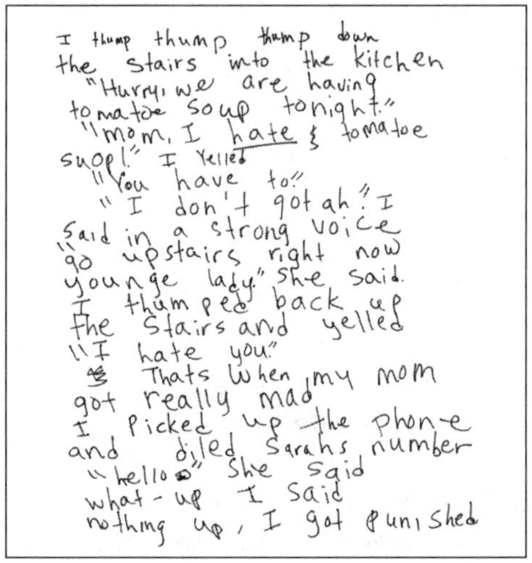
I thump thump thump down the stairs into the kitchen "Hurry, we are having tomatoe soup tonight." "mom, I hate tomatoe suop!" I yelled "You have to." "I don't got ah!" I said in a strong voice "go upstairs right now younge lady" She said. I thumped back up the stairs and yelled "I hate you." Thats when my mom got really mad I picked up the phone and diled Sarahs number "hello" She said what-up I said nothing up, I got punished

FIG. 4–2 Ariana's scene showing her character

"He and Timmy are riding their bikes and he . . . "

"So write that!" I said, dictating, "One time Timmy and Griffen . . . "

Francesca wrote this entry (see Figure 4–3).

> One time Timmy and Griffen were riding their bikes and he went by Julie Colings. Griffen quickly stopped. "Hi Griffen," she said in a loving way. "Hi Julie," Griffen said almost falling to the floor. "Well bye," Julie said. Griffen could not say another word. Then he fell on the floor . . .
>
> The next day Griffen saw some 13-year-olds skateboarding on a big ramp. Griffen wanted to impress Julie so he asked to try. Timmy told him that it was a bad idea but he did it. He landed flat on his face and the 13-year-olds teased him. Griffen was so embarrassed.
>
> Then Julie went over to him and pulled him up. "Are you ok?" she said. "Of course," Griffen said meekly. "Well bye," Julie said.

Meanwhile, I'd moved on to Felix, who'd written reams of notes about Max. "What a lot of work!" I exclaimed, and asked Felix to give me a guided tour of his entries. They seemed to have been written in a chain-of-thought style, with one detail about a character prompting the idea for a related detail. Max was at the park saying to people, "You dropped your brain," or "Your sock is untied." "He is not a bully but no bully goes

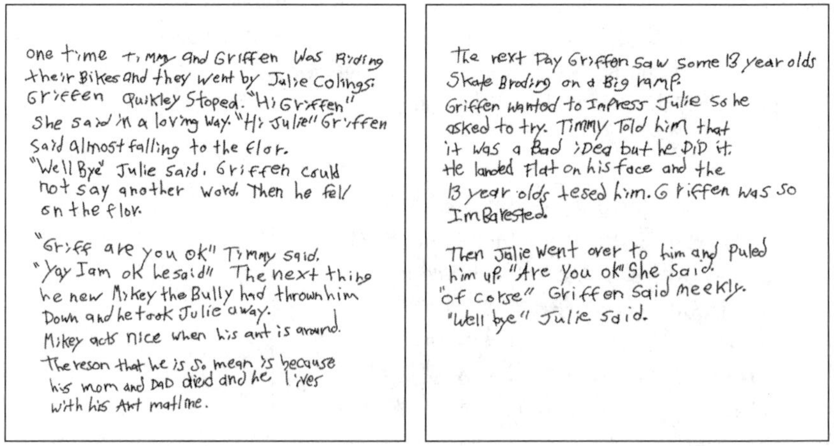
one time timmy and Griffen Was Riding their Bikes and they went by Julie Colings. Grieeen quikley Stoped. "Hi Griffen" She said in a loving way. "Hi Julie" Griffen Said almost falling to the flor. "Well Bye" Julie said. Griffen could not say another word. Then he fell on the flor.

"Griff are you ok" Timmy Said. "Yay I am ok he said" The next thing he new Mikey the Bully had thrown him Down and he took Julie away. Mikey acts nice when his ant is around. The reson that he is so mean is because his mom and DAD died and he lives with his Ant matline.

The next Day Griffen saw some 13 year olds Skate Broding on a Big ramp. Griffen wanted to Inpress Julie so he asked to try. Timmy Told him that it was a Bad idea but he DiD it. He landed flat on his face and the 13 year olds tesed him. Griffen was so Imbaresed.

Then Julie went over to him and puled him up. "Are you ok" She said. "of corse" Griffen said meekly. "Well bye" Julie said.

FIG. 4–3 Francesca's second draft of the scene

near him. He wants to be a boxer. He goes to boxing lessons." The details about Max clearly conveyed complexity. Felix wrote, "Max is very scared because there's this new kid. He's as strong as a bulldozer. He might cream Max." In addition, Max is scared of clowns and horses. Felix summarized the latter fear, saying, "Because one day Max's uncle owned a farm and they were going to ride on horses and there was a mean old one. Max still has a horseshoe scar but he puts cream on to hide it." (See Figure 4–4.)

After taking a guided tour through Felix's ten pages of entries, I asked, "What are you planning to do next as a writer?" Felix pointed out that he'd gathered entries especially about his main character, Max, and still needed to decide on his other characters and then develop them. I asked how he planned to decide on the secondary characters, and he said he figured he'd need to write about Max's parents, so he might start there.

"Felix," I said. "I want to congratulate you on the fact that you've developed a really complex, interesting character. You could have just made Max into a tough boxer, but you built in tension in your story idea, suggesting a new kid moves to town who could be even tougher than Max, and suggesting also that for all his cool, tough exterior, Max is still afraid of clowns and of horses. You've made him into a really human, complex, real sort of a person, and I can see why you're thinking of doing the same work for a host of other characters. You're really talented at developing characters, and I may want you to help others who struggle with this."

Then I said, "But Felix, instead of moving on to do similar work with a host of other characters, I think you'd profit by first trying to crystallize your story. If you worked now on a secondary character, it could be someone in the park, someone he boxes with, a person at the farm. I'd first zoom in a bit on the central tension of your story. I'd do that by taking some of the tensions you've created in your characters, and try to think through, 'What might end up being a turning-point moment for Max?' You could think about a time when he changes, maybe, or when he goes from being totally tough to being something else." Then I reminded Felix to zoom in on one particular moment, to envision it and to write the scene step by step. Before long, Felix had written these entries (see Figures 4–5 and 4–6).

Should I get on that horse? No, no, no. Do it. Stop going. I won't. I will. My little brother will make fun of me. He will tell everybody in school. I am scared of horses. What happens when it moves? Nothing. How do I stop it? Oh no, it goes faster. Stop, stop, stop, kablam. I am not getting on a horse ever! It smells, it's ugly, everything is bad. I'd rather babysit three-year-olds. I will hate horses for the rest of my life. Why did I get on that horse?

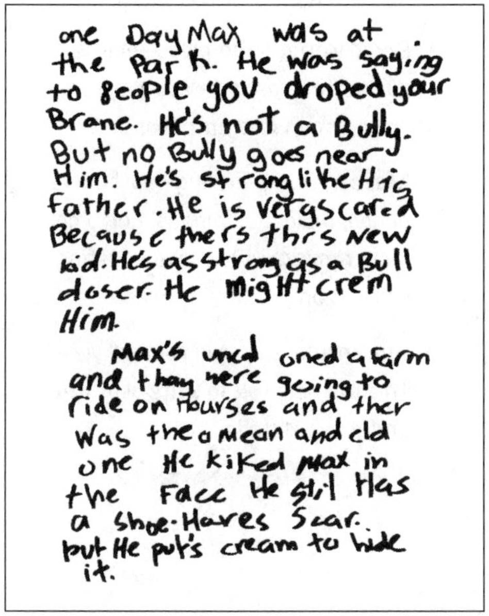

one Day Max was at the Park. He was saying to people you droped your Brane. He's not a Bully. But no Bully goes near Him. He's strong like His father. He is very scared Because thers this New kid. He's as strong as a Bull dozer. He might crem Him.

Max's uncl oned a farm and thay were going to ride on rourses and ther Was the a Mean and cld one He kiked Max in the Facc He stil Has a shoe-Haves Scar. but He put's cream to hide it.

FIG. 4–4 Felix's entry in which he develops the character of Max

scared to get on Horse
get on Horse
By axsadent said word to make Horse go
got off Hors
got mad
no More Horse rides

FIG. 4–5 Felix's timeline

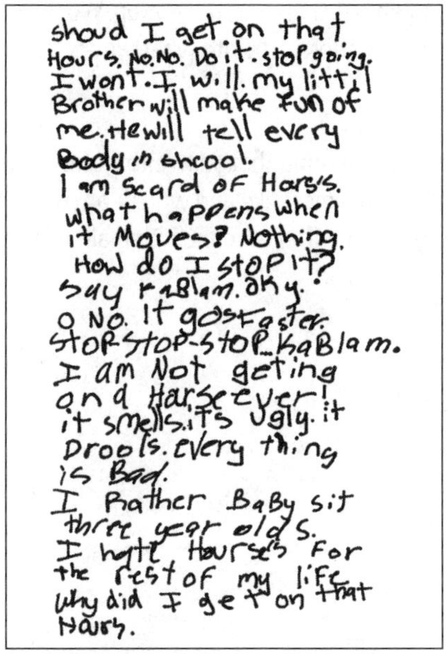

shoud I get on that Hours. No. No. Do it. stop going. I wont. I will. my littil Brother will make fun of me. He will tell every Body in shcool. I am scard of Harsis. what happens when it Moves? Nothing. How do I stop it? say raBlam. oky. o No. It gos Faster. stop stop stop kaBlam. I am Not geting and Harse ever! it smells its Ugly. it Drools. every thing is Bad. I Rather BaBy sit three year olds. I hytt Hourses For the rest of my life. why did I get on that Haurs.

FIG. 4–6 Felix puts his character, Max, into action—riding a horse.

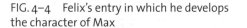

Mining Past Learning to Apply to Current Pieces

Share the work of one writer who used what he learned about writing in previous years. Explain that all writers can do likewise and invite them to begin.

"Ramon just did some important work that all of us could learn from. His story is about Marco, who knows his grandfather will leave soon for Jamaica and who wants to feel more connected to his grandfather before the old man leaves. Ramon didn't come right out and say any of this; instead he put his character, Marco, in the kitchen, cooking his grandfather some scrambled eggs as a way to do something for him. Ramon stretches out the action in the cooking scene, like all of you learned to do with your personal narratives. Marco cracks the eggs on the edge of the bowl and is afraid they'll slurp down the side of the bowl, and he's worried that the shells will go into the bowl and the breakfast will be ruined. But this is the really smart thing: when I asked Ramon how he'd thought to do this smart work, he said, 'I just wrote it like a small moment!'

"Based on Ramon's suggestion, I've found an old chart and hung it up. Would you get with your partner now and talk about that Small Moment story chart and your efforts to write what we are calling a *scene*? Because really, a scene in a fiction story *is* a small moment.

"If you see qualities of good personal narrative writing that you've forgotten to try to do, I don't suggest revising your writing. Instead, I suggest you take an entry you almost like and write it all over again, an entirely new version, this time using all that we already learned to help you write it as an effective small moment."

> **Qualities of Good Personal Narrative Writing**
>
> - Write a little seed story; don't write all about a giant watermelon topic.
>
> - Zoom in so you tell the most important parts of the story.
>
> - Include true, exact details from the movie you have in your mind.
>
> - Begin with a strong lead—maybe use setting, action, dialogue, or a combination to create mood.
>
> - Make a strong ending—maybe use action, dialogue, images, and whole story reminders to make a lasting impression.
>
> - Stay inside your own point of view. This will help you to write with true and exact details.

Plotting with a Story Arc

S OME PEOPLE IMAGINE THAT WRITERS put a pen to paper and out pours a story, or a novel, or a play, from beginning to end. In fact, that is how the writing process is often depicted in movies, giving the average person a romantic but false version of how writers work. We are fortunate to know from our own processes and through learning from countless writers over the years that the process involves as much organization as inspiration. This unit of study offers a perfect opportunity to teach children the power of rehearsal, and specifically, it gives us a chance to teach children that writers organize their ideas before they embark on a draft.

In this last session before drafting, we again remind writers of a template used by countless authors to structure the plotlines of their fiction—the story arc. The role of the story arc is as old as the idea of story. For a story to be a story, and not just a listing of events (much like a flat timeline might be), the events and the characters have to start in one place, and climb, facing obstacles and challenges, coming out changed on the other side. As an organizing tool, the story arc acts like a timeline or an outline. It allows the writer to step outside the details of the story to see the big picture. Some writers imagine that there is some sort of pivotal movement at the apex of the arc that changes everything. Other writers see not one big moment or conflict, but rather a series of events that end up in a change for the character of some sort. The goal of the story arc is to help the writer to be able to see the big picture shape of his story—to make sure it will move and evolve as the events unfold and not be a plodding list of moments linked together only by chronology. It might help for you to consider either designing your own story arc for a story of your own invention or spending some time looking at the story arcs of published books. Try to steer your students from the common misconception that a story arc means that they need to have dozens of little scenes to make up the arc. An arc can be made up of simply two or three scenes. Think of the classic "boy meets girl, boy loses girl, boy gets girl" as a perfect example of story arc. Not that you need share that example with your students!

This session also emphasizes that story arcs are tools for revision. Because children will be writing in scenes and not in summaries, they'll probably need to revise their story

IN THIS SESSION, you'll teach children that writers sketch out possible plotlines for stories, often in story arcs that represent traditional story structure.

GETTING READY

✔ Story arc on chart for *Fireflies!* by Julie Brinckloe (see Teaching)

✔ Story arc of shared class story, created in active engagement

✔ "How to Write a Fiction Story" anchor chart (see Link)

COMMON CORE STATE STANDARDS: W.4.3.a,b,d; W.4.4, W.4.5, W.4.10, RL.4.1, RL.4.5, RL.4.10, RL.5.5, SL.4.1, L.4.1, L.4.2, L.4.3

plans by zooming in on just two or perhaps three key moments. Encourage students to try many versions of their story arcs. The more they try, the more likely they will land on a story structure that works for them. Remind them that tomorrow they will begin drafting and they will want the best possible story arcs to carry with them.

"*This unit of study offers a perfect opportunity to teach children the power of rehearsal, and specifically, it gives us a chance to teach children that writers organize their ideas before they embark on a draft.*"

Before this session, you would be wise to reread the fiction mentor text your students are most familiar with. In this session it is *Fireflies*. You might direct students to notice the structure and how the events of the story move from one moment to the next. As many long time workshop teachers can attest, it is very helpful for students who are relying on a mentor text to learn about writing to know that text as well as readers.

Plotting with a Story Arc

CONNECTION

Remind children that once fiction writers have brought their characters to life, they use knowledge of the characters' wants and struggles to develop a possible plotline.

"Writers, a few days ago, I told you that fiction writers don't just go from choosing a story idea to writing a draft. Instead, fiction writers have strategies for bringing people to life, strategies like thinking about the internal and the external characteristics of the main character, the protagonist. They go through their lives thinking, 'What would my character do in this situation?' They give special attention to what a character yearns for and struggles with.

"Writers postpone thinking about what happens in a story, about the plot of a story, until they've done this other work. They postpone thinking about the sequence of events because eventually they take all they know about their characters—especially their understanding of what their characters yearn for and struggle with—and they use this information to create a plan for their stories.

"You'll probably remember that when you wrote your personal narratives in third grade, you got ready to write by remembering what happened and plotting the sequence of events on little timelines or perhaps with story arcs."

Before now, children may have drafted scenes that put their characters into motion and revealed them as people, but those scenes will probably not comprise the start of their story. Before a fiction writer can write her lead, the writer needs to know the character, to imagine him or her in action, and to have drafted, chosen between, and revised multiple plotlines for the story. Today, then, children will consider a variety of ways their stories could unroll.

❖ **Name the teaching point.**

"Today I want to teach you that after you develop your characters, you draft possible story arcs. And I want to teach you something new about plotting your story, something that will help you whenever you write fiction from now on! Fiction writers plan by plotting the arc of the story—and specifically, by aiming to intensify the problem.

"Writer Patricia Reilly Giff says that the fiction writer's job is to make every part so interesting that the reader can't wait to turn the page. She says some writers call that 'plotting,' but she calls it 'making the problem worse and worse!' Story arcs can help you do that because they remind you that it's not just one event after another, with no real change or climb. It's like each scene in the arc is a whole new movement for your character. That's what makes readers want to keep reading, to find out how the character will get to the other side of this arc.

Notice that I teach story arcs within the context of a bigger focus—thinking about how the story will go in general (across the pages). Only after emphasizing that the character will get himself or herself into a growing mess of trouble do I mention that this is signified by the rising slope of the story arc. I'm trying to be sure the graphic organizer functions as a symbolic representation for the story itself.

"The story arc also shows you that something is going to happen, and things are getting tough, and then something happens as the story arcs that changes things or that solves your character's problem. After that, things change, your character is different, and there isn't a feeling of anticipation anymore."

TEACHING

Explain why a writer would use a story arc to help plan a plot. Teach children that writers are not always sure of what might happen in their story when they first set out to draft a plan.

"Writers, in reading workshop, we discussed how stories have a way they usually go. And we learned that usually the main character has wants, and something gets in the way of the character getting all that he or she wants. So the character encounters trouble, or a problem. And today we learned that usually after encountering the problem, the character has to deal with that problem somehow, giving movement to the story—making sure the story isn't just going from one event to another in a flat way, but rather, each scene builds on the one before it.

"Let's take a look back at a story we have been studying, *Fireflies!*, and how it could be outlined using a story arc," I said.

"You'll remember that when I read aloud *Fireflies!* to you, we talked about how the story went, how the events fit together, what its shape is. If it were to be written up on an arc, it might look something like this," I said, turning to a chart where I had recorded the main events of the story on an arc.

> The narrator gets ready to catch fireflies
> He goes out and catches fireflies with his friends
> He comes home and puts the fireflies next to his bed
> He watches their lights start to fade
> He doesn't want to let them go
> He lets them go

"When Julie Brinckloe wrote this story, she probably knew that it would be about a boy catching fireflies and having to decide whether or not to set them free. But she probably didn't know, when she started to write the story, exactly what would happen on every page. I bet she imagined one way the story might go, and another, and another.

"Authors always know that the trouble will grow and that characters will make choices—some of which probably won't work out. And authors know that *somehow*, in the midst of all the trouble, *somehow* there will be *something* that makes a difference. I bet Julie Brinckloe didn't start her book realizing all the little details. She probably didn't know before she started writing that the boy wouldn't just let the fireflies go free right away, that he would wait until they almost died before he let them go.

I'm especially aware that I'm oversimplifying the resolution part of a story, setting children up to believe that in every story characters achieve all that they want—which is far, far from true.

44

"When we plot our Luz story, I know that our character will struggle to achieve what she yearns for. Our character will make choices. Some of those choices may not work out. We don't know which ones, exactly. But we do know that something will happen that makes a difference. Our character will find a way to resolve the struggle, or she will change her sense of what she wants.

"And we know that just as a story arc climbs and then changes, Luz will take actions, and things will happen that will result in a change."

ACTIVE ENGAGEMENT

Demonstrate planning a possible plotline based on the story idea the class has been following.

"So let's try planning our Luz story, the one that Ramon helped us start, keeping the story arc in mind. In the draft we've already begun, we have Luz lying in bed, practicing sleeping without a light on so she can sleep in the dark at a slumber party. Then she gets up to turn on the closet light. Before fiction writers move forward to plot the whole story, it helps to rethink the start of it. Do you want to keep what we have so far as the very beginning? (This does show Luz's fears.) Or we could alter the beginning, perhaps in a way that more dramatically shows what she wants, and only then shows her fears.

"Talk with your partner and think what the scene in our arc should be. The starting scene must bring Luz to life, show what she yearns for, and show the trouble (which we already know will be her fear of sleeping in the dark and of being embarrassed in front of her friends). And remember, things need to climb and get harder before things change, so think about how we'll then make Luz's problem get worse. Turn and plan the start of our story arc."

Everyone started to talk. I moved among the partners. Marissa said, "Let's think of a different beginning, one that shows she wants friends. We could have Luz decide to hold a slumber party. Then she gets worried who'll come."

I nodded. "But try to think about that in terms of actions. What exactly might you show Luz *doing* when she decides to have a slumber party? How does the movie in your mind actually go at this starting scene?"

Marissa answered, "She realizes her birthday is just two weeks away. Then she starts writing invitations."

I nodded. "But you can't *tell* that she realizes her birthday is coming. What could she do? Imagine this as a movie. What would the character be doing that shows her realizing this?"

Marissa jumped up with excitement. "She looks at a calendar?"

Convene the class. Report on overheard ideas for how the story could begin.

"Writers, I heard some great ideas. Some of you suggested we alter the start to show first that Luz is hoping lots of friends come to her birthday party. Marissa thought the story could begin with Luz looking at a calendar, realizing

In this minilesson, you'll notice that the teaching component is brief because most of the teaching is embedded in the active engagement. I mostly told and reviewed, and I did not show—an exception from the norm.

The story arc is useful because it provides a concrete image for thinking about a complicated idea. When teaching students about the story arc, I draw a hill shape on a chart and model the plot points that move the character toward a moment when he or she solves a problem, confronts someone, changes, or learns something.

Anne Lamott, in Bird by Bird, *reminds us of the relationship between character development and the story arc. "Find out what each character cares most about in the world," she writes, "because then you will have discovered what's at stake" (1995, 55).*

Notice that in this active engagement children are not only working on the teaching point of the day. They're also synthesizing all they know to collaboratively author a story. This is an unusual active engagement for this reason.

John Gardner, one of our leading novelists and the author of The Art of Fiction *(1991), describes writing fiction by saying, "One of the chief mistakes a writer can make is to allow or force the reader's mind to be distracted, even momentarily, from the fictional dream." The writer encourages the reader to dream by presenting as many concrete details as possible. I'm trying, in this intervention, to elicit those concrete details and to remind writers that the story is carried by scenes, not summary.*

her birthday was approaching, and beginning to address invitations. Would you be willing to have our story start like Marissa suggests?" I asked, and when children agreed, jotted an abbreviated version of Marissa and Ramon's points on the class story arc and retold those scenes from the story.

Set children up to imagine what might come next, then convene the children and add their ideas to the story arc.

"What could come next? Remember, you'd need to *show* (not summarize) her struggle and that the problems need to get worse. Turn to your partner and plan."

Again I listened in, and after a bit I again paraphrased what I'd heard a child suggest. Soon the story arc contained these scenes.

◆ Luz looks at a calendar and starts writing lots of birthday invitations and gets worried people will find out about her fear of the dark.

◆ Her friends don't like her games.

◆ Her plan to leave the closet light on fails.

◆ She has to face her fear of the dark OR her fear of being embarrassed.

Model for the students that the story could also go another way.

"Great. We have one fantastic story arc. But, just like any other part of the writing process, we know that we should give it a few goes before we decide on the perfect arc. I heard a few other ways the story could go too. I heard Hannah and her partner saying that the story could start right at the party." I drew a line under our first story arc and created a new arc with these points.

◆ Luz welcomes everybody to her party and shows people around, avoiding the closet.

◆ Her friends don't like her games.

◆ She can't leave the closet light on, or she'll give herself away.

◆ She decides to tell someone that she's afraid.

"The first job of a story's beginning is to start at the right time. It should not start when things are quiet, when nothing's happening, when things are much the same as they always have been. After all, the whole reason we tell the story is because something about life is new and different, something's happening that stands out—and your responsibility, as the writer, is to begin the work at that point of change" (The Artist's Torah, Ebenbach, 60).

Philip Gerard, in his chapter "An Architecture of Light: Structuring the Novel and Story Collection" suggests that stories have a "signature" that can be stated in a single sentence. The signature for Moby Dick *is "Madman goes hunting for a white whale." This line defines what Gerard refers to as the "structural arc" of the story. He writes, "Think of the signature as the cable that hauls the rollercoaster cars up the long hill of suspense, round the hair pin turn of reversal, down the stomach-clenching fall"* (152).

Most importantly, Gerard says that although writers begin with our structural arc and our characters clearly in mind, "almost everything will change" (153).

LINK

Remind writers that when fiction writers plot story arcs they do so knowing the problems will get worse before they get better.

"So, writers, I hope you've been reminded today that the time comes when fiction writers plot their stories. They are usually not sure exactly what will happen next, but they plan the start of the story against the shape of an arc, remembering that they can't just write any old thing next. In our Luz story, after she makes the invitations, we can't have her grandmother arrive and the family go to dinner, forgetting all about her being afraid of the dark and the slumber party! Instead, when we ask ourselves, 'What will happen next?' we already know that Luz's struggles to master her fear of the dark and to have friends will have to get worse before they get better."

Encourage students to try multiple story arcs, each one improving on the one before.

"Writers, I know many of you are pretty sure that you know exactly how your story should go, but it's important that you make sure to try a few different story arcs just to make sure you have the best one you can make. Push yourself to come up with two or three different ones, each one better than the one before it. I've added this newest strategy to our "How to Write a Fiction Story" anchor chart.

"Off you go! Draft your story arcs, and do so making the problem worse and worse, like writers always do!"

> ### How to Write a Fiction Story
>
> - Develop a strong story idea, character(s), and setting.
> - Spend time planning how the plot will go, making sure there is an arc to the story, trying again and again until the plan feels just right.

Building Story Arcs

I DREW MY CHAIR FIRST ALONGSIDE CALEB, who had taped his plan for his story onto the corner of his desk and was now staring at a half-written page. "You've put your story arc just exactly where Rachel, in 'Eleven,' "put that red sweater," I said. "It's on the tippy top corner of your desk, could hang over the edge like a waterfall, I bet you'd push it there! Are you trying to get it out of sight, out of mind?"

Caleb laughed and assured me that he wasn't mad at the story *arc*, just at the story. I glanced at the graph, noticing that instead of marking specific Small Moment scenes in it, he'd labeled general trajectories he'd planned for the story (see Figure 5–1).

But it seemed he was preoccupied with other worries. "So what's troubling you?" I asked.

"I want to show Spencer walking to school, worrying about Humphrey, the bully. But I just keep telling what's in his brain: 'I'm worried. I'm so worried. I'm really worried.' There isn't any way to *show* his worries except if he looks up and down the block like James Bond or something," he said.

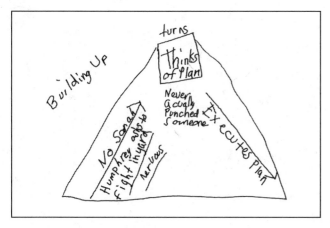

FIG. 5–1   Caleb's story arc

MID-WORKSHOP TEACHING
Finding Story Arcs in Published Stories

"I need to stop you for just a moment and tell you something really wonderful that's going on right now. I just saw Ari get up quietly from his seat and grab his folders. Then I noticed he was going back and rereading some of the realistic fiction short stories we've been reading as a class. I wasn't sure what he was doing at first, but then I talked to Ari and realized he was doing something so smart. Ari, can you tell people what you were up to?"

Ari held up his notebook to show a rough story arc. "I was getting a little confused as I tried to put my story into an arc. So I thought, well, if most stories have a story arc, I'll go and see what other writers did. I went back to look at 'The Marble Champ' by Gary Soto, and I noticed that the story starts with Lupe getting her thumb all ready for the marble competition, in lots of different ways. So I decided to look for what would be the top of the arc in 'The Marble Champ' and to make a story arc from that story. I think Lupe's last battle where she wins the championship is the top of the curve. Because after that she got everybody's cheers, and the trophy, and her family gave her that party, and then everything seems to calm down."

I thanked Ari, and then said to the class, "Writers, if you can pull yourselves away from work on your own story, it'd be helpful for you to try what Ari did. Consider looking for a story you can use as a model for your own story. Plot the story arc in the text you select as a mentor text. And remember, you need to continue thinking and writing about your characters even as you plot out possible story lines."

"Caleb," I responded. "You are doing what every fiction writer—really, what every writer—does. You've identified the writing problem that your story line poses. Some stories are hard because there are lots of characters, some are hard because time jumps backward and forward. Yours is hard (or at least the start of it is hard) because you want to show what your character is thinking and feeling, and yet he's walking all alone. So the problem you are struggling with is this: how does an author reveal a character's thoughts and still show, not tell? It is really smart for you to identify the problem!"

Then I said, "What I do when I encounter a problem is that instead of thinking about what the final solution will be, I switch my brain over and think, 'What strategies could I use to at least get me started on this?' So that means, for example, I'd probably sit here and just list optional ways to solve the problem. I'd brainstorm possible ways to go about solving it. How could you *maybe* solve it?"

Caleb generated a couple of ideas, culminating in the idea to add Sarah, Spencer's friend, into this section of the story. Soon he'd begun a new draft of the lead (see Figures 5–2).

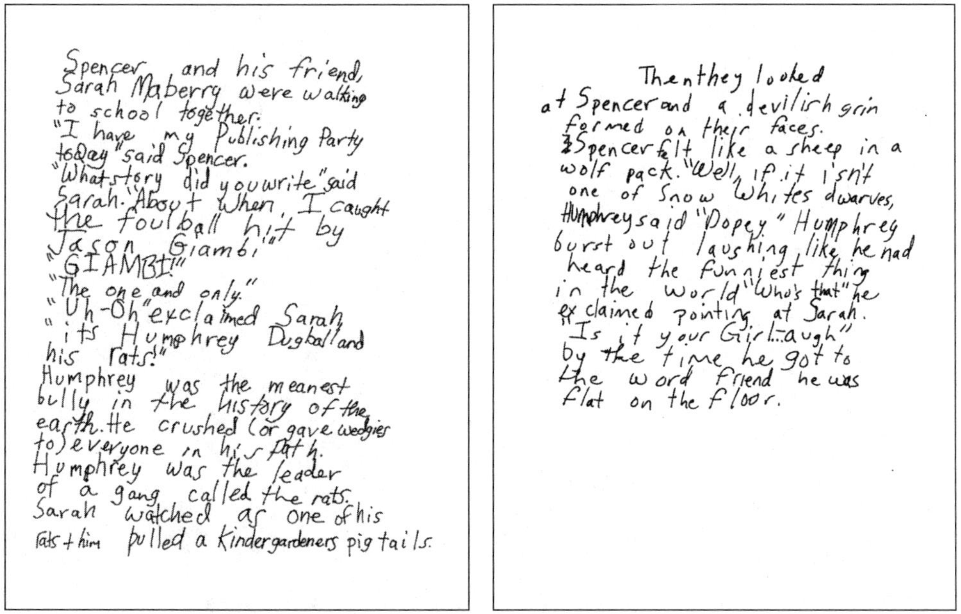
Spencer and his friend,
Sarah Maberry were walking
to school together.
"I have my Publishing Party
today" said Spencer.
"What story did you write" said
Sarah. "About when I caught
the foul ball hit by
Jason Giambi."
"GIAMBI!"
"The one and only."
"Uh-Oh" exclaimed Sarah
"its Humphrey Dugball and
his rats!"
Humphrey was the meanest
bully in the history of the
earth. He crushed (or gave wedgies
to) everyone in his path.
Humphrey was the leader
of a gang called the rats.
Sarah watched as one of his
rats + him pulled a kindergardeners pig tails.

Then they looked
at Spencer and a devilish grin
formed on their faces.
Spencer felt like a sheep in a
wolf pack. "Well, if it isn't
one of Snow Whites dwarves,
Humphrey said "Dopey." Humphrey
burst out laughing like he had
heard the funniest thing
in the world. "Who's that" he
exclaimed pointing at Sarah.
"Is it your Girl..augh"
by the time he got to
the word friend he was
flat on the floor.

FIG. 5–2 Caleb has added a second character into his lead.

Spencer and his friend, Sarah Mayberry were walking to school together.

"I have my publishing party today," said Spencer.

"What story did you write?" said Sarah.

"About when I caught the foul ball hit by Jason Giambi."

"GIAMBI!"

"The one and only."

"UhOh," exclaimed Sarah, "It's Humphrey Dugball and his rats!"

Humphrey was the meanest bully in the history of the earth. He crushed (or gave wedgies to) everyone in his path. Humphrey was the leader of a gang called the rats.

Sarah watched as one of his rats and him pulled a kindergartner's pig tails. Then they looked at Spencer and a devilish grin formed on their faces. Spencer felt like a sheep in a wolf pack.

"Well if it isn't one of Snow White's dwarves," Humphrey said. "Dopey." Humphrey burst out laughing like he had heard the funniest thing in the world. "Who's that," he exclaimed pointing at Sarah. "Is it your Girl . . . augh" by the time he got to the word 'friend' he was flat on the floor.

Once Caleb had written this lead, we again conferred. I pointed out that with the arrival of Humphrey, he'd definitely created some tension, but he hadn't really had a chance to develop Spencer's character or to show what Spencer wanted before Humphrey arrived on the scene. With that in mind, Caleb decided to revise his story arc. "Fiction writers do that a lot," I told him. "They shift back and forth between planning possible story arcs, writing a scene or two, rereading and rethinking what they've written, and revising their story arcs."

Next I gathered a group of children together for a strategy lesson. "I want to talk to all of you together," I said, "because each of you has a great plan for a *novel.*" I added, "But I want to remind you that you are writing a very short story, and before you get much farther, you need to do some rethinking. When you plot out your story, the first point on it will probably belong to one Small Moment story, to one vignette. And then you'll probably leap ahead to a second and maybe a third moment, but by then the story will need to be complete." Then I suggested we all look together at Felix's tentative plans, using that as a case in point. Felix had already made a timeline that began with Max winning his first boxing trophy. Then Felix shows that Max practiced to win more, followed by Max having a fight with his nemesis, followed by Max's first loss and the arrival of a girlfriend (see Figure 5–3).

"You need to go back to that question," I said. "What does Max most want? Fear? Struggle toward?" The group of children helped Felix revise his plans and sketch a story arc, and then they each brought out their own work. Soon the children had stories that were at least somewhat focused!

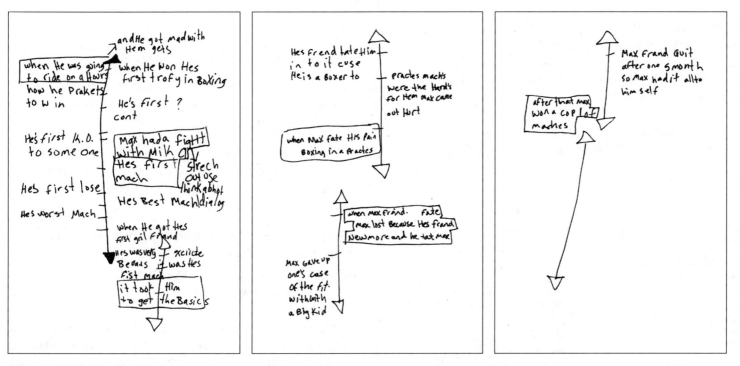

FIG. 5–3   Felix's timeline

Choosing the Story Arcs that Map Our Stories the Best

Guide students to choose their strongest story arc.

"I saw tons of very intriguing story arcs being worked on today! I really can't wait to get a chance to look more closely at them. I also noticed that many of you made more than two or three. No matter how many you made, though, you will need to choose one that you think will make the best possible story. Can you, right now, read through your arcs and put a star on the one you think is strongest? The one you think will make the best story? If you're having a hard time, feel free to get your partner's opinion."

Explain that story arcs can be maps for writers' imaginations, allowing them to picture with detail how each moment might go.

Once I noticed that most students had their eyes on me, I called them back. "I know for many of you it was a hard choice. You have a couple of really good options. What a great problem to have! The good news is now that you have a story arc that you really like, it's a bit like having a map to someplace you want to go. You know how sometimes when you go someplace, like an amusement park or a museum, there's a map that allows you to see everything that is there? Well, if you're anything like me, you look at each place on the map and imagine exactly what that place will look like and also how you will get from one place to the next.

"Here's a little tip. You can do that with story arcs too. Except story arcs don't keep you from getting lost in a museum. Story arcs help writers make sure that they don't get lost in their stories. Even more importantly, story arcs help you to let your imaginations explore a little bit about how each scene might go and how to get to the next scene. We can imagine those things without fear, because our story arcs will help us keep from going too far off. Tomorrow we will begin drafting, so it would be really good practice to help you get ready for drafting by allowing your minds to follow the map of your story arcs. Can you right now look at a point on your story arc, and tell your partner how you imagine that scene playing out in your story? Where will it take place? Who will be in it? What will they say? What will they do? How will the character get to the next scene?"

Drafting and Revising with an Eye toward Believability

Show, Don't Tell

Planning and Writing Scenes

IN THIS SESSION, you'll teach children that writing scenes is, in a sense, the same as writing Small Moment stories. Writers often begin by putting the character into action or by laying out the character's exact words and then unfolding the moment step by step.

GETTING READY

✔ A snippet of conversation between children about their writing, illustrating that it's time to write (see Connection)

✔ Chart paper booklet for mapping out the class story

✔ Two retellings of *The Three Billy Goats Gruff* or other familiar fairy tale, one retelling as a summary and the other retelling as a scene from the story (see Teaching)

✔ Drafting booklets or draft paper for students

✔ "How to Write a Fiction Story" anchor chart (see Link)

COMMON CORE STATE STANDARDS: W.4.3.a,b; W.4.4, W.4.5, W.4.10, RL.4.3, RL.4.5, RL.5.5, SL.4.1, SL.4.2, SL.4.4, L.4.1, L.4.2, L.4.3.a

TODAY BEGINS A NEW BEND IN THIS UNIT. Your children will shift from planning to drafting. This is the place where the rubber hits the road. It is important to build up students' excitement over their move from developing to actually drafting. The more enthusiasm they have for drafting, the better they will be able to approach any challenges offered by the work. You'll help them use their story arcs as guides in creating story booklets, transferring one event from the arc onto one page of the booklet, and then you'll help them story-tell (not summarize) their plotlines. Above all, you'll help them see that "show, don't tell" pertains to an entire draft, not just to one selected passage.

It is easy to tell writers, "Show, don't tell." But as a writer there is never a day when I don't struggle to follow this seemingly simplistic adage. Donald Murray has referred to "show, don't tell" as the most important quality of all dramatic writing. Instead of simply coaching students to "Show, don't tell" try to practice what you preach and *show them* what "show, don't tell" really means. Remind your students that they practiced this work in years past when they wrote personal narratives or Small Moment stories, as well as when they wrote fairy tales.

In this session, you'll once again say to students, "Writers bring characters to life by setting them in motion." You'll show children that instead of saying, "Leo was mean," a writer shows Leo kicking his cat. Instead of saying, "Sasha was upset," the writer shows Sasha tearing out of the room, calling, "See if I care!"

Your minilesson alone can't be your only vehicle for teaching children that we come to know people through actions. Watch your children, and spot one child making a generous gesture. Point out to the class that this child's actions reveal who he is as a person. "I watched Felix lend Paige his best pen, and I learned something about Felix through his actions," I recently said to the class. "I learned how generous Felix can be." Actions reveal character.

Of course, you'll also want to pause in the midst of reading aloud to talk about the character's behaviors, and point out that in similar ways, children are using actions to bring their characters to life on their pages.

Show, Don't Tell

Planning and Writing Scenes

CONNECTION

Use an overheard comment about writing to illustrate that there comes a time when writers need to move from planning to drafting.

"Writers, while you were lining up to come in this morning, I heard Emily tell Rachel that she can't figure out exactly what her character will do all along the way in her story. Emily *knows* her character wants to dance a solo in her dance recital and that every time she performs in class, she messes up, but Emily can't decide exactly *how* her character messes up."

You'll want to refer to a conversation you hear your own children having. The important thing is that you keep your ear to the ground, and that you hear evidence that your children's work on their stories is becoming the "talk of the town." Engagement matters tremendously, and it deserves your attention.

Remind children that when the time comes to write, writers can use paper in a way that flows from the organization they've set out. In this case, tell children that writers can use a separate page for each scene on their story arc, and demonstrate by transferring dots on the class story arc onto the early pages of a booklet.

"So I told Emily something that I want to teach you—that yes, there comes a time when writers need to stop planning and write. Sometimes it's easier to plan once we are already writing. Often the best details are those that come out of our pens, surprising us.

"So today I want to remind you that when we want to write a story, it helps to think carefully about the paper we'll use. In this case, I suggest we write our stories in drafting booklets that have one or two pages for the opening scenes of the story and then several pages for the heart of the story, and a page or two for the ending scene. You may want to write a few words, or a sentence at the top of each scene as a description of what that scene will be about. Then you know where to start and where you're going, roughly. Writers always try to make their materials support the plans they have for writing.

You'll probably use the word scene *synonymously with* small moment. *By* scene, *we mean a bit of continuous drama—as in one part of a play. In your own mind, think of a scene as a Small Moment story, and keep in mind that it includes a flow of related minievents.*

"We already know that narratives are made up of scenes, or Small Moment stories. Many fiction writers get themselves ready to write a draft of a story by gathering a booklet of paper and thinking through plans for what they'll probably write on each page of the booklet. I usually give myself a different page, a different piece of paper, for each scene on my story arc. Then I just start writing my scene, jump right into the action, like I would for a Small Moment story, because really, that's all short stories are: a few small moments, or scenes, stacked on top of each other."

You could, of course, decide against encouraging your children to write in story booklets, steering them instead toward notebook pages. We chose the booklets because they are a concrete way to encourage children to take their time, stretching out the story. But there is nothing sacred about writing in booklets.

Looking at the first page of a chart paper booklet (on which I'd already written a scene title), I said, "Marissa helped us realize we could start the story with Luz looking at a calendar, realizing her birthday is two weeks away, and sending out invitations. We realized she'd definitely be dreaming of all the friends who'd come, but she'd be nervous too."

Then I said, "I copied the lead Marissa helped us write onto one page of our drafting booklet." Then I turned to page 2 and, looking at the story arc, I said, "I think time will need to jump ahead until it's the day of the sleepover and Luz is getting everything ready and starting to worry about her fear of being revealed, so I wrote, 'Luz got ready for her party' on a fresh page. After I finish setting up my whole draft, I'll come back to this page and write this scene, or Small Moment story. But for now, let me move on to thinking about what might happen next in the story.

"Writers, after you've planned out your story, you'll want to work on a lead. Before you do, I want to remind you that throughout most of your story, you'll be writing in scenes, not summaries."

> Luz looks at a calendar and starts writing lots of birthday invitations.
>
> She starts to worry about her fear of dark coming out.
>
> Her friends don't like her games.
>
> Her plan to leave the closet light on fails.
>
> She has to face her fear of the dark OR her fear of being embarrassed.

❖ **Name the teaching point.**

"Today I want to teach you that when writers want to create a scene, they need to create drama. Writers sometimes use a line of dialogue—making a character talk. Or they describe a small action. They make the character move or react physically to what is going on in the scene."

TEACHING

Illustrate the difference between summary and scene by telling a familiar tale in two contrasting ways.

"Let me remind you of the difference between writing summaries and writing scenes," I said. "Listen while I tell the story of 'The Three Billy Goats Gruff' in a summary way, like a stream of words rushing past."

> *It's a story about three goats who are trying to cross a bridge to go eat some grass on the other side, and there's this troll who wants to eat them. So as he goes across, each goat tricks him by promising he can eat the next goat, who is even bigger. The troll's greedy, so he waits for the next one, but the biggest goat pushes him in the water, so they all get across safely. The end.*

"Didn't you feel like that story just rushed by you? Didn't you want me to slow down and give the troll a voice and make some sound effects and put in some suspense to help you see and hear what is happening?

I told this story in a purposely hurried, monotone way, emphasizing the summary feeling. I do this for two reasons. First of all, it is easier to tell a story using story language and dramatic flair once the storyteller or writer has some sense for the bare bones of the story. Telling the story in summary fashion acts rather as a timeline, scaffolding the storytelling that will follow. I also summarize the story to define what a story is by highlighting what it is not. A story is not a discussion, a summary.

"Now listen as I write-in-the-air a scene from that story."

> "That's the greenest green grass I've ever seen in my life," said Third Goat. "Can we go over to that hill to eat some, pleeeeeeese?"
>
> "Yeah, we're hungry!" said Second Goat. So First Goat placed one hoof gingerly onto the little wooden bridge that would carry them over the rushing river to a delightful afternoon snack. The bridge felt good and sturdy. "Nothing's stopping us! Follow me!" And First Goat stepped out onto the bridge toward the grassy hillside.
>
> "No No NO!" boomed a voice. "Who dares to cross my bridge?" Suddenly, First Goat felt the hot breath of a troll on his muzzle!

"Can you hear the difference between that stream of words, just telling, telling, telling what happened, and then the sound when my characters talked in their character voices?"

Explain that this storytelling is what will be written for each scene in their story booklets.

"So you can just imagine that it would never work if I went back to the page in my story booklet that says 'Luz got ready for her party' and just wrote under it":

> Luz had a hard time picking what to wear and how to get her apartment ready. She thought about it and decided to just pick an outfit she liked and hung all the decorations up.

The kids laughed at the ridiculousness of that suggestion. I shook my head, as if I had never seen anything like it before. "No, I would want to write this scene exactly like a storyteller would, telling every little piece so that my readers feel like they are standing right beside Luz." I picked up my marker and returned to my draft to write a few lines.

> Luz stared at the clothes hanging in her closet until her eyes were blurry. Nothing looked good to her. She wanted to look cool, grown-up. But all her clothes looked like little kid clothes, or else were too ratty to wear to a party. She bit her lip, "There's got to be something I can wear."

ACTIVE ENGAGEMENT

Set children up to story-tell a moment from their stories to each other. Then share one child's summary, inviting the class to reimagine it as a story.

"Let's try it together. Will each of you think of a moment from your story arc—perhaps the moment that could become the start of your story? And will you turn to your partner and take turns saying your little moment first like a summary of what's happening?

"Okay, great! Let's listen to Caleb's summary, and see if we can help him reimagine this as a story."

As I stretch out a moment from the story, I use my voice purposely again, this time to give body to the words and help children really hear the difference.

There is a reason why I appeal to the listener's sense of sound, of voice. I believe some children need to learn about story almost viscerally, from soaking it up. Mem Fox describes how she learned story, saying, "It came from the constant good fortune of hearing great literature beautifully delivered into my ear, and from there into my heart, and from my heart into my bones." Mem goes on to write, "All this makes me wonder whether we, as teachers of writers, focus too much on the mind: have we forgotten, or did we ever know, the explosive power, the necessity of focusing also on the ear?"

It might be hard for children to mentally shuffle through their entries, settling on one in which they summarized a tiny moment rather than storytelling it. For this reason, I know from the start that I'll soon draw on one child's example and ask all children to help the one child reimagine a moment he's summarized, writing it as a scene.

This guy named Spencer really wants to do great in school 'cause he wants to go to the same college as his big brother, but his friends think he's a geek for reading.

"Whew! That story flew by, didn't it? I want to hear what Spencer sounds like and what the other guys say to him and what books he's reading, don't you? Before you try to turn this summary into a scene, remember that during our personal narrative work you learned that it's easiest to do this if you begin with a line of dialogue or with a small action."

Remind children that when you turned the summarized fairy tale into a real story, you started it with dialogue. In this way, help your children have success storytelling their classmate's summary.

"Remember that I began my 'Three Billy Goats Gruff' scene with a line of dialogue? I said, 'That's the greenest grass I've ever seen in my life!' When a character talks first thing, it can make the scene come alive *instantly* in the reader's ears and mind.

"A second way that writers begin their scenes sometimes is with a small bit of action. Usually the story doesn't start with the main action, giving everything away in the first sentence, but with a tiny action that causes the reader to picture that movement in his or her mind's eye. So, for instance, I could have begun my Billy Goats scene by having First Goat put out his little hoof to test how steady the bridge was. So it would sound like this."

> First Goat gingerly placed one hoof onto the wooden bridge and leaned his weight into it. It seemed sturdy enough. "Let's cross to the other side and eat some of that greeny, green grass," said First Goat.

Ask each child to try telling the story idea as a story, not a summary.

"Okay, now let's all try to write-in-the-air and help Caleb turn his summary into a little scene. You can choose to make the first sentence a line of dialogue or a small action to pull your readers in right away." I listened in on the children. "You've got it! I can picture so many of the scenes I heard, as if they were on movie screens in front of me! Let's hear the way Caleb rewrote his own scene."

> Spencer peeked out from behind the science portable and looked both ways. Good. No one in sight. He sat back against the wall of the portable and pulled his football jersey out of his backpack. He opened the jersey and there, hidden safe and sound, was a piece of heaven: Harry Potter.

Debrief by reminding writers to show their characters by putting them into action.

"Can't you see Spencer peeking out to see if any of those tough guys are around? That's the way to bring the reader right into the heart of the scene. Show us what your character is doing or saying."

You'll notice that this active engagement section involves another round of demonstration. I made the decision to do this because I think children need lots of scaffolding to go from summarizing to storytelling. There are no set laws for how minilessons must progress. The most important thing is that these lessons are helpful—and our job as teachers is to do whatever is needed to make them so.

If you examine active engagements, notice the blend of support and of space I try to give children. You'll notice that I scaffold some aspects of these little practice sessions, supporting and channeling children's work so they are able to have success with the one new tool or strategy I just taught in the minilesson.

LINK

Send children off to work, reminding them of the many points you've made today. And tuck in a reminder to carry these lessons with them always.

"So, writers, your job today is first to transfer your story arc onto a story booklet, and then to use that booklet as a support for story-telling your story. Try telling it so that each page or two of your booklet contains a Small Moment story. When you are ready, start working on your lead. Make sure when you start writing a scene today that the scene sounds like a story. Create a kind of word movie with dialogue and action. I've added this new bullet to our class anchor chart. Let's get to work, writers!"

> ### How to Write a Fiction Story
>
> - Develop a strong story idea, character(s), and setting.
> - Spend time planning how the plot will go, making sure there is an arc to the story, trying again and again until the plan feels just right.
> - Draft the story scene by scene, only using summary when needed.

Children will understand right away what you mean when you tell them you can picture their scenes being on movie screens. Their world of entertainment is largely one of moving images: television, video games, movies, etc. You can take this image further by talking about the sounds of your children's writing, the tones of voice you imagine their characters having, the ways in which they move, their facial expressions. "All this," you might say, "came from the words you chose and the way you decided to put them together!"

Moving from Summary to Story

YOU'LL WANT TO MAKE SURE that every student is now drafting scenes rather than using writing as a way to think about and plan the scenes they'll soon write. Bits of story should be taking shape; they should pop off the page at you as you confer today. It might be helpful to remind students of their last narrative unit in third grade, fairy tales. If at all possible, you might bring out copies of their published tales from last year to further jog their memories.

If students have trouble moving from entries that are *about* the story to entries that *sound like* story, you may find that it helps for you to model. Listen to the child's story, tell the child your observation about his or her work, and then say, "So I imagine it might sound like this," and rewrite the child's summary into the start of a story. Pause after just a bit to say, "Of course, I'm just making this up and *you* know how the story really goes. So now you try it. Tell it like a story." Help the child get started writing-in-the-air.

If the child says a summary statement, quietly prompt for more specifics. You'll find that when students rehearse bits of a story out loud, with you coaching right beside them, saying things like "What did she do? What did he say back?" students get started saying aloud beautiful stories. Jot down what the child says as a way to synthesize it, and then say it back to the child. The writer will hear the difference between the first and the later version.

I got home. I was exhausted. I went to bed.

becomes:

I flicked on the light so that I could see my way to my bed. It looked like it was miles away from where I was standing. I closed my eyes. I wanted more than anything to be carried to my bed. Instead, I had to walk. I dropped my backpack on the floor with a thud. Then I used my feet to pry off first one shoe, then the other.

The idea of bending over to untie them was just too exhausting. I trudged to the edge of my bed, step by step. "You can make it, just a few more steps," I told myself. Then I was there. I began to fall onto my bed, unable to even pull the covers back. My eyes closed as I fell. The last thought I had before I fell asleep was, "I should have taken off my jacket."

MID-WORKSHOP TEACHING
Matching Writing with Story Arcs

"Writers, I want to remind you that when we worked on our Luz story, we had our story plans out beside us, and before we picked up our pens and stepped into Luz's shoes, we first checked our story arc so we'd keep in mind the main event that we knew would happen next. Before we wrote the story of Luz bringing out the stack of games, we checked our plans. As we wrote, we kept in mind the overall game plan—one page about playing games, another page in which Luz's worries over being liked get worse and worse. Make sure you're keeping your own story arc beside you as you write and that as you move on to another moment on your story arc, you are starting a fresh small moment, a new scene."

Then I added, "Remember that as you move from page 1 to page 2 of your story, your character's troubles should escalate. Things get worse and worse.

"Caleb has already started to move into the next scene in his story about Spencer, the boy who decides to face up to the big bully and meet him on the playground. Listen to the beginning of this first scene, how he sets up the problem. There is going to be a confrontation with that bully." (See Figure 6–1.)

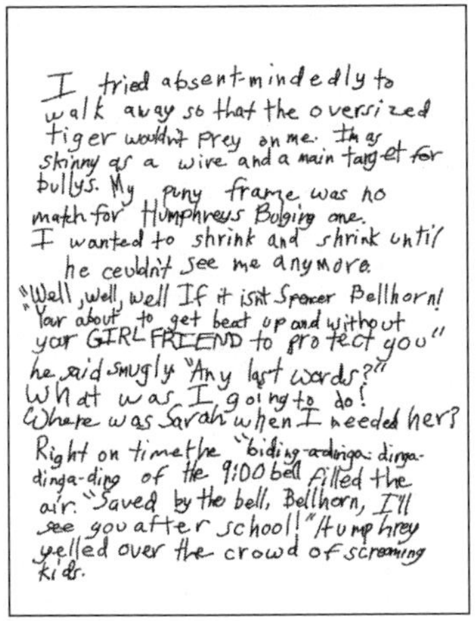

I tried absent-mindedly to walk away so that the oversized tiger wouldn't prey on me. I'm as skinny as a wire and a main target for bullies.

My puny frame was no match for Humphrey's bulging one. I wanted to shrink and shrink until he couldn't see me anymore.

"Can't you just see them? Caleb has really set this scene up, and it feels dramatic. What will happen? Will the bully hit him or not? Listen to the next scene that Caleb made." (See Figure 6–2.)

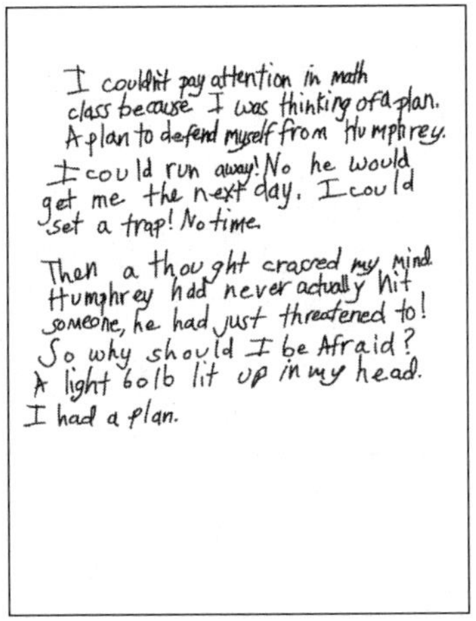

I couldn't pay attention in math class because I was thinking of a plan, a plan to defend myself against Humphrey. I could run away! No he would get me the next day. I could set a trap! No time.

Then a thought crossed my mind. Humphrey had never actually hit someone, he had just threatened to! So why should I be afraid? A light bulb lit up in my head. I had a plan.

"Can you hear how Caleb is making a plan for how to stand up to the bully? Make sure that as you write your stories, you keep in mind where the story is going, but that, like Caleb, you take your time getting there."

FIG. 6–1   A snippet from Caleb's draft

FIG. 6–2   Caleb's draft, page 2 of his story booklet

Your conferring today will be crucial. As important as the adage "show, don't tell" is to all writing, it's even more important to fiction. Fiction writer Shirley Jackson ends her "Notes for a Young Writer" by summarizing all that she's said in the article (*Come Along with Me* 1995). She concludes,

> *Just remember that primarily, in the story and out of it, you are living in a world of people. Suppose you want to write a story about what you might vaguely think of as "magic." You will be hopelessly lost, until you turn your idea, "magic," into a person, someone who wants to do or make or change or act in some way. Once you have your character you will of course need another to work in opposition, a person in some sense, "antimagic;" when both are working at the separate intentions, dragging in other characters when needed, you are well into your story.*

Help children reread their own work, noticing times when they tell the reader something that they could instead have shown. For example, Sofiya's story about a girl named Elizabeth who is afraid of snakes includes a fair number of places where she summarizes or talks about the character and the events. You and Sofiya could find those places and work together to rewrite them (see Figure 6–3).

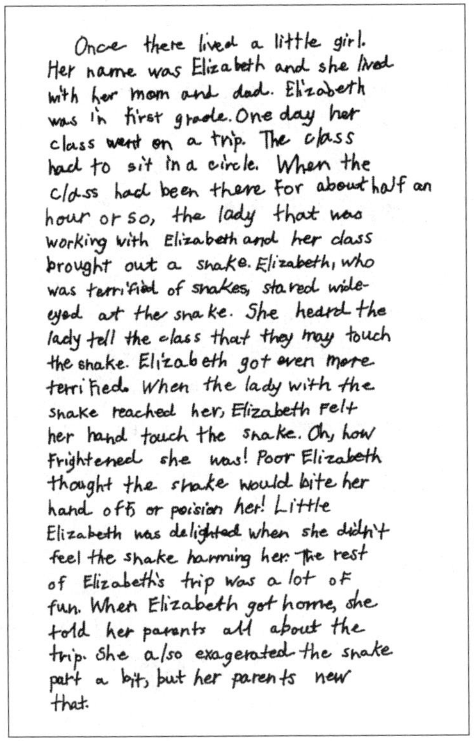

FIG. 6–3   Sofiya's draft contained bits of summary.

Once there lived a little girl. Her name was Elizabeth and she lived with her mom and dad. Elizabeth was in first grade. One day her class went on a trip. The class had to sit in a circle. When the class had been there for about half an hour or so, the lady that was working with Elizabeth and her class brought out a snake. Elizabeth, who was terrified of snakes, stared wide-eyed at the snake. She heard the lady tell the class that they may touch the snake. Elizabeth got even more terrified. When the lady with the snake reached her, Elizabeth felt her hand touch the snake. Oh, how frightened she was! Poor Elizabeth thought the snake would bite her hand off, or poison her! Little Elizabeth was delighted when she didn't feel the snake harming her. The rest of Elizabeth's trip was a lot of fun. When Elizabeth got home, she told her parents all about the trip. She also exaggerated the snake part a bit, but her parents knew that.

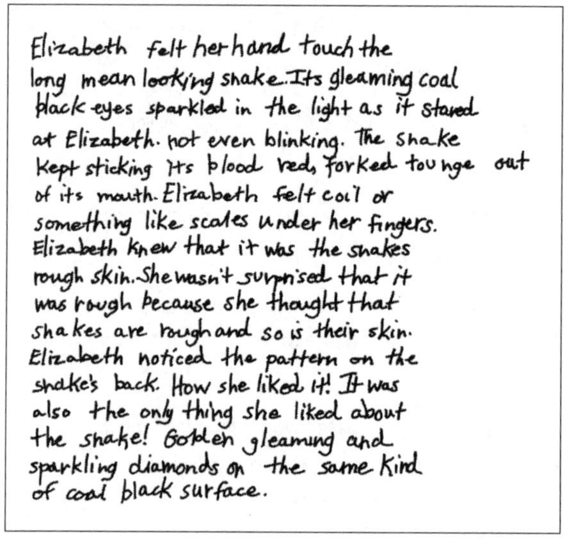
Elizabeth felt her hand touch the long mean looking snake. Its gleaming coal black eyes sparkled in the light as it stared at Elizabeth. not even blinking. The snake kept sticking its blood red, forked tounge out of its mouth. Elizabeth felt coil or something like scales under her fingers. Elizabeth knew that it was the snakes rough skin. She wasn't surpised that it was rough because she thought that shakes are rough and so is their skin. Elizabeth noticed the pattern on the snake's back. How she liked it! It was also the only thing she liked about the snake! Golden gleaming and sparkling diamonds on the same kind of coal black surface.

FIG. 6–4 Sofiya tried to rewrite so that her summaries became scenes.

In her next draft, Sofiya left off the most obvious instances of telling/summarizing, as you can see in Figure 6–4. What an important step ahead!

Elizabeth felt her hand touch the long, mean-looking snake. Its gleaming coal-black eyes sparkled in the light as it stared at Elizabeth, not even blinking. The snake kept sticking its blood-red, forked tongue out of its mouth. Elizabeth felt coil or something like scales under her fingers. Elizabeth knew that it was the snake's rough skin. She wasn't surprised that it was rough because she thought that snakes are rough and so is their skin. Elizabeth noticed the pattern on the snake's back. How she liked it! It was also the only thing she liked about the snake! Golden gleaming and sparkling diamonds on the same kind of coal black surface.

Acting in Scenes to Get Ready for Drafting

Ask several students to direct fellow classmates in the scenes they've written to see what revisions, if any, are needed to make them "camera ready."

"Writers, I wish we had the movie cameras rolling on some of these scenes you've got going! But why don't we pretend that we *do* have movie cameras filming our scenes. Let's try acting out a couple of your scenes to see how they look and sound, to see how that helps us revise them!

"I'm going to choose five students to be the directors of their little scenes." I named them. "Will you find actors for your scenes? You have five minutes to give them the directions so they know what your characters are saying and doing, and then you all can rehearse the scene once, really fast! Then another group of kids will watch the scene you develop and see if it feels ready for filming or if the scene needs some revision. Okay, choose and rehearse fast!"

Reconvene the class. Tell a story about children resolving to do superbly well, even while knowing today's best draft will be revised.

"Ariana and Gabe and Francesca are working on a dance for the talent show. They're practicing every day after school for this whole week. Do you suppose that on Monday they grab any CD and start doing any old dance moves, saying to themselves, 'We don't need to make this good 'til Friday?'

"No! Ariana and Gabe and Francesca worked really hard so that when they met on Monday, they had already chosen the song they thought would work and the moves they hoped would be perfect. As the group practiced, I hear they came up with even better dance moves—but that doesn't mean that on Monday they aimed for anything less than their best!

"The same needs to be true for all of you as you move forward in your drafts. I know you will aim to make this draft of your lead gorgeous and spectacular and significant. We've learned that writers first plan how their stories might go, sketching out possible lines of development on one story arc after another. They try on leads and use those leads to test out what their stories might be like if they write in one voice or another, if they start in one place, at one time, or another."

If you've never had your students practice acting out parts of stories or using their bodies and voices like this before, you may find this share a bit chaotic. But when students are accustomed to role-playing and to performing Reader's Theater, like these students are, this provides a powerful way to give body and voice to the words on a page. When writers see real human beings trying to carry out the action of the scene, they realize quickly that they have important revision to do so the scene works better. (And the good news is, this comes at the end of the workshop, and you can end it early if you feel you need to!)

READING THE WORK OF OTHER AUTHORS FOR INSPIRATION

Sometimes when we are starting a new story, we stop and take some time to get inspired. We reread some our favorite fiction stories and we look for new stories we've never read before. We do this to find techniques that other authors have used that we can emulate, sure, but we do this for another even more important reason. We read other writers' work because it can change what we're feeling inside. When I reread parts of some of my favorite books, like *Because of Winn-Dixie* or *Roll of Thunder, Hear My Cry*, I get goose bumps. I get excited because those books are just so good. I want to write stories that are that good; I want to write stories that give people goose bumps the way Kate DiCamillo and Mildred Taylor give me goose bumps.

Writers, give yourselves the time to be inspired by the fiction writers you know and love. Tonight, pull out a book or two that you've read and loved. Don't limit yourself to chapter books, either. Often some of the best stories are in picture books. Look through these books and put a sticky note wherever you find a place you love, one that gives you goose bumps. Read that part again and again. Read it aloud. Then, put the book aside and bring out your draft. Reread what you've written so far. Perhaps you'll find yourself drafting or even revising!

Session 7

Feeling and Drafting the Heart of Your Story

I N THIS SESSION, you'll set children up for something quite magical. When writing, we plan and chart, deliberate and select. But then the day comes when we do none of this. Instead, we "let it rip." We "go with the flow." We write fast and long, our eyes glued not to charts admonishing us to do one thing or another and not to mentor texts that demonstrate what's possible, but instead to the drama that unfolds before us as we follow our characters into the thickening plot.

Frankly, it's not easy to figure out how to pass along the equation for the magic that happens when writers find that words and characters lead them toward meanings they didn't even know they knew! To some extent, I always approach this particular minilesson knowing my teaching will be hopelessly inadequate. But we carry on, as best we can, knowing that children can learn from their words as they appear on the page, if not from the minilesson.

In this session you will try to equip children to experience the power of getting lost in one's own writing the way one might get lost while reading a book. One way writers do this is to empathize with their characters, imagining themselves within another's feelings, situations, and thoughts. By stepping into the character's skin, right into the story, the writer watches and listens and feels what is happening as the story unfolds—writing the story down as it happens.

Set children up to expect that as they write, their character's problems will get worse and worse and the stakes will rise. Teach them to hold onto their hats, expecting quite a ride! In this session, then, we'll teach children that writers draft by empathizing with their characters and letting that empathy determine the course of the story.

IN THIS SESSION, you'll teach children that fiction writers create their best drafts when they experience the world through their character's skin, letting the story unfold as it happens to them.

GETTING READY

✔ Example of a well-known text, such as *Fireflies!*, in which students have probably experienced "becoming" the character, to reference during Teaching

✔ Current lead for the class story

✔ Current story arc for the class story

✔ Idea for a scene for the class story that you can use to demonstrate writing by pretending to be the character (see Teaching)

✔ Narrative Writing Checklist, Grades 4 and 5, along with clipboards for students (see Share)

COMMON CORE STATE STANDARDS: W.4.3.a,b; W.4.4, W.4.5, W.4.10, RL.4.3, SL.4.1, SL.4.4, L.4.1, L.4.2, L.4.3, L.4.5.a

Feeling and Drafting the Heart of Your Story

CONNECTION

Celebrate that your children have created story arcs and characters and, best yet, they've begun bringing these to life on the page.

"It's a rather amazing process, isn't it? You plan, list, choose, sketch—like the old woman making that gingerbread boy. She probably thought, 'What will I use to show his eyes?' 'Will his shirt be a button-down shirt?' 'Will he wear suspenders?' But then the day comes when the gingerbread boy springs to life, calling out, 'Run, run, as fast as you can. You can't catch me, I'm the gingerbread man. I am, I am!'

"You have each created a gingerbread child who has sprung to life. Hannah's character, Jane, is standing in Central Park near the carousel, with her two friends circling her, taunting, 'Jane is scared, Jane is scared.'

"The blood rises to Jane's face. She feels circled, caught, so she snaps back, 'At least I'm smarter than you guys!' and she huffs away. The amazing thing is that Jane's creator didn't know that Jane would snap back like that. One thing led to another, that's all; Jane was caught and she dug deep into herself and found a kernel of self-respect and shot back with 'At least I'm smarter than you guys!'

"This is the magical power of writing fiction. Your characters, like that gingerbread man, spring to life, and suddenly you, as writers, are following them, trying as best you can to catch up."

❖ **Name the teaching point.**

"So today what I want to teach you is this: before writers actually get going on a draft, they think a lot about ways to make a draft into a really good story. But once they're actually in the midst of the story, most of them try, above all, to lose themselves in the story. They become the characters, and writing is a bit like a drama, happening to them."

William Faulkner has said, "There are some kinds of writing that you have to do very fast, like riding a bicycle on a tightrope." Another time, he used a different analogy to convey the same message, "A writer writing is like a man building a chicken coop in a high wind. He grabs any board he can and nails it down fast." You are setting children up to draft, fast and long—and more than that, you are setting children up to produce a draft that they regard as temporary and improvable.

TEACHING

Remind children that when reading, we lose ourselves in a story, becoming the character. Explain how this is true for writing as well. Give an example.

"You all know how, when we read, we feel almost like we become Gilly or Opal or Melanin Sun or the narrator in *Fireflies!* We read the words and suddenly we are that boy at the dinner table, looking out the window onto our backyard at dusk, seeing the dots of light flicker by the dark shape that is our tree house—seeing through his eyes and living in his self. We hardly need the words of the story to tell us that the boy pushes away his plate and asks, 'Can I be done?' and then rushes to get a jar for catching fireflies."

Tell children that readers can more easily walk in the shoes of a character if the writer has done this first.

"Readers can do that. We can read words on the page and suddenly be in the shoes of the character because writers first do the same. Gerald Brace, in a book called *The Stuff of Fiction*, says it this way."

> It is not enough for a writer to tell us about a person or a place; he must give us the illusion of being the person ourselves . . . the basic failure in much writing is the failure of the writer's imagination: he is not with it . . . not trying hard enough to live from moment to moment in the very skin of his characters. (1969)

"You, as writers, need to try to do this work—live in your characters' skins as you draft your stories!"

Demonstrate to show how you go from envisioning to enacting to drafting.

"And so today I'm going to reread the latest lead to our Luz story. At one point we'd said we wanted to start it earlier, as she writes invitations, but now we've settled on this lead. I revised it a bit since you last saw it. Today I'm not going to be rethinking the lead so much as writing more. To do that, I'm going to pretend to *be* Luz." I reread the latest draft, written on chart paper:

> On the day of my slumber party I put everything I would need into a corner of our family room. I propped my sleeping bag up against the corner, and my pillow on top of it. Above the pillow, I laid out my cute new pajamas. Then I added my secret night-light to the pile. I was afraid of the dark and nobody knew it.
>
> I checked all my stuff at least three times. I made sure my secret nightlight was pushed all the way to the bottom of my pillowcase where no one would see it. Then I walked over to the table and rearranged the napkins. Everything on the table was yellow. Yellow wasn't my favorite color, but a lot of the girls coming to the party wore yellow all the time, so I thought they'd like it. And like me.

It could be a fruitful inquiry to look at all the minilessons focused on drafting in all the Unit of Study *books. I believe fast-writing works to help students draft. You may not, in which case you may want to suggest that some people draft slowly and cautiously. Regardless, there is a cyclical curriculum underlying these units, and you can learn from studying it—and also from questioning it! Any one line of work is but one choice among many.*

So far, I have given a little lecture on the virtues of envisioning and role-playing. I could shift now to the next phase of the minilesson. Instead, I demonstrate what I just described in the hopes that this will provide more ways to support children. You can decide whether to explicitly tell, to demonstrate, or to do as I have done.

"Let your story move as naturally and as easily as possible," Shirley Jackson urges young writers in "Notes from a Young Writer" (Come Along with Me, 1995). "Suppose you are writing a story about a boy and a girl meeting on a corner; your reader wants to go to that very corner and listen in; if, instead, you start your boy and girl toward the corner and then go off into a long description of the streetcar tracks and a little discussion of the background of those two characters—you will lose your reader and your story will fall apart."

First Marta came in. Then Joy and Tish walked in together, helping each other carry all their sleeping stuff. I helped carry things to the corner of the room where my mom and I decided we would keep the stuff until it was time to go to sleep.

"So what are we going to do first?" Joy asked.

I looked around at all my friends. I was so excited that my party was finally happening that I almost forgot the games I had planned.

"I'm going to keep in mind that the next dot on the story arc says, 'Her friends arrive and don't like her games,' and I'm going to remember that Luz wants desperately to feel popular," I said, referring to the story arc.

"But mostly I'm just going to try to be Luz." I picked up my pen and began scrawling on my pad of paper, saying aloud the words as I wrote them. Pulling back from writing, I said to the children, "I just that second made up the idea that the games were brand-new and Luz pretended they were junk. I have no idea what, exactly, will happen next, so I'll reread what I just wrote and just let something come to me."

Soon I'd added (and voiced) this scene.

"What do you wanna do?" I asked, waving with feigned carelessness to the stack of games on the table. "They're all old," I said, hoping I'd taken the price tags and cellophane off each of them.

"TWISTER?" Tish said, her voice incredulous. "My mom played that when she was a kid. That's such a stupid game."

I felt the blood rise to my cheeks. "I know," I said. "I don't know why we even have it."

ACTIVE ENGAGEMENT

Recap specific tips you hope children gleaned from the demonstration.

"Writers, do you see that when we write—when any fiction writer writes—we keep in mind the big plan for how a story will probably go, but we let the details emerge from the specific, exact actions we take? Usually, our scenes involve two characters, and one does or says something and then the next one reacts."

Set children up to extend the class story by putting themselves into the unfolding scene. Then call on one set of partners and add their work to the class story.

"To continue writing our Luz story, you need to *be* Luz, gesturing with disgust at the stack of games, pretending you agree that they're junk. You need to keep in mind that Luz desperately wants the party to go well. She's got it all planned—the games she's dismissing were her best hope for keeping everyone happy.

The emphasis in this minilesson is on showing, not telling. You may determine that other qualities of good writing will help your children more. Scan students' work as they draft. The emphasis in the minilesson grew from the fact that despite all our best efforts, some students were still summarizing when they should have been writing scenes or small moments. That said, there are times when summary is the best tool a writer has at her disposal.

"Right now, pretend *you are* Luz. Picture her. The games are out on the table. The one friend has just looked in disgust at Twister. What does Luz do (remember, actions matter, not just talk). Turn and tell your partner the next bit of the story." To get them started, I reiterated the last scene.

> "TWISTER?" Tish said, her voice incredulous. "My mom played that when she was a kid. That's such a stupid game." I felt the blood rise to my cheeks. "I know," I said. "I don't know why we even have it."

The children talked with their partners, and soon I had called on one partnership and added this to the story:

> I jumped up to put the entire stack of games into the closet. The other kids, however, surrounded me, and Joy and Marta were shaking dice to see who'd go first in a game of Mousetrap.

LINK

Remind children that drafting is a form of acting on the page, and send them off.

"Writers, I want to remind you that writing is a lot like drama. Once we've written our lead, we need to reread it and become the main character. We need to stand in the character's shoes, to see through her eyes, to blush with her, and to hope with her. This way our readers will also be able to experience the story we put onto the page."

Writing in Summaries and Writing in Scenes

AS YOU CONFER TODAY, you'll want to help writers make significant revisions in their story arcs and their leads. When working with children around both of these things today, help them envision what's happening. Often writers will need to go from summarizing to storytelling. If a child has written something like, "Elisabeth woke up and listened to her parents fight," you'll want to point out that this is still a summary. "Pretend you are Elisabeth," I said to Sofiya. "You are lying in your bed sleeping. Now you begin to wake up, just a bit. You hear something. What is it?" Coaching, I said, "Maybe you hear voices. Then what do you do? Sit up in bed and listen some more? This time you make out a voice you know—whose? Can you make out any words the voice is saying?" In this way, I helped Sofiya rewrite her draft so that she story-told in a step-by-step fashion—and relived her character's experience of that morning.

As you confer with your children, remember that you are a talent scout, searching for what each child does well so that you can solicit that child to teach his or her peers. Then set children up to lead little seminars. For example, when I read Chris's work, I was blown away by his ability to convey the reciprocity and intimacy in a friendship between two best friends. And so I called a group of children together, who, like Chris,

MID-WORKSHOP TEACHING   Revising Leads

"Writers, I've been racing around, conferring with lots of you. But your stories are so long and complex and interesting that I'm not moving fast enough. And I want every single one of you to have the chance to confer with someone about your story, so that you can revise before you get a lot farther into your draft. It's much easier to write a page or two and then look at those early pages and say, 'Whoa! Let me rethink this,' rather than writing a whole ten-page draft, then rereading it and saying, 'Whoa! Let me rethink this!'

"So right now, I want to teach every one of you how to be writing teachers for each other, and then I'm going to suggest that you each meet with your partner and try to confer in ways that help both of you rethink your lead *and your story*.

"You see, when you help each other revise your leads, you are really thinking, 'If this keeps on going and becomes a whole story, what problems might the story encounter?' I think I may have told you about the time I wanted to put a new carpet on our living room floor. But I didn't want to buy a big carpet, install it, and *then* say 'Whoa!' So I got a sweater the color of one possible carpet. I put it on the floor and

I looked at it, squinting in such a way that I imagined that sweater as a whole big carpet touching the walls, and I thought, 'How would this look if it were big?' Then I put a different sweater on the middle of the floor, stepped back, and squinted at it, imagining *that* sweater as a whole big carpet.

"We can reread the early pages of a story like I looked at those sweaters, thinking, 'What might this look like when it's a bigger text?' When you do this for your own writing and for each other, reread the draft and think, 'What will happen next in the story?' Talk and think about the story that this particular lead sets up.

"Often you'll decide that your first draft starts too far from the turning point, and you'll decide the next draft needs to zoom in on an event that is closer to the main action. On the other hand, sometimes you'll decide that you've told the whole story right at the start from beginning to end, leaving nothing for page 2 or 3. In this case, you'll need to back up and work on your story arc again. Ask yourself, 'What episode (or Small Moment story) could occur next to show the predicament? What episode could make the predicament get worse and worse?'"

were writing relationship stories, and I asked them to study Chris's writing closely, just as we'd studied texts by other authors, and to pay special attention to Chris's talent for making a relationship seem very real. He'd written, for example:

> Jerod wasn't in Boy Scouts because it met at a church; he was Jewish and his mom didn't want him experiencing another religion. Luke understood and never brought it up.

When a text provides such precise detail, readers believe the story is real. Above all, children noticed Chris's culminating simile.

> He and Jerod were like a chain. If it breaks, it's just two pieces of metal always looking for the other piece.

When I find a child who has done something marvelous, it is incredibly powerful if I let that child's good work become a subject for study. Once I saw Chris's beautiful simile capturing his characters' friendship, I asked Chris if he could help revise the Luz story so that it, too, contained a beautiful simile. We found a possible place. The text read:

> Then, just like that, the lights were out. It was dark. Luz tried to find some light, somewhere in the living room.

With Chris's help, we rewrote this. We thought, "What else looks for something the way Luz is looking for a light? Hmm, she's starting to feel a bit frantic." And we wrote:

> Luz searched the dark living room like a sailor lost at sea searches for land on the horizon.

Then Chris taught a cluster of other children to do similar work on their drafts.

Of course, children, too, need to be talent scouts. You can help them find talent among their classmates and among the authors whose books they admire. Beccah came to me with this section of *Journey*, by Patricia MacLachlan, announcing, "Know what's amazing? It's the best description in the world and it only has two adjectives in it!"

> *The first letter that wasn't a letter came in the noon mail. It lay in the middle of the kitchen table like a dropped apple, addressed to Cat and me, Mama's name in the left-hand corner.*
>
> *I'd watched Cat walk up the front path from the mailbox slowly, as if caught by the camera in slow motion or in a series of what Grandfather calls stills: Cat smiling; Cat looking eager; Cat, her face suddenly unfolding out of a smile. She brushed past me at the front door and opened her hand, the letter falling to the table. (1993)*

I looked with her at the passage, agreed with her analysis, and pointed out to her that when I was studying with Don Murray, he gave me a list of editing tips. "Check to be sure you are writing with strong precise nouns and verbs, not relying on adjectives and adverbs to prop them up—the *young* dog is a puppy, and if the man walked *quietly*, he tiptoed."

Using the Narrative Checklist to Ratchet Up the Writing

Introduce students to the fourth- and fifth-grade Narrative Writing Checklist.

"Writers, I'm going to ask you to stop working on your drafts for a few minutes and bring them, a clipboard, and a pen to the meeting area," I said, heading over to the meeting area to meet them.

The complete Narrative Writing Checklist, Grades 4 and 5 can be found on the CD-ROM.

After the students had settled, I began, "Writers, I was thinking about how important it is sometimes to talk to your partner about your writing. Talking with a partner allows you to have another perspective, a fresh perspective, on what you've been working on. Sometimes when you've been working so hard on something for a while, it's hard to know how it's going. Sometimes you think everything you meant to include is there. Sometimes you have included too much. But since you've been staring at it for a while, it can be hard to see. Today, since so many of you are done, or close to done with your drafts, I thought it made sense to give you a tool to help you study your own writing."

I placed a copy of the checklist on the document camera and went through each category, explaining and defining as needed. "You'll notice this checklist includes goals for fifth grade as well as goals for fourth. It's always helpful to have a clear vision of where you're headed—and you might even find yourselves working toward some of these fifth-grade goals this year, perhaps even now." As I read each goal, I want you to be thinking about your draft. What do you have in place, what are you getting in place, and what is not done yet?"

Narrative Writing Checklist

	Grade 4	NOT YET	STARTING TO	YES!	Grade 5	NOT YET	STARTING TO	YES!
	Structure				**Structure**			
Overall	I wrote the important part of an event bit by bit and took out unimportant parts.	☐	☐	☐	I wrote a story of an important moment. It read like a story, even though it might be a true account.	☐	☐	☐
Lead	I wrote a beginning in which I showed what was happening and where, getting readers into the world of the story.	☐	☐	☐	I wrote a beginning in which I not only showed what was happening and where, but also gave some clues to what would later become a problem for the main character.	☐	☐	☐
Transitions	I showed how much time went by with words and phrases that mark time such as *just then* and *suddenly* (to show when things happened quickly) or *after a while* and *a little later* (to show when a little time passed).	☐	☐	☐	I used transitional phrases to show passage of time in complicated ways, perhaps by showing things happening at the same time (*meanwhile, at the same time*) or flashback and flash-forward (*early that morning, three hours later*).	☐	☐	☐
Ending	I wrote an ending that connected to the beginning or the middle of the story.	☐	☐	☐	I wrote an ending that connected to the main part of the story. The character said, did, or realized something at the end that came from what happened in the story.	☐	☐	☐
	I used action, dialogue, or feeling to bring my story to a close.	☐	☐	☐	I gave readers a sense of closure.	☐	☐	☐
Organization	I used paragraphs to separate the different parts or times of the story or to show when a new character was speaking.	☐	☐	☐	I used paragraphs to separate different parts or times of the story and to show when a new character was speaking. Some parts of the story were longer and more developed than others.	☐	☐	☐

"Now some of you are saying to yourselves, 'Hmm, I haven't done enough with my draft.' And remember, we're still pretty early in the process, so there might be a lot of things you don't have yet that you will have very soon—maybe even today. This checklist will help you decide what you need to work on next, setting goals for yourself as a writer. You'll probably be paying more attention to the goals on the fourth-grade side of the checklist at this point of the year."

I find that a unit of study on fiction quickly becomes a unit of study on revision. In part this is true because writers are so eager for the chance to write fiction that they fill pages upon pages in short order. Then, too, there is so much involved in getting a story off to a good start that it's inevitable that children will write a less-than-ideal draft and that we'll want to ratchet up the level of that draft by helping children make significant revisions. One way to get your students revising is to have them reflect on their writing using a checklist, noticing what they have done and what they have yet to try. The things that they are not doing can become the very things they will revise for in following sessions. Giving them the fifth-grade checklist alongside the fourth gives students the bigger picture of what they are working toward. Additionally it makes room for more sophisticated writers, who can stretch their legs a bit and push to see what they are capable of.

Studying Published Texts to Write Leads

IN THIS SESSION, you'll remind writers of various strategies for writing effective leads. You will also remind children that writers reread literature, letting it teach techniques for writing.

GETTING READY

✔ A student's lead that invites further revision. This can be a student in your class or a fictional student.

✔ Leads of two short stories kids are familiar with. We use the leads from *Pecan Pie Baby* and *FireFlies!* (see Teaching and Active Engagement)

✔ "How to Write a Fiction Story" anchor chart (see Link)

✔ A handful of familiar short stories or picture books you can use while conferring

✔ Two examples of dialogue, one empty and one revealing, written on chart paper (see Mid-Workshop Teaching)

COMMON CORE STATE STANDARDS: W.4.3.a,b; W.4.5, RL.4.1, RL.4.3, RL.4.10, SL.4.1, L.4.1, L.4.2, L.4.3

AS YOU MOVE THROUGH all the units of study that we've detailed in this series, you'll see that time and again we ask children to draft and revise their leads. The goal in making a great lead isn't the lead itself. The goal is to imagine a work of art and then to write a lead that points the course toward and is worthy of that larger enterprise. Opening scenes set up the drama of what will follow. We plan our leads with an eye toward all that we believe is essential for the larger experience to work. The Common Core State Standards also asks students to "orient the reader by establishing a situation and introducing a narrator and/or characters" (W.3.3.a).

This session, then, aims to help children remember that after drafting a lead it's important to step back and ask, "How might this lead set up the larger text? Is that the way I want the larger text to go?" As writers revise this opening paragraph or two, they also revise the larger text.

We ask children to revise their leads because front-end revisions are vastly easier for children to embrace and more likely to lift the level of entire drafts than back-end revisions, which are much more time-consuming. And by investing a minilesson (and therefore an added day) in early revision work, we slow children's progress, making it more likely that we'll be able to confer with more children at this crucial just-starting stage. Once children are deep into the first drafts of their stories, they become more and more committed to the road they've taken, and it is harder to deter them from that pathway. Soon, children won't want us to confer in ways that help them imagine other paths their story could have taken.

When we ask children to revise their leads, we aim to remind them that writers consider and reconsider not only the content of their stories, but also their craftsmanship. When a writer shifts from planning a story to writing a draft, the writer needs to think not only about what will happen in a scene (in this instance, in the opening scene), but also about how to write the scene well. Children are much more apt to write well if, just before they pick up their pens, something occurs that stirs their hearts, that raises their hopes, that fills them with a sense of momentousness. So we tell them, "Study the work of other authors." And, secretly, we say, "Put yourself under the spell of other authors. Let their magic rub off!"

Studying Published Texts to Write Leads

CONNECTION

Celebrate that your children have begun their stories, and do so by conveying the essence of a couple of students' stories to the class.

"Writers, you'll see from today's schedule that the read-aloud we've scheduled for later will be a special one. Instead of me continuing to read our chapter book aloud, some of you will read aloud the leads to your stories. Something extraordinary is happening in this classroom, and we all need to be a part of it. Stories are literally coming to life in your drafts. You need to know each other's stories!

"You need to know that just as that gingerbread boy came to life, there are characters coming to life right in this room. You need to know that a girl named Elexa is surveying the playground, hoping against hope that the boy who stalks her hasn't caught a glance of her. Elexa sees her best friend—but oh no! She is frantically gesturing that someone is close by, and with a sinking heart Elexa realizes she's been spotted.

"You need to know that Spencer is getting ready to confront his nemesis, Humphrey Dugball, the meanest bully in the history of Butts, Missouri. And you need to know that right here in this room, Jane's friend Amy has asked her yet again to sleep over, and Jane is frantically coming up with yet more excuses."

❖ **Name the teaching point.**

"Today I want to teach you that just when writers are most fired up to write, they force themselves to pause. They pause, rewind, listen to what they've written, and revise it. They revise the lead because by doing so, they revise the entire story. Sometimes, they do this with help from a pro."

Notice that the message to children today is, "Your stories are riveting! I'm dying to learn how they turn out." It's important for children to aim toward writing riveting, absorbing stories that draw in readers. Children can learn as much from their friend's work with a draft as they learn from your work with a demonstration text. So be sure that you help them learn vicariously by following the drama of each other's progress.

TEACHING

Tell children that to write leads that draw readers into a story, it helps to study the leads published authors have written.

"You already know that the beginning of a piece of writing, any piece of writing, is called a *lead* because these sentences are the way an author *leads* readers into the text. A good lead functions like the Pied Piper. You remember the story of the Pied Piper, walking through town playing his flute? People would listen up, and soon all the villagers were following along wherever he led them.

"This morning I told Francesca that I always work hard on my lead because I want it to draw readers along. But she asked the crucial questions: how can a lead do that? What techniques do writers use?

"Of course, you know how to answer that! When writers want to learn how to do something, they study texts written by authors they admire. After they look really closely at exactly how other authors pull something off, they try the same techniques in their own writing."

Tell the class that you and one student studied the leads from familiar stories. Read one aloud, listing what the student noticed about it and then showing the resulting revisions in her own lead.

"Francesca and I decided to study leads. We first reread the lead to *Pecan Pie Baby* by Jacqueline Woodson, which you'll remember is a picture book by Jacqueline Woodson. The story starts like this."

> *Just as summer started leaving us and the leaving brought all those colors to the trees, Mama pulled out my winter clothes.*
>
> *"Time to give away the stuff that's too small," I said. "This didn't used to be a* mini-*dress."*
>
> *Mama smiled. "Let's keep it, Gia."*
>
> *And I knew what was coming next—more talk about the ding-dang baby. (2010)*

"Looking at this story reminded Francesca of things she'd learned earlier: it often helps to start with the exact words one character is saying (or with a small action); and, in a short story, it's important to start close to the main event. If there's a waterfall in the story, start when you can hear the falls. The main tension in this story revolves around Gia not really wanting her life to change and not looking forward to her mom having a new baby. Notice that the lead of the story hints at what will come later."

Set children up to listen to and then talk with partners about what one child did as she revised her lead.

"So Francesca thought about her story. She already knew that the heart of the story revolved around Griffen, the boy in her story, trying to convince his father he could take care of a pet. She remembered that often it helps to start a story with dialogue, so she decided to try a lead in which Griffen says something to his dad about getting a pet (see Figure 8–1). Listen to what she wrote."

When teaching skills, we need to anticipate that we'll often revisit earlier lessons. It's a challenge to find new ways to teach a familiar concept. In this instance, I've found a new way to describe the role a lead plays in a story.

F. Paul Wilson has said: "I don't know how it is with other writers, but most of the time when I finish [reading] a story or novel, I may be pleased, I may even be impressed, but somewhere in the back of my mind I'm thinking, 'I can do that.'" The act of apprenticing oneself to a respected and more experienced practitioner is an age-old tradition.

"Dad," Griffen said.

"Can I get a pet?"

"Well, a pet is a lot of responsibility," Dad said.

"Please," Griffen said.

"If I see that you are responsible enough you can get a pet," said Griffen's dad.

The next day, Griffen told Timmy. He was amazed.

"I bet we can show that we are responsible enough," Timmy said.

ACTIVE ENGAGEMENT

Share a second lead, this time asking the class to list to a partner what they notice about it that Francesca, and all of them, could try.

"Then Francesca and I looked at a second lead, this time from Julie Brinckloe's *Fireflies!* We were pretty sure this story would teach us more techniques, so we read it really closely. Reread it with me now, and think, 'What has Brinckloe done that we can learn from?'"

On a summer evening
I looked up from dinner,
through the open window to the backyard.
It was growing dark.
My treehouse was a black shape in the tree
and I wouldn't go up there now.
But something flickered there, a moment—
I looked, and it was gone.
It flickered again, over near the fence.
Fireflies*!*
"Don't let your dinner get cold," said Momma.
I forked the meat and corn and potatoes into my mouth.
"Please may I go out? The fireflies—"
Momma smiled and Daddy nodded.
"Go ahead," they said. (1985)

This is not a spectacular example of a lead. Francesca is a very capable writer, as you will have seen from following her progress throughout the year. Don't be surprised if your children's writing, like Francesca's, is not as impressive when they are writing fiction as when they wrote personal narratives. As this session unrolls, you'll point out ways to enrich this writing.

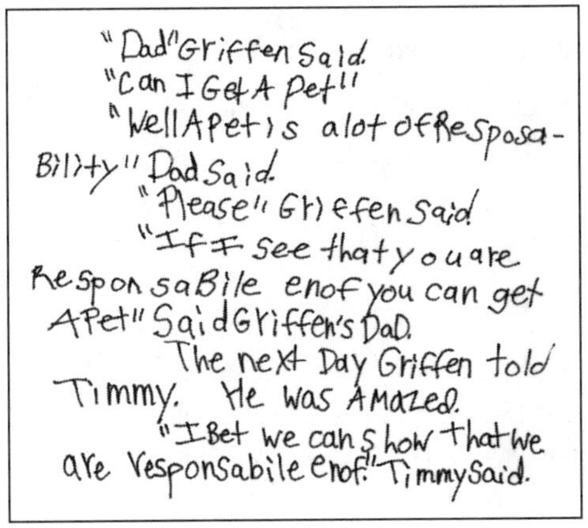
"Dad" Griffen Said.
"Can I Get A Pet"
"Well A Pet is alot of Resposa-
Bility" Dad Said.
"Please" Grieffen Said
"If I see that you are
ResponsaBile enof you can get
A Pet" Said Griffen's DaD.
The next Day Griffen told
Timmy. He was AMazeD.
"I Bet we can show that we
are responsabile enof" Timmy Said.

FIG. 8–1 Francesca's lead

You've probably noticed throughout this series that I use the same texts in my minilessons over and over again. These are texts that I have read to the children, texts that they know and love, carefully selected for their teaching potential. Returning often to the same text shows students how very much we can learn through the study of one beautiful story. Keep a stash of these texts to use as demonstrations during small-group and individual conferences, too. I've sometimes led workshops to show teachers how we can weave any one text into fifty very different conferences!

"Brinckloe's used lots of techniques here; the lead is one we could examine and talk about for hours. So let's reread it again. As you listen this time, let a section of the lead stand out for you, and then when I finish reading it, turn and point out that part to your partner. Name what Brinckloe has done that you could emulate."

I reread the lead and reminded children of what they each needed to do in their own minds. After giving them a moment or two of silence, I queried, "Ready?" and when they nodded yes, I directed them to share with a partner. I listened in as the children talked.

Convene the class to talk as a group about what they noticed in the lead. Do this to lift the level of partner talk, which will be continued soon.

After a moment, I said, "Who can get us started on a conversation about the techniques Brinckloe has used in her lead?"

Deveonna's hand shot up. "It has less talk."

"Hmm, that's interesting," I said, looking at the text. "That's a smart thing to notice. But class, do you see that if there's *less* talk, there is *more* of something else?" I asked. Then I named the larger principle. "Writers, when I try to learn from other authors, I push myself to name what a writer *has* done, not just what he or she *hasn't* done, because it's easier to emulate something positive. What *did* Brinckloe do instead of writing dialogue?"

"She takes her time showing where the story takes place; the evening is coming and the treehouse is a black shape and all?" Ramon said.

"She doesn't start with dialogue." Ari added. "First there's just the backyard, then a flicker by the fence."

"So this author first creates the setting," I confirmed, providing Ari with the words he seemed to be reaching for. "But also, even before we see the backyard, we see the narrator, sitting at the dinner table, looking outside. The backyard is growing dark. It's not the author who describes the setting, is it? It's the boy, the narrator, who notices the setting. And what do you make of the flicker? Why did the author write the setting in such a way that there is a flicker right from the start?" Then I said, "Let's again try to talk with partners, and this time really name what Julie Brinckloe has done in this lead." I sent children to talk in pairs about this.

Convening the class, I again called on a few children.

"I think there is action, but it is just the flicker of the firefly."

"I think some stories start with the setting, and with making a mood. That's what this lead does 'cause we know it's evening outside."

"You've noticed a lot of techniques!" I said, and listed a few on my fingers.

Notice that when teaching strategies, I am careful to describe each step in sequence. I don't simply suggest that children "talk about what they can learn from this author." Instead, in order to set children up to make a reading-writing connection, I ask them to reread the text, let a part stand out for them, then point to that part and name the technique the author has used in this part that they can emulate.

This is unusual. I'm asking for a child to launch a whole-class conversation within the minilesson instead of simply retelling what I heard a child do. The teaching component of this minilesson was brief, so I saved enough time for this.

You could decide to create a large chart with a favorite passage from a mentor text on the left, the words children use to describe what the author has done in the center, and examples of two or three children's efforts to write similarly in the right column. This chart could form a cohesive link, tying together several days of inquiry and apprenticeship.

- Sometimes stories begin not with a big action but with a small action, and this can be an action in the setting, as when the firefly flickers on and off.

- Some stories begin by creating a mood and a place, and only afterward does the sequence of actions begin.

- Sometimes the time and the place are revealed slowly, bit by bit, as the character sees or moves into the setting.

Channel children to use what they notice an author has done to help one child again revise her lead.

"Let's all listen again to Francesca's first lead and think whether the techniques we've learned from Brinckloe could help Francesca as she gets ready to again revise this lead. Listen again, then tell your partner if you have suggestions for Francesca."

> "Dad," Griffen said.
> "Can I get a pet?"
> "Well, a pet is a lot of responsibility," Dad said.
> "Please," Griffen said.
> "If I see that you are responsible enough you can get a pet," said Griffen's dad.
> The next day, Griffen told Timmy. He was amazed.
> "I bet we can show that we are responsible enough," Timmy said.

After the children talked with their partners, I called on Shariff, who said, "Francesca, I'm not sure, but I think maybe your first lead had *too* much talk. You could add in where you are, and put some setting in with it and take some talk out."

Hannah added, "Another idea is you could start the story earlier, before this when he's just sitting and dreaming about getting a pet, and have Griffen be alone, like the kid in *Fireflies!* Then he could go to his dad next. That'd show his wants more."

LINK

Restate the options your children have for today, reminding them of the step-by-step process they might take to revise their leads.

"So, writers, I want to tell you a surprise. Francesca and I came to the same conclusions when we studied her lead. Francesca tried two other leads; let me read them to you." (See Figures 8–2 and 8–3.)

I deliberately selected a student whose lead invited further revision. I wanted to make it easy for children to imagine ways they could incorporate more setting. I also carefully chose a student who enjoyed collaboration, was viewed as a strong writer by classmates, and would find this whole experience a positive one.

As Griffen Tomson Was walking Down the Iile of Pets at SAMs PETSHOPE He was looking at a cage of Baby Saimming Hamsters. then He remembered the time When he got his Pet Mice and how They got Smuched by the Chair. "Come on" said his Dab. "Can I get a Pet" Griffen said. "Noˈsaid Griffen's Dad. "If you Show me that You are Responsabile Said his Dad.

FIG. 8–2 Francesca's first revision of her lead

Francesca's first revision:

> As Griffen Tomson was walking down the aisle of pets at Sam's Pet Shop, he was looking at a cage of baby squirming hamsters. Then he remembered the time he got his pet mice and how they got squashed by the chair. "Come on" said his dad. "Can I get a pet?" Griffen said. "No" said Griffen's dad. "If you show me that you are responsible," said his dad.

Francesca's later revision:

> The smell in the air of the pets' fur rubbing against the cage. The smell of the dogs breath panting. Griffen could hear the hamsters squeaking as they ran. He could hear the running water in the fish tank. It felt like all of the animals were his pets. He could hear the cat's purring and he could hear the turtles walk. It smelled like dog and cat fur. He could hear the birds squawking and making loud noises. He could see the little turtles rest under their mom. He saw one little turtle all alone under its shell. He saw it go under a big rock like a cave. He wanted to take the little turtle home!

"Do you see what she learned from other authors in her own lead? Today each one of you needs to decide what you need to do. Some of you are probably realizing that to write with this sort of detail, you need to rethink your story plan, figuring out how you can zoom in more on just two Small Moment stories. Some of you may decide that you need to do some revisions that are similar to those Francesca has done. Some of you will want to study published leads for yourself, learning more techniques. All of you will be drafting and revising leads, but you'll decide how to go about doing that. You can refer to our class anchor chart if you need help. You're the boss of your own story!"

How to Write a Fiction Story

- Develop a strong story idea, character(s), and setting.
- Spend time planning how the plot will go, making sure there is an arc to the story, trying again and again until the plan feels just right.
- Draft the story scene by scene, only using summary when needed.
- Study other authors for ways to make the story better.

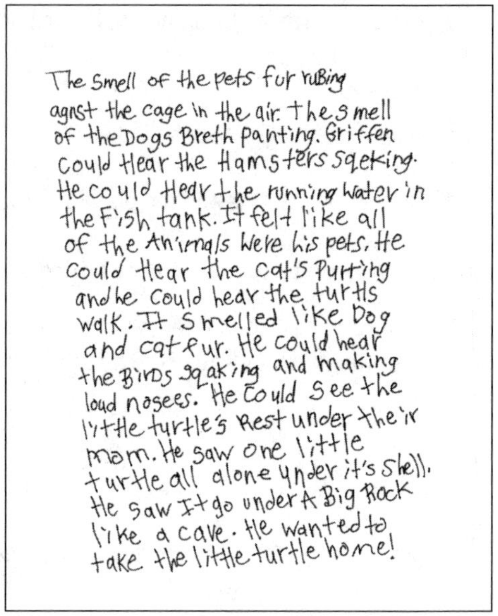
The Smell of the pets fur ruBing
agnst the cage in the air. the smell
of the Dogs Breth panting. Griffen
could Hear the Hamsters sqeking.
He could Hear the running water in
the Fish tank. It felt like all
of the Animals were his pets. He
could Hear the cat's Purring
and he could hear the turtls
walk. It smelled like Dog
and cat fur. He could hear
the Birds sqaking and making
loud nosees. He could see the
little turtle's Rest under the'ir
mom. He saw one little
turtle all alone under it's shell.
He saw It go under A Big Rock
like a cave. He wanted to
take the little turtle home!

FIG. 8–3 Francesca's second revision of her lead

Learning from Mentor Texts

AS YOU MOVE AMONG YOUR WRITERS, you may want to carry a couple of short stories or picture books with you so you can refer to these often as you work with children. Keep in mind that the same text can be used to help writers with a wide array of goals. This means that your resolve to help children use mentor texts needn't control the course of a conference. Instead, you'll want to open your conferences by asking, "What are you working on as a writer?" Presumably many children will respond that they're trying to learn from Julie Brinckloe or from another author.

Don't act as if this answers your initial interest in understanding the writer's intention. Instead, press on. "And what, exactly, are you admiring about your mentor author's text?" you can ask, channeling the child to at least point to a favorite part. Appreciate that section of the text. But then quickly shift from oohing and ahhing toward helping the child think, "What has the author done in this text that worked so well?"

That's a tricky question for a child to answer. If the child makes any attempt to articulate the replicable and transferable strategies the author has used, plan on accepting and building upon whatever the child says. Act fascinated by the child's observations. "Huh! That's so interesting!" you can say. "Explain more, 'cause you are onto something!"

On the other hand, be ready to demonstrate the sort of response you hope the writer might produce in case the child says nothing. If a child says she liked the lines "It was growing dark," "My treehouse was a black shape," and "But something flickered there, a moment . . . It flickered again, over near the fence," and if the child doesn't respond when you nudge her to articulate what Brinckloe has done that she, too, could try doing, you might help her imagine the sort of response you hope she provides. "Were you especially impressed by the way Brinckloe made us feel that her character was the one noticing the backyard? Was that it? You loved that we got to see the setting through the boy's eyes? Was that the aspect you especially liked?" Give the child some options. "Or were you impressed with the way Brinckloe made the setting, the place, more interesting by setting it into motion, having it be active?

(continues)

MID-WORKSHOP TEACHING Using Dialogue Deliberately

"Writers, can I stop you? I know by talking to many of you about your pieces and by looking over your shoulders that you are using a lot of dialogue in your stories. Give me a thumbs up if you have dialogue in your story." Most of the students gave a thumbs up.

"That's great. We know that fiction writers use dialogue all the time, so it makes sense that you're using it. I just want to give you one caution. When you use dialogue in your stories, there has to be a reason. You usually use dialogue because you're trying to show something about a character. It's important that you don't just use dialogue as filler. For example, look at this piece of dialogue." The students looked at lines I'd written on chart paper.

> "Hi" I said.
> "Hi," he said.
> "How are you?" I asked.
> "Fine, how are you?" he replied.

"Does everyone see how this part of dialogue doesn't do anything to help us learn more about the characters? It doesn't even move the story along. Instead, we can simply summarize what they said and write dialogue that deserves to exist, like this."

> After we exchanged greetings, I said what I had been meaning to tell him for days. "Mike," I blurted out. "I can't stand the way you pick on me all the time."
>
> "I had no idea," Mike said quietly. "Why did you wait so long to tell me? I would have stopped a long time ago."

The backyard grows darker, doesn't it, until the tree house is just a black shape, and then something flickers." Then restate your question. "Were you impressed that we saw the setting through the character's eyes, or that Brinckloe made the setting active, or what?" By this time, the child will probably be able to indicate which of those two options impressed her more, or she'll grasp the sort of response that was expected and contribute something of her own. Either way, ask if the writer was thinking of trying to do similar work in the next draft of her lead. It was this sort of conference that led Francesca to revise her lead (Figures 8–2 and 8–3).

Although your minilesson today was erudite and set children up for ambitious work, don't fool yourself into expecting that all your conferences will be aimed toward making good leads into great ones. Today's session gives you a final chance to check in with each student, making sure that each child has embarked on a project that is at least in the ballpark that you have in mind. You are sure to find some children who, like Jasmin, have resolutely refused to follow any of your advice! Look at Jasmin's rough drafts of some leads (Figure 8–4 and Figure 8–5).

Jasmin's first lead:

> Lora, Ashley, and Akyra all said to us,"What are you doing?" "Nothin . . . " Chaos said quickly, "For now." Chaos's eyes shifted side to side. "Really?" Akyra asked, a little suspicious. I nodded. Chaos, Death, and I zoomed up the stairs. Lora and Ashley closed the door of the basement. Even though I started to hear weird noises from the basement, I kept walking. As Lora, Ashley, Akyra, Chaos, and Death walked ahead of me I turned the flashlight and laughed maniacally, "MUAHAHAHAHAH!"

Jasmin's second lead:

- I saw Death and Chaos open the door of the basement. They walked down the stairs. I tilted my head for a second, then I followed them.
- Chaos, Death and I were stuck in the basement . . . thanks to Death. Chaos and I looked at Death. We both yelled to Death, "NICE GOIN' IDIOT!" I thought of this situation as, DEATH'S FAULT!

When I reminded Jasmin that we were studying *realistic* fiction, she immediately pointed out that her characters' names—Death, Chaos, and Spike—were really their nicknames, and that underneath the nicknames there are really just three normal fifth-graders named Marilyn, Steven, and Lilly. "And underneath the bits about zombies and so forth, what's the simple, human storyline?" I asked.

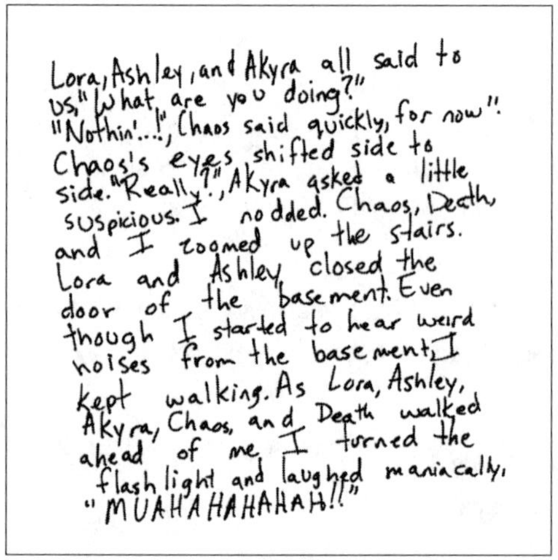

Lora, Ashley, and Akyra all said to us, "What are you doing?" "Nothin'...!", Chaos said quickly, for now". Chaos's eyes shifted side to side. "Really?!", Akyra asked a little suspicious. I nodded. Chaos, Death and I zoomed up the stairs. Lora and Ashley closed the door of the basement. Even though I started to hear weird noises from the basement, I kept walking. As Lora, Ashley, Akyra, Chaos, and Death walked ahead of me, I turned the flashlight and laughed maniacally, "MUAHAHAHAHAH!!"

FIG. 8–4 Although Jasmin's been directed to write realistic fiction, this is her first lead.

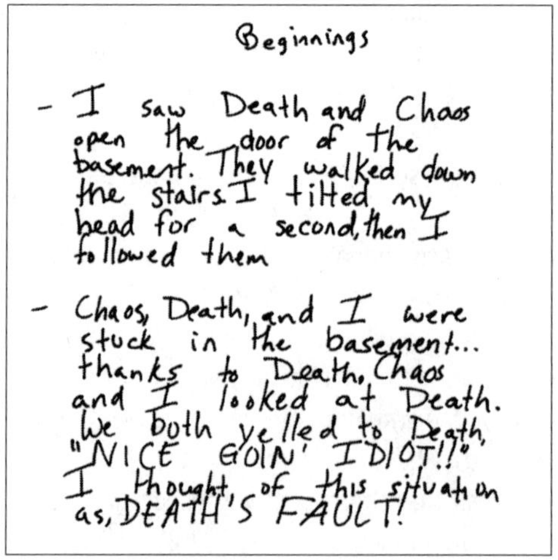

Beginnings

- I saw Death and Chaos open the door of the basement. They walked down the stairs. I tilted my head for a second, then I followed them
- Chaos, Death, and I were stuck in the basement... thanks to Death. Chaos and I looked at Death. We both yelled to Death, "NICE GOIN' IDIOT!!" I thought of this situation as, DEATH'S FAULT!

FIG. 8–5 Jasmin's revised lead is close to the first version.

After some convoluted explanation, I finally extracted the fact that Spike-Marilyn follows the other two kids but is ambivalent about their tendency to always push boundaries and get in trouble.

"This is incredible!" I said, once I finally pushed past all the overstated drama. "Now I get it! What an incredible idea. So Marilyn wants to be friends with these kids. Do they seem to her to be powerful? What's their allure?"

Jasmin and I talked a bit more, and then I put all her drafts of the Death, Chaos, zombie story inside her folder and pushed it to the side. I gave her a new blank sheet of paper and said, "You are definitely going to want to plan and write this story," I said. "Where will Steven and Lilly go? What sort of trouble will they get into?" Then I said, "Choose a place you know, a place you go to so that you can include realistic details, like Brinckloe did when describing the backyard."

This is the draft that Jasmin started that day (Figure 8–6).

> Lilly, Steven, and I walked through Chinatown. "So . . . many . . . shops," I thought. Steven pointed to the fish market. "Let's go there," he said. Lilly sighed, "Ok! What about you Marilyn?"
>
> "Whatever . . . " I responded, as I shrugged. We all ran to the fish market. I could smell the seafood. It didn't really smell so bad. Lilly swung the door open. Steven froze. "Look at the fishy goodness," Steven said. His eyes widened. I wasn't really amused. Lilly ran toward the fortune cookies.

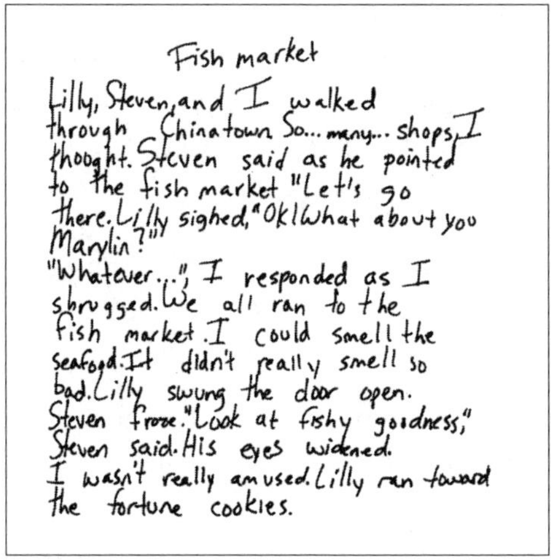
Fish market

Lilly, Steven, and I walked through Chinatown So... many... shops, I thought. Steven said as he pointed to the fish market "Let's go there. Lilly sighed," Ok! What about you Marylin?"

"Whatever...," I responded as I shrugged. We all ran to the fish market. I could smell the seafood. It didn't really smell so bad. Lilly swung the door open. Steven froze. "Look at fishy goodness," Steven said. His eyes widened. I wasn't really amused. Lilly ran toward the fortune cookies.

FIG. 8–6 Jasmin is now launched in a much more realistic story.

Testing Out Leads Can Help You Revise

Remind your children that as they reconsider various leads, they are actually reconsidering various ways their entire drafts could go. Ask them to write-in-the-air the way the next section of their story would go if they selected one lead or another lead.

"Writers, by now many of you have written several leads, several different first scenes. I want to remind you that each of your leads will get you started telling a different story. Would you share one of your leads with your partner, then see where your lead leads? Write-in-the-air to help your partner imagine how that particular lead will set up your story. After that, share a second lead, and again see where it leads. Use this as a way to figure out which lead sets you up for the story you want to tell."

Valerie's first lead:

> It was a dark and gray day. Kids were screaming and running inside puddles of water. All of them were screaming "Yahoo!" because school had just ended. The last day of school was sure a bad one, maybe it wasn't so bad for the other kids but it was pretty bad for Summer. She was sitting on the monkey bars wishing that school hadn't ended yet. In the back of her head she was thinking, "Oh, man, do I have to go to Catskills with Grandma & Grandpa?" Summer ran back home as fast as her feet would take her.

Valerie's second lead:

> I was sitting on the school porch thinking and thinking and thinking about school. School was ending. Kids were happy. They were going home. Some of them were going away for the summer with their grandparent or their parent, others were staying home for the summer, but I was going to the Poconos with my Grandparents and for me that was a disaster.

Leads set the path for the story to follow, so playing out each lead's story before choosing one is necessary work. The lead is not only a hook for the reader, it is also the rudder for the whole story.

> Lead #1
> It was a dark and gray day. Kids were screaming and running inside puddles of water. All of them were screaming "yahoo"! because school had just ended. The last day of school was sure a bad one, maybe it wasn't so bad for the other kids but it was pretty bad for summer Lennon. She was sitting on the monkey bars wishing that school hadn't ended yet. In the back of her head she was thinking "oh man do I have to go to Catskills with Grandpa + Grandma. Summer ran back home as fast as her feet would take her

FIG. 8–7   Valerie has written this lead in third person.

Valerie and her partner talked over the differences, and Valerie decided she liked writing in first person but wanted to create a mood as she'd done in the first lead. With her partner's help, she began writing a third lead (see Figure 8–9).

Valerie's third lead:

> Huge lightning bolts were in the dark gray sky. Thunder was booming in my ears, rain was hitting the ground like little bits of hard rocks hitting the windows. I was standing outside and getting soaking wet. I wasn't the only one who was out in the huge storm. For some weird reason I didn't like going home, at least that's what most kids thought. Well, I thought it was a good reason. Going home to your two boring grandparents wasn't fun, especially if one of them was really fussy, grumpy and mean.

"Writers, I need to stop all of you," I said, interrupting the partner conversations. "Your leads are beautiful. Listening to them, I thought if your leads weren't handwritten, it'd be hard for me to tell which leads you wrote and which leads had been written by professional writers! Remember, writers test out their leads as one way to help them choose and revise."

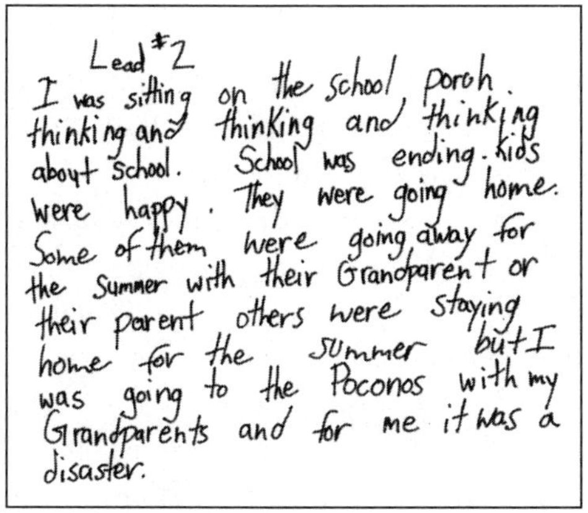

It might be convenient for you to take these three leads and turn them into a lesson that offers children an example of how they can try out different ways to draft and revise leads. You might also use these leads to hold a discussion with children about which leads work the best for which purposes. Children could also work together to revise these leads toward different ends, either as a class or in partnerships, and then compare and contrast their revisions.

FIG. 8–8   Valerie has written this as a first-person lead.

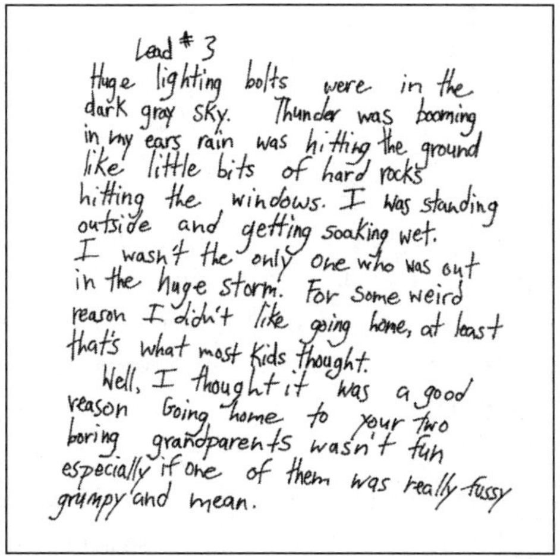

FIG. 8–9   Valeries aims to write in first person and to create a mood. She moves deeper into her storyline.

Orienting Readers with Setting

GETTING READY

✔ Anecdote or metaphor you can tell to describe the disorientation caused by lack of setting (see Connection)

✔ Scene containing almost nothing but dialogue, copied onto chart paper (see Teaching)

✔ Revised scene showing more story details, including action and setting

✔ Passage from the class story, on chart paper, for whole-class practice with setting

✔ Passage from a mentor text (we use *Fireflies!*) that communicates setting well (see Share)

WHEN TEACHERS DISCUSS PREDICTABLE ISSUES their students have had, someone invariably says, "Kids love fiction. They'll write for pages. The only problem is it's all dialogue. I can't make heads or tails of it!"

Be sure you recognize that the dialogue that swamps the pages of many drafts represents a big leap for these children. They are no longer summarizing the main events in their stories; instead, your authors are making mental movies and recording what happens in those movies—or at least they are recording the sound track to those movies! This is a gigantic step ahead, and your children are poised to write spectacular texts. You simply need to teach them one further step!

Once your children begin to ground their stories in precise settings, all of a sudden it is as if the stories become real, grounded. One character runs to the ocean's edge, then stands ankle-deep in the waves. "Come in," the character—waist-deep in the waves—beckons her sister. The sister tosses her towel on the dry sand. It falls near the water's edge, and before she can reach it, a wave washes over the towel. When writers write with setting, people carry real towels, and those towels need to be put somewhere before the character can wade waist-deep into the ocean. When we write with setting, we need to remember to put down our towels before we go into the water.

Your students have studied setting in past years, and for a variety of reasons. Today, you'll teach your students that fiction writers use settings to ground their stories. They use places, like living rooms and swing sets and forests; they use the weather, like heat waves and fog and lightly falling snow; they use times, like midnight and sunrise and lazy afternoons. Our students can often orally describe the setting of a story, but those details rarely make it onto the page. In strong stories, characters take action within a very concrete, specific world. When children learn to write with setting, they learn not only that setting allows them to anchor characters and plots. They also learn that developing setting can help them to convey tone and can hint at a character's mood, feelings, and insights.

COMMON CORE STATE STANDARDS: W.4.3.a,b,d; W.4.4, W.4.5, W.4.9.a, RL.4.3, RL.4.10, SL.4.1, L.4.1, L.4.2, L.4.3.a

Orienting Readers with Setting

CONNECTION

Tell about a time you were awakened in the dark and felt disoriented. Liken this to the disorientation some readers feel when drafts don't include enough setting.

"Last night I was sleeping, and the phone rang. When the phone woke me up, my whole room was dark and I didn't know where I was. I couldn't see anything. I couldn't tell if I was dreaming or awake. Has that ever happened to you? You wake up and for a minute, you can't remember where you are?

"When the phone rang again, I looked at where the sound was coming from and saw a light blinking, and it dawned on me that I was in my bedroom and that I'd just been woken by the phone. My eyes got used to the dark and I saw the dresser that held the phone.

"That unanswered phone call ended up helping me. Because when I was abruptly woken in the middle of the night like that and didn't know where I was, this made me realize that sometimes readers experience our drafts as if the events in our stories happen in the dark. The sounds—the voices—come out of nowhere, and readers are disoriented and need to ask themselves, 'Wait, where am I?' and 'What's going on?' and 'Where's that sound coming from?' Readers can hear the words a character says, but it's like the words come out of nowhere."

❖ **Name the teaching point.**

"Today I want to teach you that you need to be sure that you 'turn on the lights' in your stories, to show the place and the time, so that your readers don't have that disoriented feeling, asking, 'Wait, where is this? What's going on?'"

Just as writers live wide-awake lives, expecting that tiny everyday events can be grist for the writing mill, so do teachers. And of course our teaching takes on special immediacy and intimacy when we bring the tiniest little events of our lives into minilessons. Sometimes teachers don't realize they can do this. They say to me, "But I'm not a writer. My life doesn't contain writing lessons!" So I try to show them that even a phone call in the dark can bring new life to a minilesson.

TEACHING

Tell children that when writing scenes it's easy to rely only on dialogue, resulting in characters who don't seem to be anywhere in particular. Give an example of an all-talk scene in which the characters are nowhere, leaving readers struggling to feel oriented.

"Sometimes when you're writing a scene you get so caught up in your dialogue that you forget everything else. Let me give you an example. Ryan, a high school writer, wrote this." I showed a short, generic excerpt that I'd copied onto chart paper.

> I didn't know what to do. I looked at her. "Hey, are you mad at me?" I asked. "No. Are you mad at me?" she asked. I took a deep breath. "No. I don't think so," I said. "Great, then let's race," she said.

"Some things work in this scene. Characters are talking. We can tell how they're feeling. But the characters are floating. The story produces the same feeling I had when I woke up in the middle of the night and I didn't know where I was. We can't tell where the characters are, and we're not sure what they are doing."

Tell children that the student revised the scene by adding action and setting. Then show the resulting next draft.

"To make sure the lights are on for your readers, you need to always include two things: action and setting. Watch how Ryan's draft became much clearer when he added action and setting.

"Ryan didn't actually know what his characters *were* doing. When he wrote the draft, his characters were just talking. So he decided to revise his draft so his characters were walking home from school. He decided it'd be a gray, rainy day. That way, one of the characters could do stuff with an umbrella and the other character could step in puddles. Ryan expected the actions would be fillers, really, to hold up the talk, but the actions ended up revealing the real story in a very important way. Listen to Ryan's next draft."

> "Are you mad at me?" I asked as we walked down the sidewalk together.
>
> "No. Are you mad at me?" Zoe responded.
>
> A car whizzed passed us, kicking up water from the rainfilled gutters as it went. I thought about what Zoe was asking, and shifted the umbrella so that it protected her as well as me. With my other hand, I tugged on my backpack straps. My bag was heavy from all the homework our teacher had given us.
>
> "No. I'm not mad," I said.
>
> She smiled at me from beneath her yellow rain hood. "Good. Then let's race!" She took off ahead of me, splashing through every puddle on the sidewalk. The rain streamed down on her. I pulled in my umbrella and took off after her. I caught up with her, then loped easily in her wake.

I deliberately chose a very brief excerpt. I know this will more than double in size when it is revised, and I want to keep my minilessons brief. Little is gained by showing large expanses of text in minilessons.

Watch the ways in which I weave threads from earlier sections of the minilesson into the later sections, creating cohesion. I believe that all writers do this, and that the aspects of a text that reoccur are central to the text's message. This is why, when I teach readers, I put more of an emphasis on helping children see intra-textual connections (those that occur within a text) rather than intertextual (or text-to-text) connections.

Debrief, tucking some extra tips into your description of what the student did to revise. Point out that when trying to supply the setting and actions, the writer discovered important new interactions and meanings.

"Writers, do you see how the characters are not in the dark anymore? We can really picture them. We can see what they're doing and where they are. And you know what? When Ryan wrote this, his only plan was to have the two of them walking home together. He only made it be a rainy day because he figured he could describe the rain. Then, as he wrote the scene, adding in the actions, stuff started happening between the characters that Ryan never planned for at all. It just happened on the page! It surprised Ryan that his main character decided to move the umbrella over to shield Zoe, and he was totally surprised when her 'Let's race' response left him standing behind like a fool with that open umbrella! He recovered, though, and caught up with her, but didn't need to show her that he was the faster runner. All this drama came out in the story simply because Ryan realized that he needed to get his characters out of the dark and to rewrite the story, showing the characters as they moved and interacted in the setting."

ACTIVE ENGAGEMENT

Ask children to reread the Luz story from the chart paper while asking, "Will this make sense to readers?" When they encounter a passage that might be disorienting, ask them to revise it with their partner, adding setting.

"So let's try it. Let's read this section of our Luz story—I've been writing some more of it—and as we read, let's ask ourselves, 'Will this make sense to my readers? Is this clear?' If we come to a place in the story where the words seem to come out of the dark, a place where we suspect that readers might feel disoriented, you and your partner will have a chance to write-in-the-air, sprinkling references to the setting and to small actions that characters do in that setting, into our next version."

I retrieved the draft and read a section of it aloud—a section that I knew was well lodged into the setting and amplified with actions. I read:

> "Cake!" my mom called from the kitchen. All of us raced to the table, which my mom had decorated entirely in yellow.
>
> "Everything looks so cool," Marta said as she reached for a thick slice of the yellow cake with chocolate frosting. I couldn't help grinning. I had been right to choose yellow. It was a cool color. Since I didn't really have a favorite color, it didn't really matter anyway.
>
> I had barely swallowed the last bit of my cake when the other girls started to jump out of their seats to toss their party plates in the trash.
>
> "Let's go, first one there gets dibs on spots," Trish called out as she ran.

The lessons that I tuck into my minilessons are often more advanced than the teaching point itself. I know in this instance that the writing-to-discover work that Ryan has done is beyond the reach of most of the writers in this class. He is a high school student, and this is skilled work. But I do still want to expose all writers to the richest and deepest ideas, because who knows what will "click" for a child! And meanwhile, I am usually confident that my main teaching points are within reach and pertinent for everyone. The little subordinate tips one weaves into a minilesson are one of the ways our minilessons become multilevel, providing differentiated instruction.

Notice that instead of beginning the active engagement by saying, "Could you rewrite this scene so that . . . ," I instead ask readers to begin by rereading a fairly large passage of the Luz story using the lens of "Is this clear?" By backing up and starting with this, I not only get the chance to synthesize all the points I have made in this minilesson, I also demonstrate to writers how they might position themselves to do this work in the first place.

"Could you picture what was going on?" I asked. "Did you see the place?" Children gave me a thumbs up. "So let's read on," I said, and this time read the upcoming section (a part I knew was underdeveloped).

> "Here's my place," said Sarah.
>
> "I'll be near," I said. "We can talk. But let's move closer to the closet." "No, this is nice."
> "Weellll . . ." "Can we fit in?" three others said. "I'll move over," I answered.

The children talked to their partners, and after a moment I intervened. "Writers, please don't simply *comment on* how you'd go about rewriting this to add setting and actions. Write the new text in the air."

Ask one partnership to share their new version, and set up other children to act out the new version.

"Let's listen to Francesca and Jamal. While they write-in-the-air, I'll record it. But can I have someone who will play the part of Sarah and act out what they say, and someone who'll be Luz? Are there three of you who'll be the three others who want to join?" Soon the improvisational drama was ready to begin, and the children began improvising the new story. "The first character to do something is Sarah," I said, and gestured for her to step forward on the "stage." "What exactly is she doing?" I asked Jamal and Francesca. With that, they began spinning out a story while the actors moved about accordingly.

If you look back on the instructions I gave children, you'll see that I originally told children to write-in-the-air to show how they'd revise this. If our words are going to mean something, we need to speak up when children ignore our instructions.

> Sarah got her sleeping bag and found an empty spot of rug behind the sofa. She unrolled her sleeping bag. Then Sarah said, "Here's my place."
>
> I grabbed my stuff, and sat on the floor beside Sarah. "I'll be right here," I said. "We can talk." But as I said that, I knew I wouldn't be able to sleep there. I couldn't see the closet where the light was on, so I knew I had to move. I tried to talk Sarah into it, and said, "Let's move closer to the closet."
>
> Lying down, Sarah said, "No, this is nice."
>
> I wasn't sure. I looked over to a nice spot right beside the closet, and was about to try again to get Sarah to move closer to the closet. Then three other girls came. "Can we fit?" they asked.
>
> "I'll move over," I said, and picked up my stuff and went over to the empty place.

Ask the class to end the scene in a way that is informed by the acting.

"What could happen to end this scene?" I asked. "What might Luz watch that group of girls doing together?"

"They could all be huggin' each other and all so she feels left out?"

"Okay, but remember, we have them arranging their sleeping bags and getting ready for bed. Could they do those actions in a way that accomplishes the same thing in the story?"

These seemingly innocuous little prompts actually are fairly controlling. My question channeled the text in ways that made it much better. The children believe they've written this on their own, but meanwhile I've been directing.

Soon the class had written this ending to the scene.

> I watched as the group of girls figured out how to arrange their sleeping bags so they could all be close to each other. I heard Eliza say, "This way we can whisper together all night."
>
> I turned my back away from them, toward the closet where the light shone.

Debrief, highlighting the sequential steps you hope writers use with their own texts. Emphasize that revisions that begin as corrections can become entirely new creations.

"Writers," I said, "you've done some amazing revision. You reread this part of our draft and realized that readers might feel disoriented, as if the scene were taking place in the dark. So you sprinkled in a little information about the characters' exact actions in the setting, and as you did this, you—like Ryan—ended up surprising yourselves and finding that things are happening between the characters that we didn't even realize when we planned the story!

"This is what writers do. Our revisions start out as corrections, and they end up as creations!"

LINK

Remind writers that today they'll shift between drafting and revising, and that to revise, they'll want to reread their drafts with specific lenses.

"Writers, today you'll continue to draft and revise your stories, shifting between the two processes. And when you revise, you'll reread for all the goals that have become important to you. You'll make sure your characters feel real. You'll keep an eye on the deeper meaning of your story. You'll make sure you don't leave your readers in the dark. If there is a section of your story that seems disorienting, you can revise it like you've done today, adding more setting and actions to the scene. Please be sure that if you expect to *correct* your draft, you do so knowing that revisions that begin as corrections often take on a life of their own and become creations. Let your characters do things to and with each other that you'd never expected they'd do. Run along behind them!"

You may want to look at several minilessons and notice all the different ways in which we debrief after teaching. My hunch is that even though the debrief segments are usually brief, you'll find they are almost always sequentially organized, retelling a sequence of steps as one would in a how-to text. Although these sections where we debrief are summaries, they are also examples of how a writer can organize thoughts.

Weaving Together Action, Thought, and Dialogue

BECCAH WAS BUSY AT WORK adding in sentences here and there to her story. I approached her and said, "Beccah, I can see that you are busy revising your story. Can you tell me about the work you're doing?"

"Well, I realized that I don't have a lot of setting in my story, and so I'm trying to add in some setting so that my reader knows where my characters are."

"That sounds like great work, Beccah. Can you show me a place where you've done that?" I asked as I scanned Beccah's draft.

Beccah turned to the last page of her story and skimmed the page. "Right here," she said. "This is the part where Chloe and Samantha walk away from Niki and leave her standing alone. The first time I wrote it, it went like this."

> "Sorry, Niki," Chloe said.
>
> "Let's go," Samantha said, smirking at Niki.
>
> Together they turned and walked away from Niki. Niki just stood there.

"And then I revised it by adding in setting. Now it goes like this."

> "Sorry, Niki," Chloe said.
>
> "Let's go," Samantha said. They all stood in the hallway looking at each other.
>
> Doors were opening and closing as kids went to class.

MID-WORKSHOP TEACHING   Using Mentor Texts in Revision

"Writers, I want to tell you about the smart discussion Henry and I just had. He decided to study how Julie Brinckloe lets us know where and what is going on in *Fireflies!* and so he noted all the tricks he saw her use that he could use. This is Henry's list."

Sentences from Text

1. On a summer evening I looked up from dinner, through the open window to the backyard.

2. On a summer evening I looked up from dinner, through the open window to the backyard. It was growing dark. My treehouse was a black shape in the tree . . . fireflies flickered.

3. • forked food into mouth

   • asked to go out

   • found a jar

   • polished it . . .

4. First he's at kitchen table near window. Then he runs to cellar. Then he runs back upstairs. Then he returns to house . . .

Strategy Brinckloe Uses

1. tells where narrator is/what he's doing right away

2. tells big feeling of place, weather, time, right away

3. She tells a whole sequence of actions, of events.

4. Every action has a place.

"If you aren't sure that readers will know exactly what's going on in your stories, look at your draft and ask whether you do the same things that you find in the mentor text you study. Henry realized he hadn't done many of them. Now he knows just what his work can be. You can try the same thing he tried, now and anytime you write."

I thought to myself, "Yes, Beccah has certainly added setting to her story. Even this little bit helps orient the reader." But I also thought about the fact that so many of my students saw revision as adding in a word or a sentence here and there. I wanted to celebrate this kind of revision, but I also knew many of my students were capable of much deeper work. In this case, for example, I knew I could teach Beccah that people are affected by their environments and that adding setting to a story can be a tool for revealing what a character is feeling. This could teach Beccah about how to add in setting in a more effective way, but it could also teach her that revision is about helping oneself see more deeply into a character or situation, and that it entails more than adding a sprinkling of sentences. Beccah looked up at me and waited.

"So you've let the reader know that your characters are in the hallway, and you've added in details that show what's going on around them. That works for sure," I said, and then added, "As I read this, I could see that you are ready to do even bigger revision work. What do you think?"

"Okay." There was hesitation in Beccah's voice.

I continued, "You know, Beccah, when story writers revise their writing, they are often trying to show a little more of what their characters are experiencing on the inside as well as the outside. That's what we saw Ryan do, right? He added setting but did so in a way that brought out his characters." I looked at Beccah. "When you add setting to your writing, this gives you a powerful way to reveal your characters. What happens on the outside definitely affects us on the inside, right? A rainy day might make us feel down, a stadium filled with screaming Yankee fans might make us feel excited. So, when you add setting to your writing, you need to think about how the details you add can help your reader understand what your character is experiencing on the inside."

Turning to Beccah's draft, I said, "So let's look at the part of your story where Niki is watching her best friend, Chloe, walk off with her archenemy, Samantha. How is Niki feeling here?"

"Well." Beccah reread the part and then said, "She's feeling all alone, and sad. She's feeling like, 'Wow, I just lost my best friend.'"

"Hmm, so she's standing in the hallway feeling alone. Let's think about how you might use the setting to show that Beccah feels alone."

I knew as I said this that I could always show Beccah a published text where the author does this, and there are so many—*Fireflies!*, *Owl Moon*, *Fly Away Home*. I chose, instead, to coach Beccah as she thought through her work. You'll decide how to proceed depending on how much scaffolding you believe students need.

Beccah spoke up, "Well, maybe I can show that she's feeling lonely and the halls are all empty because everyone has gone to class and she's just standing there with no one to talk to or walk to class with."

"So how might you write that? Let's turn to your draft." We both reread the part that Beccah was working on. Then Beccah said, "Well, maybe it can go like this."

> "Sorry, Niki," Chloe said.
>
> "Let's go," Samantha said to Chloe. Niki watched as they walked through the blue metal doors. She looked around, but the halls were empty. She was all alone with no one.

"Yes, Beccah, that definitely works. You are on your way! You are letting the setting reveal how Niki is feeling. Always ask yourself how your revision work is helping you dig a bit deeper into whatever you want to say—and you are definitely doing that. Nice job!"

As you confer with children, show them that it helps to shift between action and thoughts, not just record a stream of thoughts. So if I wanted to describe my worry when my son, who recently got his driver's license, returned home late, I'd write in a way that intersperses thoughts with actions. To do this, I'd create a set of tiny actions that mirrored my thoughts and feelings.

I looked at the clock: 6:08. "Where could Miles be?" I thought. I went to the door and glanced out at the empty driveway, then at the road. Empty. "What could have kept him?" I worried. I went to the phone, picked up the receiver, and heard the dial tone. "Good. The phone's working and there have been no calls," I thought, and recalled last summer's awful phone call.

A few children in your class may well write in running commentary that sounds almost like free association, as Laurel has here (see Figure 9–1).

"Oh my god, Jessie is that you?"

"Lex? Oh my god. I haven't seen you in such a long time."

"I know," Jessie said. "So what's up?"

"Nothing."

"Like fifth grade?" Jessie asked.

"It's different."

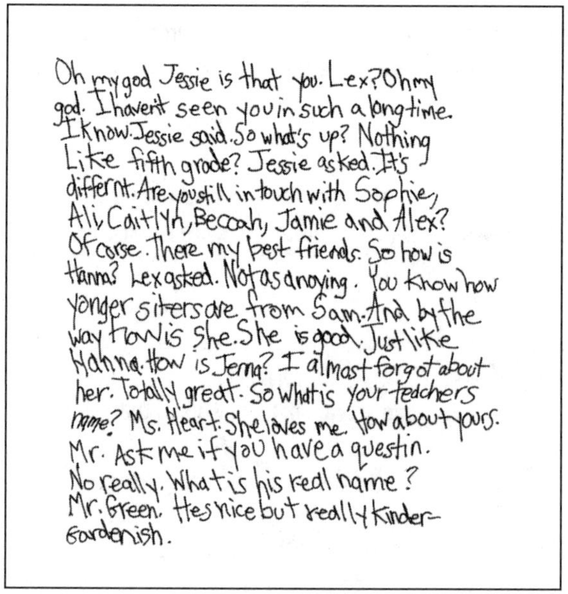

Oh my god Jessie is that you. Lex? Oh my god. I haven't seen you in such a long time. I know Jessie said. So what's up? Nothing Like fifth grade? Jessie asked. It's differnt. Are you still in touch with Sophie, Ali Caitlyn, Beccah, Jamie and Alex? Of corse. There my best friends. So how is Hanna? Lex asked. Not as anoying. You know how yonger sisters are. from Sam. And by the way How is She. She is good. Just like Hahna. How is Jenna? I almast forgot about her. Totally great. So what is your tedchers name? Ms. Heart. She loves me. How about yours. Mr. Ask me if you have a questin. No really. What is his real name? Mr. Green. Hes nice but really kinder-Gardenish.

FIG. 9–1 Laurel has been freewriting her story and needs to instead focus on a small moment or two.

"Are you still in touch with Sophie, Ali, Caitlyn, Beccah, Jamie and Alex?"

"Of course. They are my best friends. So how is Hanna?" Lex asked.

"Not as annoying. You know how younger sisters are from Sam. And by the way how is she?"

"She is good. Just like Hanna."

"How is Jenna? I almost forgot about her."

"Totally great."

Freewriting will end up being a wonderful skill that children can lean on, but writing always involves some coloring inside the lines (or working within the constraints) as well as some free expression. For now, these children's writing skills will come out best if they take each scene of their story and then plot the main sequence of actions (not the thoughts) on a timeline. Some children may want to make double timelines, with one timeline summarizing the actions and the other the parallel thoughts or comments. Then ask children to write, alternating between dialogue, action, and setting. See Laurel's second draft (Figure 9–2).

"Let's go look at the animals first so then on the sky ride, we can retrace where we were," Jessie said. "Ok," her mom said. They were zooming along 70 mph. Hanna and her mom were singing "Ninety-nine bottles of beer on the wall. Ninety-nine bottles of beer! Take 1 down pass it around ninety-eight bottles of beer on the wall." When they got to sixty-six Jessie yelled, "Enough! Let's play the quiet game whoever talks first loses. Ok 1, 2, 3." They stayed quiet then their mom said, "I hear that they have rides and games where you can win prizes." "And?" "We are there." They jumped out of the car and ran for the animals.

When conferring with children who struggle to pin down their free associations, I'd be apt to share my draft with them, or even to show a child how I might rewrite his or her draft. We might read a line or two and ask, "Where exactly were you? What exactly were you doing?" After the child answered, I'd say, "I asked those questions because you might want to shift between retelling your very specific actions and recording your thoughts. For example, your draft might go like this." And then I'd get the child started

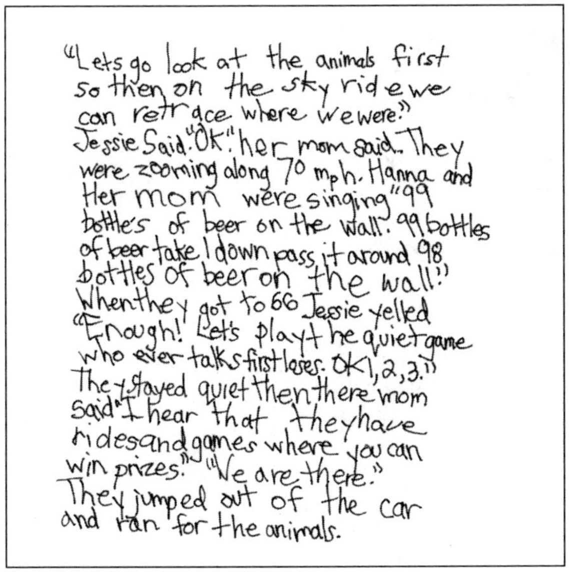

> "Lets go look at the animals first so then on the sky ride we can retrace where we were." Jessie Said. "Ok" her mom said. They were zooming along 70 m.p.h. Hanna and Her mom were singing "99 bottle's of beer on the wall. 99 bottles of beer take I down pass it around 98 bottles of beer on the wall." When they got to 66 Jessie yelled "Enough! Let's play the quiet game who ever talks first loses. OK 1,2,3." They stayed quiet then there mom said "I hear that they have rides and games where you can win prizes." "We are there." They jumped out of the car and ran for the animals.

FIG. 9–2   This time Laurel has situated her story into a few more concrete episodes.

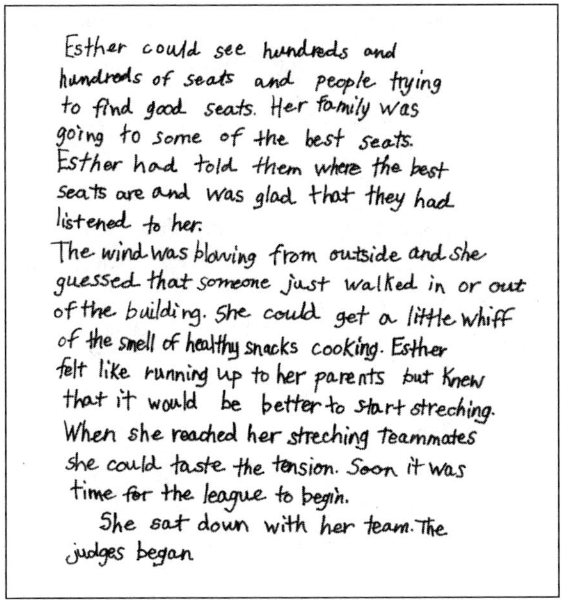

> Esther could see hundreds and hundreds of seats and people trying to find good seats. Her family was going to some of the best seats. Esther had told them where the best seats are and was glad that they had listened to her.
> The wind was blowing from outside and she guessed that someone just walked in or out of the building. She could get a little whiff of the smell of healthy snacks cooking. Esther felt like running up to her parents but knew that it would be better to start streching. When she reached her streching teammates she could taste the tension. Soon it was time for the league to begin.
> She sat down with her team. The judges began

FIG. 9–3   Notice that Sofiya's draft shows her protagonist experiencing the setting.

by showing how I might start the draft, weaving between action and thought, action and dialogue. I often summarize this teaching by saying to children, "For every thought or piece of dialogue, you need to add a narrative or action." I realize this sounds like a recipe, but for students who've resisted your more generalized suggestions, this can help.

I recently pulled students who struggled with creating setting into a small-group strategy lesson. I gave each student a copy of the Luz story with a lot of white space between each paragraph. Then I modeled how to add some setting to the Beccah section, adding the sentence, "Beccah got her sleeping bag and found an empty spot behind the sofa." As I modeled this, I wrote it onto my copy of the story, in the white space where it belonged.

Then I asked children to work with a partner, filling in some other setting details for the next paragraph, where the narrator speaks. I coached the partners, encouraging them to use actions and setting to help us picture what the characters were doing and where characters were.

Soon I shifted them to do similar work, adding details that allowed them to show the characters in their own pieces. I checked back with them as they continued the work

after I left, prompting them. "Remember how you and Shiv worked on helping us see the room here? You wrote that 'Luz spread out her sleeping bag on the floor beside Beccah.' You said, 'Luz couldn't see the closet from where she was because the sofa was blocking her view.' Those details helped us picture this place. Are there other places in your draft where readers will be in the dark?"

When I conferred with Sofiya, she'd written this opening scene to her story about a gymnastics tournament (Figure 9–3).

> Esther could see hundreds and hundreds of seats and people trying to find good seats. Her family was going to some of the best seats. Esther had told them where the best seats were and was glad that they had listened to her.
>
> The wind was blowing from outside and she guessed that someone just walked in or out of the building. She could get a little whiff of the smell of healthy snacks cooking. Esther felt like running up to her parents–but knew that it would be better to start

stretching. When she reached her stretching teammates she could taste the tension. Soon it was time for the league to begin.

She sat down with her team. The judges began to introduce the teams.

I asked Sofiya what she had tried to do in this draft, and her answer didn't surprise me. She'd tried to create a sense of place. "What really blows me away," I said, "is that even though you are only ten years old, you already realize that you can't leave the story and the character behind to show place. You need to have your character, have Esther, see and experience the place."

In this conference and in most of my conferences, I try to let children's work spark me to new realizations. I try not to simply admire the fact that a writer has done as instructed, but to also name what the writer has done that feels especially individual and original and new. This means, then, that conferences are one important source of new insight in my teaching.

Although I supported Sofiya's work with setting, which was her goal, this doesn't mean I didn't see some problematic aspects to her work. I noticed that Sofiya had been guided by an effort to include sensory details and was amused to see that as a result, even in the gymnasium, she had the character smelling healthy snacks (clearly Sofiya was trying to include all her senses, and her repertoire of smells is a bit limited!). However, I decided that commenting on this wasn't as important as helping Sofiya understand that although she was wise to describe setting, writers need to guard against being waylaid from their main direction and message. "Your readers can't get so detoured by all the sights and sounds around the main character that they lose hold of the main story," I said, and reminded Sofiya that her lead needed to go with her story arc and that she needed to remember what her story was mostly about and to highlight that in her lead. We can rephrase the question, "What's my story about?" to ask, "What does my character want? Struggle with?" This is a conference that is crucially important at this stage in the unit.

Sofiya's next lead shows that, above all, this is a story about Esther wanting desperately to do well at the contest (see Figure 9–4).

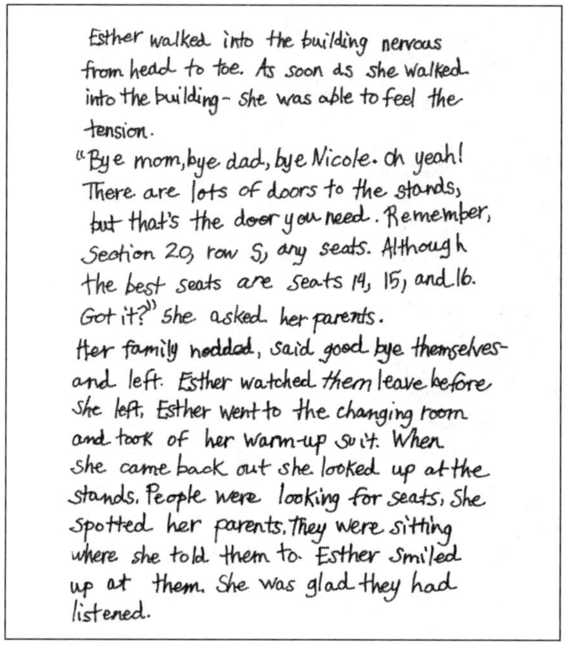

> Esther walked into the building nervous from head to toe. As soon as she walked into the building–she was able to feel the tension. "Bye mom, bye dad, bye Nicole. Oh yeah! There are lots of doors to the stands, but that's the door you need. Remember, Section

FIG. 9–4 Sofiya's next lead

> 20, Row S, any seats. Although the best seats are seats 14, 15, and 16. Got it?" she asked her parents. Her family nodded, said good bye themselves and left. Esther watched them leave before she left. Esther went to the changing room and took off her warm-up suit. When she came back out she looked up at the stands. People were looking for seats. She spotted her parents. They were sitting where she told them to. Esther smiled up at them. She was glad they had listened.

As she progressed, her writing partner reminded her that she needed to show, not tell. This too is a piece of advice you may find yourself offering at this stage of the unit. You could use the before and after samples of Sofiya's writing to help illustrate. Here is how Sofiya tried to show instead of tell (Figure 9–5).

> Esther slowly walked into the huge gymnasium with her parents and sister, Nicole. She was nervous, slightly trembling, and her teeth were gently chattering, making a quiet clicking noise.

> Esther slowly walked into the huge gymnasium with her parents and sister, Nicole. She was nervous, slightly trembling, and her teeth were gently chattering, making a quiet clicking noise.
>
> "Bye mom, bye dad, bye Nicole. I have to run if I want to be able to stretch and practice the routines" Esther told her family as she held the door to the stands open. Her family wispered good luck and nodded.
>
> They all went through the door that Esther was holding. There, they split up. Esther's parents and Nicole went excitedly to the stands that weren't even close to being thronged, while Esther ran to the changing room.
>
> When she got there- Esther took off her warm-up suit in the same speed that a cheetah runs. Then she skipped to stretch. There she warmed-up, stretched, and practiced the routines over and over again. Suddenly, a loud bell rang from the judges table.

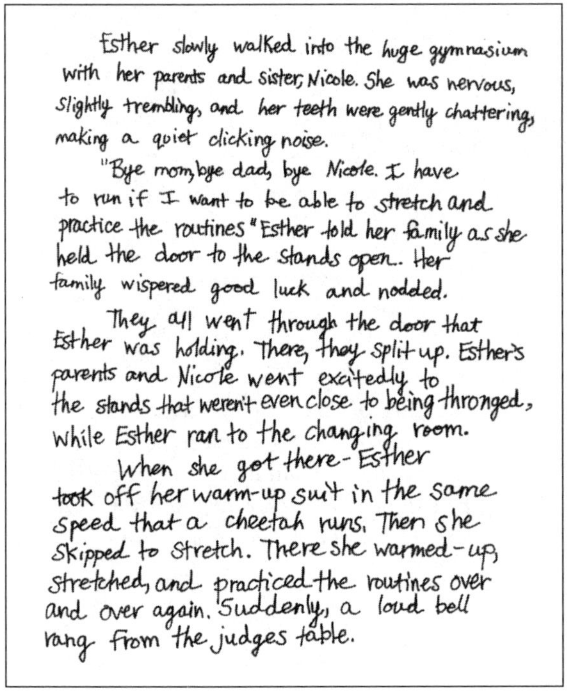

FIG. 9–5   Sofiya trying to show not tell

"Bye mom, bye dad, bye Nicole. I have to run if I want to be able to stretch and practice the routines," Esther told her family as she held the door to the stands open. Her family whispered good luck and nodded.

They all went through the door that Esther was holding. There, they split up. Esther's parents and Nicole excitedly went to the stands that weren't even close to being thronged, while Esther ran to the changing room.

When she got there Esther took off her warm-up suit in the same speed that a cheetah runs. Then she skipped to stretch. There she warmed-up, stretched, and practiced the routines over and over again. Suddenly a loud bell rang from the judges table.

Of course, once any one child has done some significant revisions, this becomes material for a small-group strategy lesson. We could then simply pull together a small group of children, and, using the one child as an example, lead the whole group through a similar work process.

Studying a Mentor for Setting Techniques

Celebrate that children have used today's teaching point to influence their revisions and drafts.

"Today, writers, some of you have been drafting and some of you have been revising, and that is exactly how it should be in a writing workshop. And I am impressed that whether you have been drafting or revising, you have been remembering not to leave your readers in the dark. You have been sprinkling little bits of the scene and descriptions of the action into whatever happens in your story."

Ask children to share, and ask listeners to signal when they feel well oriented to what is occurring in the story and when they feel they need more setting.

"Right now, would you find a place in your draft that you have recently written, a section of your story where you are pretty sure you've provided enough orienting information so that readers can truly make movies in their minds as they listen to your story?" I gave children a moment to find those sections. "Now would you get together with someone who is *not* your partner, someone who is a stranger to your story, and read this section aloud? And those of you who are listening, try to follow the writer's words and to dream the dream of his or her story. Show with your thumb up when you can really picture what's going on, and signal with your thumb down (as you listen) when it is harder for you to make that movie in your mind. Do this with one writer's draft, then the other writer's draft. If you have more time, look back on the drafts together and talk about revisions you might make."

Remind children they can attend to the setting of any writer's story to learn techniques for writing well about setting.

"Today you learned that writers help readers by describing what things look like in the room, the town, the place where the story is happening. The good news is that you don't need to be in a writing workshop to learn tips like this one. Whenever you read a chapter book, you can read with the eyes of a writer, thinking, 'How has this other author pulled off her story?' So right now, let's practice reading with the eyes of an insider. For now, let's look back on a section of a book we almost know by heart by now, *Fireflies!* Listen to this bit of the story and think about what Julie Brinckloe does, in the midst of telling action and dialogue, to show the scene."

The sky was darker now. My ears rang with crickets, and my eyes stung from staring too long. I blinked hard as I watched them—Fireflies! Blinking on, blinking off, dipping low, soaring high above my head, making white patterns in the dark. We ran like crazy, barefoot in the grass. "Catch them, catch them!" we cried, grasping at the lights. Suddenly a voice called out above the others, "I caught one!" And it

You can, of course, certainly ask students to share any part of the writing work they have been doing. You will want to angle the share to best support whatever direction you most feel children need to take in their writing.

This share has two sections to it, and of course you could select just one or the other. Always curtail your minilessons and shares if you need to do so in order to be sure that children have at least half an hour (preferably forty minutes) of actual writing time in school each day.

was my own. I thrust my hand into the jar and spread it open. The jar glowed like moonlight and I held it in my hands. I felt a tremble of joy and shouted, "I can catch hundreds!" Then we dashed about, waving our hands in the air like nets, catching two, ten—hundreds of fireflies, thrusting them into jars, waving our hands for more. (1985)

"Okay? Thumbs up if you think you saw a technique that the author used to bring out the setting in the story."

"She told what sounds there were outside," said Yasmin. "And also she described what the light was like, how it was getting darker so you could see the fireflies' lights."

"Yes! And can't you just picture what the yards and street looked like—darkness, but these little jars filled with pin-pricks of lights being carried by racing children? So from this day on, remember to read whatever book you are reading with the eyes of a writer, an insider, and notice how your author does whatever it is you are trying to do in your own story. Then use whatever the author has done to inspire you as you continue writing or rewriting your story."

Notice that I describe the techniques Fireflies! has used in ways which make them accessible and replicable. It's a bit of a trick to learn to do this, but well worth learning.

SESSION 9 HOMEWORK

NOTICING SETTING ON TELEVISION

Tonight I'm going to ask you to do something you probably haven't heard me ask before. I want you to spend a little time watching television. It can be a movie or a TV show, whichever your grown-ups say you can watch. I'd like you to watch a little bit with your writer's notebook in your lap. As you watch, look for the setting. Try to watch a part where the setting stays the same for a little bit. Watch, for example, a scene in a living room or in a park. While you're watching, jot a few notes about what you notice about the setting. Can you tell what the weather is? What time it is? Day or night? What colors do you see? What's high up in the setting? What's low? What does the camera show with more detail?

Once you've jotted a few notes, I'd like you to think about which parts of the setting helped you, as the viewer, understand the story more deeply. Then make some notes on your draft, suggesting ways you can weave more setting details into the draft when you come to school tomorrow.

Writing Powerful Endings

IN THIS SESSION, you'll teach children that writers of fiction do their best to craft the endings that their stories deserve. In particular, they make sure their endings mesh with and serve the purposes of their stories.

GETTING READY

✔ Example or anecdote to illustrate what a good ending can do for a story (see Teaching)

✔ Chart entitled "Key Questions Fiction Writers Consider in Revising Endings," prepared on chart paper (see Teaching)

✔ Ending to the class story that you and your students will write together (see Active Engagement)

A FEW SUMMERS AGO, I was glued to the gymnastics competition at the Olympics. I watched gymnast after gymnast throw his or her body across the floor or pommel horse or balance beam. No matter how complicated and flawless their routines were, if they did not "stick" their landings, their performances felt ruined.

It is the same way with stories. We've all had the experience of falling in love with a story and then the ending is either too sudden or unbelievable or just plain unsatisfying. We all know, too, that our students often fall into these same traps when they are writing their own endings.

Today, our goal is to teach children that in real life solutions don't usually fly in from outer space (or from left field). No one arrives on the scene at the final moment, solving everything. Each of us, as a person and as an author, can find small solutions in the everyday truths of our all-too-human existence.

The Common Core Standards ask students to "provide a conclusion that follows from the narrated experiences or events." This is a simple thing to do if students truly have understood the concept of the story arc—that the ending is where the story has been heading all along. We want students to internalize cause and effect, not just in their science, math, and reading life, but also to see how when they are in charge of the cause, they need to make sure the effect (in this case, the ending of a fictional story), follows a logical and satisfying path.

There is no one way to write a wonderful ending. An ending may be happy, sad, funny, or thoughtful. It may contain dialogue and action, or it may be a bit of setting. What all good endings have in common is that they address something essential in the story. Today's session, then, aims to show children that writers and characters alike can find turning points in the details of their lives. Today's session also marks the end of this bend, a bend that focused primarily on the blurry lines between drafting and revision, and preparing to move on to preparing for publication with an eye toward the audience.

COMMON CORE STATE STANDARDS: W.4.3.a,b,d,e; W.4.5, RL.4.5, SL.4.1, L.4.1, L.4.2, L.4.3.a

Writing Powerful Endings

CONNECTION

Acknowledge that some children will soon draft an ending to their stories, and share author quotes that spotlight the importance of an effective ending.

"Writers, before long some of you will write your way toward the ending to your first draft. I know some of you, as you've been writing, have been rehearsing possible endings. That's smart because we all know from television shows that end 'to be continued' that endings, like returning home from a journey, give us closure that is so important. They bring the story full circle. They are crucial. 'The opening line is a promise,' Jane Yolen has said, 'and the ending is a pay off to that promise.'

"Rick DeMarinis puts it even more strongly, 'My poetry writing teacher years ago said the ending of a poem is like a ski jump. There's the long accelerating downward glide, and then whoosh, you are thrown ballistically into space. You've been firmly fixed to earth, and now you're not.' He asks, 'Is that too much to ask of a poem or a story? Not at all,' he answers. 'That's exactly what we must ask'" (*The Art and Craft of the Short Story*, 2008, 40).

❖ Name the teaching point.

"Today I want to teach you that writers take their time with endings, weighing and considering, drafting and revising until they find one that fits. They know that a just-right ending will feel as if it is tailored exactly to fit their particular story. They know this ending will tie up loose ends, resolve the unresolved difficulties, and bring home the story's meaning." I added this to our class anchor chart.

TEACHING

Share something you know about how good endings go.

"When I taught very young children, I remember working with one child whose story told about a disastrous picnic but then ended with a hasty 'and we lived happily ever after.' The young writer—she was probably five—had just grown tired of her story and plopped that ending onto it. So we talked about ways she had actually appreciated the rained-out picnic after all, and I said, 'You'll definitely need to change the end of your story!'

◆ COACHING

No doubt, you've noticed that we make connections between the students and professional writers. Now, as we near the final two bends of the unit, when students' energy might be flagging, making those connections is more important than ever.

How to Write a Fiction Story

- Develop a strong story idea, character(s), and setting.
- Spend time planning how the plot will go, making sure there is an arc to the story, trying again and again until the plan feels just right.
- Draft the story scene by scene, only using summary when needed.
- Study other authors for ways to make the story better.
- Make sure there is trouble in the story, and write an ending that resolves that trouble.

"I came back later and she'd crossed out 'we lived happily ever after' and was instead writing of 'the end' in bubble letters. Each letter of 'The End' was carefully decorated with stars and stripes. 'I'm fixing up "the end,"' she said cheerfully to me.

"We laugh, but the truth is—many of us aren't all that different from that five-year-old. We don't have a clue how to resolve our stories. We may not slap a 'they lived happily ever after' ending onto our story booklets, but in our own way, what we do is not much better. The three girls gang up on Kayla, putting cockroaches and trash in her locker and spraying whipped cream on her face. How does that story end? The principal arrives on the scene like Superman, flying in from nowhere, and brings the three mean girls to his office where they see the light of day.

"I want to teach you one bit of advice that I think can make all the difference when you draft and revise your endings. This is it: the ending is there all along, in the problem. There is never a need for another character to zoom in from outside the story to save the day!"

Offer an example that illustrates a principle of good endings.

"Let me show you what I mean. Let's go back to that story of the three girls who gang up on Kayla. It's not a sweet story. In fact it is a tragic one, but it needs an ending nevertheless. The mean girls hide around the corner in the hall, watching when Kayla pulls open her locker door. They see her step back as the trash plops out onto the floor, reeking. The mean girls laugh at the cockroaches as one drops onto Kayla's sweater. One of the girls, to top it off, approaches with a can of whipped cream in hand, ready to spray it in Kayla's face.

"What might happen?" I said. "I've discarded the idea of the principal or the therapist or the parent arriving from outer space to teach a lesson. I'm trying to find an ending—a solution—that's right here in the midst of the problem. Hmm." I paused for a long while. "I'm trying to think what could happen in that awful moment to change things."

Then I said, "Perhaps the girl with the can of whipped cream goes to spray it, brings the nozzle close to Kayla's face, and for a moment, she looks in Kayla's eyes. She sees Kayla, the person, and she sees herself, too, and drops the can onto the floor.

"Or, then again, perhaps a cockroach drops onto this girl's arm, perhaps she is terrified, perhaps Kayla reaches out to help her, and the turning point comes in that gesture.

"To write an ending, it'll take lots of drafts, of course. These are just early ideas, but I wanted you to see that the solution is often in the details of the problem, and that turning points often involve a word, a gesture—on the outside. Because the real turns happen on the inside."

Introduce a list of a few ways writers make sure endings are of good quality.

"Here are a few key questions fiction writers consider when revising their endings and imagining how they might go." I referred to the chart I had prepared.

You might say, "It makes me think of how Fire-flies! ends. We were all sort of surprised the first time we read it, but at the same time we all thought—that ending makes sense. I can't imagine it ending any other way. Of course, that ending probably didn't come to the author on the first try. She probably revised and revised until she got it just right, just like you are going to do. In fact, I'm pretty sure she thought about a few things before she wrote the perfect ending. And you guys will be doing the same thing."

Key Questions Fiction Writers Consider in Revising Endings

- Can the reader see evidence of the main character's evolution?
- Does my ending make sense or come out of nowhere?
- Are the loose ends tied up? Have I answered the reader's key questions?
- Have I revealed everything I need to for the story's purposes?

ACTIVE ENGAGEMENT

Ask students to think about the class text in relation to one of the considerations set up in the demonstration. In this case, ask them to consider whether the class story's purposes are fulfilled in the ending.

"So, writers, let's work together and see if we can imagine some possible endings to our Luz story. You'll remember that the ending will always relate to the story's real message," I said. "So we need to remember what the story is really, really about." I flipped through drafts that we'd written on chart paper.

"Hmm. So, writers, it seems to me our ending needs to somehow address Luz's fears of sleeping in the dark and also of being ostracized by the girls. Would you and your partner think about two possible endings?" The children turned to talk, and after a bit, I asked one of them to share her idea. Sofiya said, "I think Luz can be lying there in the dark getting really scared and then another girl—maybe Marta—whispers, 'Do you have a flashlight?' and it turns out *she's* afraid of the dark too."

Turning to the whole class, I said, "Sofiya had a suggestion for an ending. We need to think, 'Does it address—even resolve—Luz's fear of the dark?' 'Does it link to her desire to be popular?' 'Does it show that she's changed internally?' I'm not sure if it does the last of these but it certainly links to her fear of the dark. And there's no Superman swooping in to save everybody!" Then Henry said, "I want Luz to get over being afraid of the dark. I want her to realize that there's nothing to be afraid of. Maybe we can have someone make a noise, and Luz and Marta realize it's a robber and they are really brave even though it's dark and they catch him."

I said, "I know Henry's not alone in thinking that in a story, a character should change—so it makes sense that Luz conquers her fears, catches the robber, and so forth. But I want to remind you that we all, as people, change and grow in small ways. This is realistic fiction, and realistically, Luz isn't going to get over her fears in the blink of an eye. So, Henry, can I steer you toward appreciating the much, much smaller changes that human beings actually make?"

LINK

Acknowledge that you know students will be in different stages of writing today, but if they are ready, they can move into revising their endings.

"I know you are all in different places right now. Some of you may begin to write the first draft of your ending today, and for others of you it'll be tomorrow. No matter where you are in your work, when you get to the ending, remember that writers always consider whether their ending matches their story. And they look for solutions and resolutions that come from the grit, the specificity, the truth of the story. More than this, you need to remember that endings matter. Write a few different endings. Weigh which one you like best."

You could also muse, "Are the loose ends tied up? Have I answered the reader's key questions? I'm not sure about that. Is Luz still afraid of the dark? I bet people might want to know that. The story isn't only about fitting in. It's also about getting over your fears. I'm going to make a note of that right here in the margin."

Notice that I did not explicitly teach the students how to write and experiment with different endings. I assumed that the students would hold on to that strategy from our earlier work on leads and revision. If you feel that your students need that work explicitly taught, by all means do.

Reining in Last-Minute Additions

WHEN YOU CONFER WITH CHILDREN TO HELP THEM imagine possible endings, you'll find that many of them propose endings that writers refer to as *deus ex machina*. The term means "god from the machine," and it refers to an ancient Greek drama in which all the conflicts of a play are miraculously solved by an actor dressed as a Greek deity who descends from the clouds to resolve everything with a timely wave of the hand. Many children will choose a quick-fix ending because they don't want their stories to go on and on or because this gives them an easy way to resolve their story's main conflict. But students' writing becomes unrealistic because the story ends abruptly or because the student has something happen that is out of left field.

I sat down next to Joey, who was quickly writing furiously down the page. I waited for him to find a stopping point and then asked, "So, Joey, it looks like you've hit upon something big. Whenever I write fast and furiously, it's usually because I've had a great idea, and I want to get every word down. What have you hit upon?"

Joey looked up with a smile across his face. "I've figured out a new way to help my character with his problem, and I wanted to get it all down before I forgot." "That's huge! You must be so relieved," I said as I picked up Joey's paper, reminding myself of his story. It began like this.

> Gary stood in front of the store window looking at the brand new BMX bike. It was candy-apple red and had shock absorbers on the front tires. He imagined himself riding this bike, doing wheelies, jumping off ramps. He imagined himself zooming down huge hills in Central Park and zooming past people. He was like a statue standing in front of this bike. How would he be able to afford it?

"So, Gary's problem is that he wants a new bike, but he can't afford it." Joey nodded.

"How have you decided to help Gary buy his bike?" I prepared to jot as Joey spoke so that I would have his words clear and straight in my mind.

Joey looked at his writing. "Well, I'm going to have an old lady who lives in Gary's building give him the money. The old lady hears Gary talking to his mom one day about the bike and how much he wants it, so this old lady decides to help Gary by giving him the money. Then, at the end, Gary goes and buys the bike."

I listened as Joey told his story, and jotted notes. "So let me make sure I have this straight." I looked down at my notes. "An old lady who lives in Gary's building is going to give Gary the money to buy his bike. Then, at the end, he goes to the store to buy the bike?"

MID-WORKSHOP TEACHING   Partnering in Revision

"When I was walking around, conferring with you, I was thrilled to see that many of you are sharing your ending ideas with a partner. I think that's a great idea. It makes me think that you know something that professional writers know. It helps to have fresh eyes look at a piece. After all, you've been looking at the same piece for a long time. It's hard to see all the things there are to see in it. Just like it's sometimes hard to see that your desk is messy because you look at it every day. It's only when someone else sits at your desk for a few minutes that you realize—oops—it's due for a cleaning!

"Remember, you need your partner to look not just at the ending itself, but also at your piece as a whole. If you haven't yet asked for a reader, do so soon."

"Yes, that's right."

"Well, I take my hat off to you, Joey, for working so hard to solve your character's problem. You know, it's not easy to solve a character's problem in a short story, because you don't have lots of time to do so."

"Yeah, I know. That's why I like my new ending, because Gary gets the money and can go buy the bike."

"Can you show me where this old lady comes into your story arc?" I asked, flipping the pages of Joey's notebook to find his plans.

He quickly found his most recent story arc and pointed to the top of the arc. "She comes in at the middle of the story. Gary begs his mother to buy him the bike. Then, one day, this lady hears him and she tells him that she'll give him the money."

As Joey spoke, I thought to myself that there were a couple of ways that this conference could go. I could teach Joey to look at the events that had already happened in his story and then show him how he could use something that had already happened to lead to a solution. Or I could teach Joey to introduce this new character earlier and think about how her story might unfold so that it doesn't feel as if she's come out of thin air. With those options in mind, I pressed on. "You know, Joey, having this new character in your story can add a whole new dynamic. It adds so many possibilities for how your story might unfold. So that was a very smart thing to do. But I want to give you a very important tip. Writers don't just add in characters at the last minute and have them fix all the problems that the character faces. When a solution zooms in from outside the story, this can throw a reader off and make your writing seem unrealistic. Instead, writers weave characters in from the beginning—and then sometimes those characters end up being heroes of the story." I paused so that Joey could take in what I'd said. "So let's look at your story arc. Where might it make sense to have the neighbor come in? Remember, we want it to be somewhere close to the beginning. Introducing her in the middle is too late."

Joey looked at his story arc and read out a point close to the beginning. "Well, here is the first time my character asks his mother for the money to buy the bike. So maybe they can be in the hall or on the elevator and the woman is there and she hears it."

"That could totally happen. Absolutely! Now you need to imagine a realistic reason for her to eventually give him the money. It feels unreal that she just gives him the money. What's her motivation for that?"

Joey thought. "Maybe she needs some chores done and she asks him to help her. He spends a couple of weeks doing chores for her and then he earns the money to buy the bike?"

"Yes, Joey, that's a realistic possibility. So before you start writing, go back and revise your story arc so that you are sure to weave your character through the whole of your story. And after this, try to be sure your solution grows out of the details of the story."

You will also find that some students, as they near the end of their stories, seem to feel insecure and therefore reach to add a little pizazz. Viktor did just that with his story about a boy who overslept for the ELA test (New York State's standardized language arts test). During the last phases of revision, he added pages and pages onto his draft. "I've been reading other people's stories and I realized my story was just not that exciting. So I decided to create more tension. So now, my character doesn't only miss the ELA test, but his father gets in a car crash," he explained (see Figure 10–1 and 10–2).

I acknowledged that the car crash definitely added drama, but then continued, "You know, Viktor, a car crash is really very serious and important. In short stories, like what we've been working on, there is only room for one big event. For example, in our Luz story, we have the slumber party. We wanted to say that it was okay to be different and to be afraid of things, and the slumber party helps us show that. What important thing are you trying to say in your story?"

Viktor stopped and thought for a minute, then admitted that he was trying to talk about how stressful taking tests can be. "Maybe I should save the car crash part for another story," Viktor said, and I concurred.

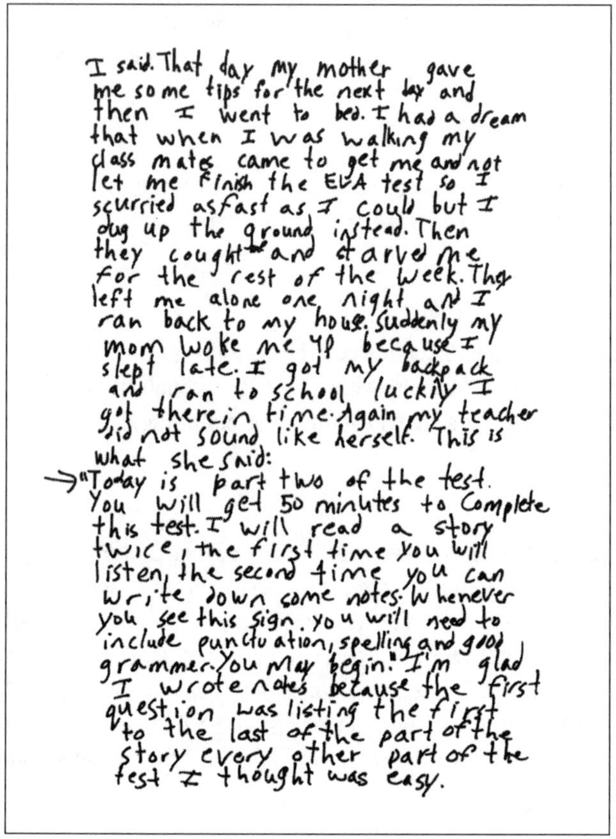

I said. That day my mother gave me some tips for the next day and then I went to bed. I had a dream that when I was walking my class mates came to get me and not let me finish the ELA test so I scurried as fast as I could but I dug up the ground instead. Then they cought and starved me for the rest of the week. They left me alone one night and I ran back to my house. Suddenly my mom woke me up because I slept late. I got my backpack and ran to school luckily I got there in time. Again my teacher did not sound like herself. This is what she said:

→ "Today is part two of the test. You will get 50 minutes to complete this test. I will read a story twice, the first time you will listen, the second time you can write down some notes. Whenever you see this sign you will need to include punctuation, spelling and good grammer. You may begin." I'm glad I wrote notes because the first question was listing the first to the last of the part of the story every other part of the test I thought was easy.

FIG. 10–1   Excerpt from Viktor's original draft

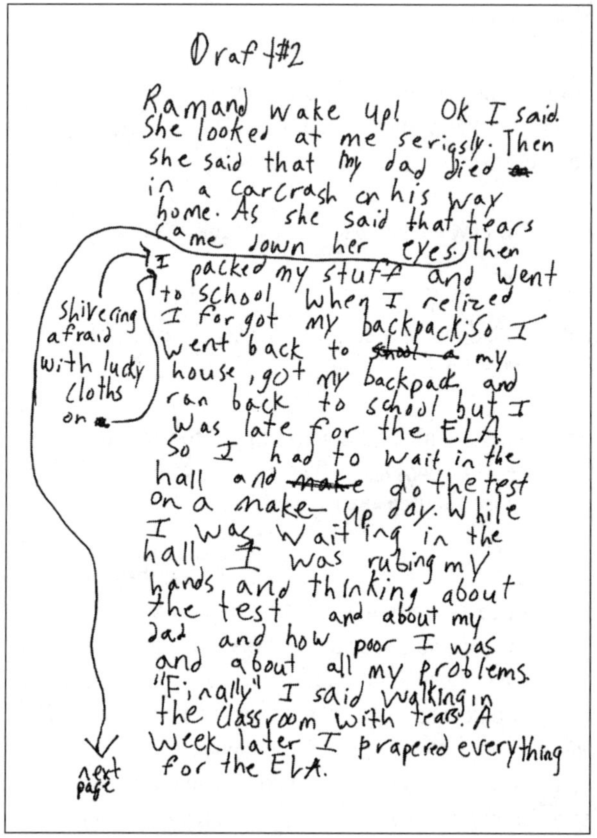

Draft #2

Ramand wake up! Ok I said. She looked at me serigsly. Then she said that my dad died in a carcrash on his way home. As she said that tears came down her eyes. Then I packed my stuff and went to school. When I relized I forgot my backpack, so I went back to my house, got my backpack, and ran back to school but I was late for the ELA. So I had to wait in the hall and do the test on a make-up day. While I was waiting in the hall, I was rubing my hands, and thinking about the test and about my dad and how poor I was and about all my problems. "Finally" I said walking in the classroom with tears! A week later I prapered everything for the ELA.

shivering afraid with lucky cloths on

next page

FIG. 10–2   Excerpt from Viktor's revised draft

Learning about Endings from Colleagues

Share the story of one child's writing process that led her to write a more powerful ending.

"Writers, I want to tell you about something exciting that Deveonna realized today. Deveonna realized that she didn't need a miracle to happen at the end of her story. Let me explain. You'll remember that Deveonna's story is about a popular girl, Alexa, who feels as if she's been stalked by a somewhat nerdy boy, Max. In the opening scene of Deveonna's story, Alexa hides behind a tree so that Max won't find her—though of course he manages to spot her and is on her like glue. He comes close, and Alexa's friend cries, 'Run!' Later, Alexa decides she's going to confront Max and tell him she wants her privacy. She wrote" (see Figure 10–3):

> I sat in reading class, and started to doodle all over my reader's notebook. Even when the class was reading out loud, all I could hear were the ticks and tocks of time getting closer to when I'd tell Max. I think to myself, "My next class is with Max." I think, "I hope I'm strong enough to tell him."
>
> On my way to lunch I was so busy practicing what I'd say that I didn't realize I had bumped into Max. He said, "I'm so sorry, Alexa." I tell him, "I don't want any one helping me, or even following me."

FIG. 10–3 Deveonna's opening scene

"At first Deveonna wanted to write, 'He said fine, and that day after school we played chess and became best of friends.' But then she wrote in her notebook, 'I don't like that. Everything is just so peachy like one of those corny shows on TV for little kids.' So she tried another ending. Will you listen to it, and afterward, be prepared to list across your fingers four things that Deveonna has done in her writing that really work? This time she wrote" (see Figure 10–4):

> I had bumped into Max, dropping my books. He said, "Sorry Alexa," and bent to pick up my books. He gave them back to me, then I said, "Well thanks, but you know the following around thing has to stop."
>
> I looked into the eyes that had once been jolly, that had now turned into eyes filled with tears. With my human research I could tell not only that he was sad, but I felt the exact way.

Why? I thought back to when I was the new kid. I didn't do the exact same thing, but I knew it was hard to make friends. I thought to myself, "How could I do this to him?" I thought, "But the deed is done." I turned away, too sad to look. Then I looked back and I realized I was the only person left in the hallway.

Ask children to consider what they've learned from this child's process and begin considering how to improve their own endings.

"Turn and tell your partner four things Deveonna did that really worked," I said, and the room erupted into talk. After a bit, I intervened. "If you wrote an ending today, share that ending and talk about how it works—and how it could be better still."

Let students know that today was the last day the class will be studying drafting. The next session will focus on revision and moving toward the finishing stages of their pieces.

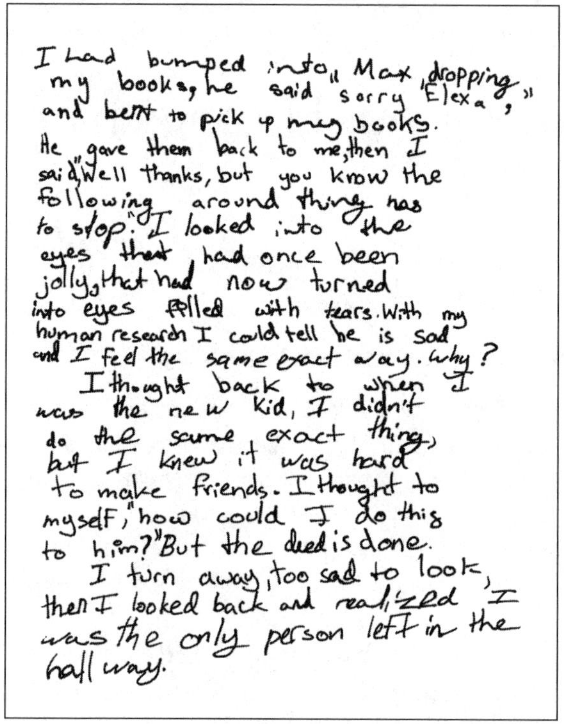

FIG. 10–4 Deveonna's ending

Once student's conversations had started to wind down, I gathered students back. "I know most of you put the finishing touches on your drafts today. Some of you have already moved on to major revisions. Today marks the last day we will work on drafts as a class. Tomorrow we begin the exciting work of revision—and move even closer to sharing these pieces with audience."

Revision

Rereading with a Lens

IN THIS SESSION, you'll teach children that when revising, writers don't simply reread; they reread with a lens. Writers vary their lenses according to what they value for their work.

GETTING READY

✔ A pair of glasses to demonstrate how revision is like rereading with a lens (see Connection)

✔ Latest version of the class story, on chart paper, to demonstrate revising through a lens (see Teaching)

✔ Former student's draft, prepared for projection or on chart paper for whole-class practice

✔ "How to Write a Fiction Story" anchor chart (see Share)

COMMON CORE STATE STANDARDS: W.4.3, W.4.4, W.4.5, W.4.8, W.4.10, RL.4.3, RFS.4.4, SL.4.1, L.4.1, L.4.2, L.4.3

I N THIS SESSION and the ones that follow it in this bend in the unit, you will rally children toward a serious commitment to revision, editing, and publishing for an audience. To start that work, you'll pull out all stops in an effort to support revision. You'll teach revision strategies in the minilesson, confer toward revision in your conferences, and celebrate revision in your mid-workshop teaching point and your share. But above all, you'll convey the assumption that, of course, children will revise.

Children generally come to us resisting revision. They often regard it as punishment for writing badly. In the earlier grades I usually introduce revision by telling children that when we are really proud of our work, when it is the best writing we've ever done, we revise it. Revision is a way to make our best better. Later, I invite the youngsters to reread texts they've written, looking for whether any of them are "good enough that they deserve to be revised." My message is clear: revision is a compliment for good writing. Lousy writing is abandoned; good writing is labored over, developed, refined, and polished.

It's important to teach and model this stance toward revision, but it is also important to equip youngsters with tools that will allow them to revise to good effect. Too many children add a clarifying phrase or insert a detail and regard that as revision!

In this session, you will teach children that revision begins as rereading, and suggest that writers can reread with any one of many lenses. This is not a new point. We can reread asking, "What is this story really about? Have I brought out that deeper story? Have I made my characters vulnerable enough to seem human?" While it is true that revision is a Common Core State Standard (W.4.5), we want students to revise because they see the value of it for their readers, but also for themselves. This is their chance to make sure that the piece they are intending to write is the one that ultimately ends up on the page.

The larger message is that revision begins with rereading and that writers can be deliberate and strategic, selecting a lens based on whatever they value, and rereading with that lens.

Revision

Rereading with a Lens

CONNECTION

Celebrate that some of your students have finished drafts of their stories, and remind them that reaching the end allows writers to reread and revise with new perspectives.

"Hurrah! Many of you are coming to the final pages of your story booklets. And the good news is that once you reach the ending of your story, you have a chance to look over the story and to make the whole of it fit together into a single coherent piece."

❖ **Name the teaching point.**

"Today I want to remind you that even when we move heaven and earth to write our drafts really well, we will each shift from drafting to revision. And specifically, I want to teach you that revision means just what the word says—revision. To see again."

Then I leaned toward the children as if conveying a secret and said, "I want to teach you that when you revise it really helps to reread with glasses." I put on a pair of glasses for effect. Then, pulling the glasses off, I said, "You don't *really* need to wear glasses to be a writer. But you do need to put on special lenses, lenses that allow you to reread your writing with one particular question or concern in mind. We sometimes call that 'reading with a lens.' You might, for example, reread looking specifically to see if your character development satisfies you, or to see if you've shown the passage of time effectively, or to study the way you've used varied sentence lengths and punctuation to create rhythm and suspense in a story."

You will notice that here, as in most minilessons, I deliberately weave a certain amount of flexibility into the form the work of the day might take. I don't say, "You must look at your writing through two lenses." Instead, I say, "You might look at your writing through this lens, or this lens, or another lens that reflects something that is important to you in your writing." By doing this, I reinforce the idea that writers have to make decisions about their stories, and that the work is not the same for every writer. I entrust these decisions to students, and they feel more invested in the process than they would if I kept a tight hold on the reins. This is one way in which we can help writers become independent.

TEACHING

Explain that, especially when writing longer texts, many writers shift often between writing and revising. Tell children that you will revise what you've written so far, and ask them to notice that you start by rereading the draft through a lens.

"Let me show you what I mean when I say revision starts by rereading with a lens. Before I do, let me join you in noticing that our class story isn't finished yet. We've written three pages for our story booklet, and I want to point out that when I'm writing a long text, I usually don't wait until I'm all done before I begin to revise. I'd rather rewrite three pages than revise the whole book! Many writers do that."

Demonstrate rereading the draft through a lens. Explain what rereading through another lens could look like.

"So I'm going to revise the draft we've written so far. And to do so, I'm going to use a special lens. I'm going to read just a bit of it with an eye toward one issue I choose. I could choose any issue that especially matters to me."

"Remember earlier, we said that it is really important to think, 'What am I trying to show?' and to ask, 'What is this story *really* about?' So I am going to reread our Luz story, thinking, 'Have I really brought out the idea that this isn't just a girl-has-a-sleepover story?' This is a girl-who-worries-no-one-will-like-her story, a story that revolves around Luz's worries over whether her friends will laugh that she needs a night-light."

I reread the class story, underlining places that illustrated the deeper meaning. With the class's approval, I decided aloud that the class had, indeed, brought out that understory. "Did you see how I reread the draft, looking at it simply through the lens of whether I'd shown what the story is *really* about?" I asked. "As writers, you can choose any lens you want, and you usually reread and revise several times with several lenses."

Now demonstrate that you can alter the lens with which you reread your draft, thereby seeing new aspects of it.

"One revision lens that writers use is a lens that a writing friend of mine calls the 'Cardboard Character Alert.' Anne Lamott says that our stories are only as good as the characters we develop. Even if we have the most wonderful plot, we need the characters to take us on the journey. We loved reading *The Great Gilly Hopkins* because Katherine Paterson created characters to take us on the journey. Writers reread to be sure that their characters, especially their main characters, look and act so real that the reader feels like the character could walk right off the pages of the book into the living room.

"Remember we talked about making sure the character had some good traits but also some not-so-good traits? If they don't, they seem fake. They are only as real as cardboard. So when I reread our story, I'm checking that we haven't made Luz be the sweetest, most sensitive girl, the greatest artist, a straight-A student, and the perfect daughter to her parents, or else readers might go, 'Ugh! No one's like that!' I find things about Luz that are not perfect—including that she is afraid of the dark. This makes her more like a flesh-and-blood person!

I often try to show children that when I check for whether I've done something, I sometimes find "yes," and I sometimes find "no." I do not want all my "checks" to lead to the same answer!

Early on, children thought about their characters' external and internal features, and about their characters' strengths and weaknesses. Now I lead children to revisit that early work. This, again, is a rhythm you should anticipate. Plan on the fact that the qualities of good writing that you really want to highlight in a unit will need to be introduced during the first few days of the unit and recycled later in the unit. You could, of course, harken back to this early work and even suggest that children use strategies they learned earlier to breathe life into the characters they've now settled upon.

"But when I put on the Cardboard Character Alert lens, I might decide we could flesh out Luz even more by giving her little traits—things only she thinks, says, and does. For instance, I might describe the way Luz eats in such a way that she'd seem unique. Maybe we could say she likes to eat foods that look pretty together. She is an artist after all, right? So maybe she tries to arrange food on her plate so it looks like a painting, with purple, orange, and green foods set carefully next to each other.

"So during this revision stage, a writer puts on just one lens, then another lens. We might reread asking ourselves, 'Did I show what this story is *really* about?' or 'Did I develop idiosyncratic character traits?' This rereading often prompts revisions—even before the first draft is written."

ACTIVE ENGAGEMENT

Set children up to try reading a text through the lens of a Cardboard Character Alert. Encourage them to imagine revising the draft based on what they notice when they reread it.

"Why don't we try putting on the Cardboard Character Alert lens to look at this part of a draft story by a former student? Now, really go for it! With your partner, find the places where the character feels only as real as cardboard instead of as real as your Uncle Charlie." I put up a transparency with part of a draft by a former student and read it out loud to the class.

> Rex was the star quarterback of the sixth grade football team. He could kick faster and farther than anyone else on the team, and he was big too and no one could push him over. He could just catch the ball and plow through to the endline without interference. With Rex on the team, no one else ever got to play that position.
>
> "I think you should give someone else a chance to play quarterback, Rex," said his friend. (Rex had lots and lots of friends and also he was real good at school, so his teachers all liked him best too.)
>
> "Okay," said Rex. Because he was really nice too.

"Do you have your Cardboard Character Alert glasses on? What do you see?" Pulling in to listen to partners, I heard Caleb say, "No one is all that good at everything." He added, "I mean, who could be the star at sports *and* at school-work? He is too perfect."

"Yeah," Felix agreed, "and if they were, probably they wouldn't have any friends 'cuz people would hate a person who is so great. Hey! Maybe that could be Rex's big problem! He could be so super great at everything, but in his true heart, he's real lonely and just wants a good friend. So he has to change something. Break a leg or something!"

Make sure you gather examples of student writing that will help you illustrate your teaching points. Especially keep an eye out for notebook entries and drafts in which the writer has some "typical" issue that you could teach into. For example, this piece about Rex could also be used to teach students how to add setting to their stories, how to add physical details to create a picture of their characters, or how to add a main character's internal thinking. When you find student pieces that are very flexible in this way, make copies for your colleagues. And, if you don't have any pieces from former students on hand, you can use a piece from a different classroom or a piece that you have written yourself to illustrate your teaching point.

"Fantastic!" I said. "You're already thinking like terrific writers, and you're beginning to revise this piece of writing." Then I convened the class. "You were coming up with great ideas. Of course, it is easier to fix up someone else's stories instead of your own!"

LINK

Send children off to reread their own writing through a specially chosen lens, and remind them to do this throughout their lives.

"Today, like professional writers, you are going to reread your writing with lenses. You might look at your own writing and ask, 'Have I brought out the real thing this story is mostly about?' You might reread asking, 'Can I make my characters seem less like cardboard cutouts?' Try other special lenses you invent to serve your purposes as well, and let your rereading lead you to revision.

"For the rest of your life, remember that writers do all they can to write great drafts, but then they return to those drafts, rereading them with different lenses in mind, expecting to revise them."

Helping Reluctant Revisers

IN TODAY'S MINILESSON, we encouraged writers to reread drafts with a particular lens in mind. You won't be surprised when I remind you, similarly, that we, as teachers, can also look over our children's work with a particular lens in mind. It is important to remember this because otherwise, we tend to believe there is something objective and universal about whatever it is we see when we look at the work being done by our writers. A researcher once pointed out, "We do not see with our eyes or hear with our ears but with our beliefs."

The good news is that we can each make ourselves aware of the lens we tend to use when viewing kids and their writing, and this allows us to make decisions. I might say, "I usually read my children's writing trying to understand the content of their pieces, but for today, I want to look mostly at the length of their writing and at whatever efforts I see them making to elaborate or to write long." There are countless lenses worth adopting for a time. Try noticing what children seem to think good writing entails. Try categorizing the scale of their revisions or noticing what does and does not prompt them to revise.

For today, I suggest you deliberately focus your attention on one thing, however, and that is the rereading your children do in the midst of writing. Ask children if you can watch them reread and hear what they are thinking as they reread. Your focus will surprise and please children; they'll expect you to be driving them directly toward revision. The secret truth is, most significant revision must begin as rereading, and children often don't realize this.

In any case, you will probably see that children need you to demonstrate and coach them before they understand what it can mean to read or reread with a lens. For example, you could reread, paying special attention to places where the dialogue seems especially lifelike and true. Then you can show children how you mull over what you find, thinking, "Why are these sections of dialogue so lifelike?"

Usually it is powerful to reread, searching for instances of a particular quality of writing, and then to ask, "What is it that I did here that worked so well?" By identifying and thinking about sections of a draft that work well, a writer gathers the strength and wisdom to tackle sections that work less well.

MID-WORKSHOP TEACHING   Revising the Story's Sound

"Writers, you are finding so many places to flesh out your characters! The room is getting noisy with all those 'real' characters walking off the pages! Can you take off your character lenses for a moment and look at me? I want to share with you the smart revision work that Max is doing. Max has found another lens with which to view a draft. What do you call it, Max? Oh, your 'Sound Check' lens!

"Max told me he put on this lens to reread his story for how it sounds. That is just what professional writers do too, Max! Often they even read their stories out loud to a friend or to the mirror or into a tape recorder, just to see if they've missed words or to see if the language and the rhythm of the sentences flow and make sense. We need to read with our ears as well as our eyes!

"This lens helps us make sure our story sounds good. Consider trying Max's lens—rereading to revise the sound of your story."

Revision

Explain to students that part of revision can also be reminding themselves of the basics and making sure that those are in place as they move forward.

"Writers, you have come up with so many ways writers can reread and revise their work! While it's great that we're getting all fancy with our lenses, I want to also give you a word of caution—this is something you've heard me mention before in this unit. It is very easy to get carried away when writing fiction. There are so many opportunities for showing off all that we can do, that sometimes we might do a little too much. It is important that you also keep the most important things about what you know about writing narratives, or stories, at the forefront of your minds."

I flipped the chart paper to reveal our "How to Write a Fiction Story" anchor chart. "Right now, I'd like you to tell your partner, just list across your fingers, a few key things that you think are crucial to remember when writing a story. In other words, what are the things that a writer absolutely must do in order to be able to write a story? Focus on the main things, not all the razzle-dazzle, but the stuff a writer *must* do."

Point out that they already know a lot about writing stories, and that they can use what they know from now on, every time they write a story.

"Wow! You really have your basics down, don't you? Yes, you know lots of fancy things, but you also have managed to keep the most crucial things in mind, too. Remember, these are things to do not just today, but any time you are writing stories."

How to Write a Fiction Story

- Develop a strong story idea, character(s), and setting.
- Spend time planning how the plot will go, making sure there is an arc to the story, trying again and again until the plan feels just right.
- Draft the story scene by scene, only using summary when needed.
- Study other authors for ways to make the story better.
- Make sure there is trouble in the story, and write an ending that resolves that trouble.

Making a Space for Writing

I N THIS SESSION, you'll rally children's commitment to the project before them: that of seriously, deeply revising their writing.

When I begin work on a new writing project, my first step is not to write or even to read. Instead, my first step is to clean my office! After that, I set out all the things I will need to write or, in this instance, to revise.

When I began work on this series, for example, I put the previous series, Units of Study for Primary Writing and Units of Study for Teaching Writing Grades 3–5, on the far corner of my desk. Then I gathered together the books that bring my distant teachers close to me: books by Don Murray, Annie Dillard, Bill Zinsser, John Gardner, Don Graves, and others. I pinned a few letters from readers on my bulletin board; those letters and others like them have made me care desperately about this work. On my bulletin board I tacked a calendar of deadlines and my brilliant editor's list of tips to remember.

Children, too, need to be encouraged to build spaces in their lives that allow them to write and to revise as well as possible, and they need to be encouraged to fill those spaces with items that can inspire and cajole and guide them as writers. By physically setting up the space in which we work, we take control of our own writing processes. As we make our writing spaces, we make ourselves. And for teachers, whose ultimate goal is to help children grow to be passionately committed, zealous writers who author richly literate lives, nothing could matter more than this.

Today, by sharing with children my own tricks of the trade, I speak to them as fellow insiders in the world of writing. And by inviting them to surround themselves with items that carry reminders of their resolutions, I encourage children to review all they have already learned and also to renew their vows to lessons that may have slipped out of view.

IN THIS SESSION, you'll teach students that writers create their own intimate work spaces inside their writing notebooks and their homes.

GETTING READY

- ✔ Anecdote you can tell about one writer's special work space (see Connection)

- ✔ Something special from your own writing life—a quote or object—whose significance you can share (see Teaching)

- ✔ Charts of writing tips and strategies created earlier in the year and, if possible, borrowed from previous years' teachers, for reference

- ✔ Narrative Writing Checklist, Grades 4 and 5 (see Share)

COMMON CORE STATE STANDARDS: W.4.3, W.4.4, W.4.5, W.4.8, RL.4.1, RL.4.3, SL.4.1, L.4.1.e, L.4.2, L.4.3

Making a Space for Writing

CONNECTION

Tell students that you prepare for a writing project first by cleaning your desk. Explain that many writers set up work spaces, putting items nearby that remind them of their resolutions.

"Writers, I think each one of you is off to a great start revising your fiction story. When I turn the bend in a writing project, in addition to sketching plans for that writing, I do one other very important thing. I clean my desk. Every writer is different, and you may decide that your needs are different from mine. But many, many writers take the time to set up spaces in which they can do their best work."

Tell the story of one writer who set up his or her writing space in ways that convey messages about writing.

"The author Annie Dillard turned a tool shed into a study, pushing a long desk against a blank wall so that she'd have nowhere to look but at the page. She says, 'Writing a first draft requires a peculiar internal state which ordinary life does not induce' (*The Writing Life,* 1990, 47).

"Annie Dillard has also pinned a photograph above her desk. It's a photo of a little Amazonian boy whose face is sticking out of river rapids. White water is pounding all around his head, and his dark eyes are looking up. 'That little boy is completely alone,' Dillard says. 'He's letting the mystery of existence beat on him. He's having his childhood and I think he knows it and I think he will come out of the water strong and needing to do some good (*The Writing Life,* 1990, 58)."

Debrief. Help your students see the generalizable principles in the example of one author who organized a writing space.

"Do you see how Annie Dillard has built a place for her writing, a place that reminds her of what she wants to remember as she writes? She makes sure her place whispers a message to her—and for Annie Dillard, the message is this: Wake up. Wake up to the mystery and power of your own life. Put it on the page."

❧ **Name the teaching point.**

"Today I want to teach you that most writers set up spaces in which they can do their best work. They put items and words into those spaces that remind them of all they resolve to do and be as writers."

This minilesson doesn't require such extensive detail about Annie Dillard's writing space. I relish detail and trust that it conveys larger principles, but you may decide to abbreviate this session—it could easily be done. Obviously, you'll want to tailor all your teaching to your children.

Tell students that you like to look back on ideas learned from previous writing, bringing those lessons to bear on current writing.

"What I like to do as a writer is to look back on my writing life and to think about all I learned before today that I resolve to remember. When we're working on one piece of writing, we need to bring with us all the lessons we've learned from all the pieces of writing we've ever written. Because the way we grow as writers is like trees, with one ring inside the next, or like those little wooden dolls."

TEACHING

Share the dream that each child might have a writing shed (akin to Annie Dillard's) and suggest that instead, all of them can set up their notebooks and writing spaces to convey messages about writing well.

"Wouldn't it be great if instead of putting up portable classrooms outside this school, they instead put up tool sheds— one for each of us? Then the writing workshop could be like those writing colonies I read about. We could convene for a meeting, and then each of us would head to our very own writing shed to read and write all morning. In some writing colonies, a basket lunch is left outside each writer's door so as not to disturb the writer's muse!

"It'd be great if we could each set up a writing shed for ourselves, but in this classroom, we can only set up our writing spaces, our notebooks, our folders—items that can carry bits of advice to us."

Explain that before you return to the class story or your own story, you'll first set out items that remind you of advice you want to recall. Select a quote from a book or an item from your writing life, and share the significance of whatever you select.

"So before I work any more on our class story and before I work on my own fiction stories, I'm going to choose a few items to keep near me as I write—items that carry advice for me. First of all, I want to keep one passage of 'Eleven' by Sandra Cisneros, near me—the bit about how the narrator pushed one hand through one sleeve of a sweater that smelled like cottage cheese. Do you remember that passage? It told how she stood there with her arms pushed back, with the sweater itchy and all full of germs that weren't even hers. I know I shared that passage with you to show that a writer can describe an event in passing ('she put on the sweater') or can stretch it out, telling the story bit by bit. But for me, I love this passage also because it has a ring of truth. The details feel as if they are true details, and I want to remember the power of writing the truth, even when I'm writing fiction. So I'll tape that passage inside my notebook and remember that advice today and always as I write.

"I think I'll also tape this calendar inside the front cover of my notebook," I said. "I want to remind myself that I can't spend too long planning for writing, or I won't have enough time to revise. I think it will be helpful to me in making decisions to have the calendar saying, 'Just get on with it.'"

Notice that I repeat my teaching point here, this time in a more poetic fashion. I hope that by doing so, I increase kids' energies for this work.

I deliberately selected a passage that will be familiar and memorable to children, and layered it with a somewhat new message. This is a small way to tuck another pointer about good writing into my minilesson. "I think I'll also tape this calendar inside the front cover of my notebook," I said. "I want to remind myself that I can't spend too long planning for writing, or I won't have enough time to revise. I think it will be helpful to me in making decisions to have the calendar saying, 'Just get on with it.'"

ACTIVE ENGAGEMENT

Help writers leaf through and revisit old charts and mentor texts, thinking, "Does any of this belong in my writing space?"

"So, writers, today and tonight, would you think about ways you can make a space for writing both here in the classroom and at home—a space that carries messages *you* need to remember?"

"Right now, I'll revisit some of the items in our classroom that *might* contain lessons for you, and as I do this, will you jot your own notes so that when I'm done, you can tell your partner whether any of these items (or others you can recall) might belong in your writing space?" I displayed some charts from earlier in the year and pulled out charts that they probably hadn't seen since third grade from their personal narrative work and read off a few items.

◆ Ways to Get Ideas for Personal Narratives

◆ Qualities of Good Personal Narrative Writing

◆ Monitoring My Writing Process

◆ Lessons from Mentor Personal Narratives

◆ When to Use Paragraphs

I continued flipping back through charts from past years' units until I reached the current one.

Ask children to talk to a partner about items they might put in their notebooks or writing spaces that can help them recall previous lessons on good writing.

"Would you turn and tell your partner if you've seen anything so far that reminds you of a message that might help you do your best writing and revision work today? Remember, writers grow like rings on a tree. When we write fiction, we still have the layers of all we've learned from earlier units of study. Which words or objects might you put into your writing space? Turn and talk."

LINK

Put today's lesson into context by reminding writers of the many ways they can prepare themselves for writing well.

"So, writers, from this day forward, remember you can prepare yourselves for writing by looking back over lessons you learned earlier in your writing lives and the texts that have taught you a lot. Writers often select passages or charts or quotations or objects to keep near them as they write, and they do this as a way of holding close the lessons they've learned."

Writers live with a constant, eyes-wide-open awareness, gathering ideas from the world like collecting berries in a basket. We must remind students of this often by modeling and discussing these habits. So, in addition to jotting down ideas from class writing charts during this lesson, encourage students to write or paste meaningful passages, writing advice, photographs, or other inspiring pieces into their notebooks or folders to create a rich writing space. This lesson gets to the real work that authors do to support their writing.

This session calls for you to refer to charts from previous years' writing workshops. If possible, ask third-grade teachers if you can borrow the charts they have used that year for their narrative teaching. If you're lucky, that teacher might even have saved some of her charts from last year. Alternately, you could talk to some of your third-grade colleagues, or look at the third-grade narrative units of study to make your own versions of the third-grade charts. If that's not possible, you might consider making arrangements to gather the third-grade charts at the end of the school year to use in the future. While this doesn't address the need to have familiar charts now, it can ensure you have plenty to choose from for next year.

This is sophisticated work, and it takes self-awareness for students to identify exactly which lessons or skills they need to keep at the forefront of their minds as they write. Think of the writing as a building. Placing the supports at random would do little to make a sound structure. Just as one needs architectural knowledge to effectively brace a building, writers need a certain amount of savvy about themselves to determine which words or objects will offer them the support they need.

Learning from Our Writing Patterns

THIS MINILESSON INVITES EACH CHILD to create an individualized work plan, one tailored to whatever particular work that child needs to do. In your conferences, you may want to help children take a larger look at themselves as narrative writers, asking, "What lessons did I learn in past years that really paid off for me?" and "What worked really well in my earlier stories that I'll want to remember as I revise this new story? What didn't work too well for me in my earlier stories that I could address this time, in this piece?"

To help children look back at and learn from prior work, encourage them to see the continuities between their earlier narrative writing and their current work with short fiction. Many students seem to forget to carry forward with them the things they learned in past grades and will be a bit surprised that you are asking them to not only remember but to build off that learning. In fact, you might want to point out to your students that chances are very good that a child will bring the same strengths and the same needs to any kind of narrative. Most of the problems that will show up in short fiction will also have been present in the child's third-grade work, particularly the work toward the end of the year.

The minilesson puts a spotlight on objects and texts that carry lessons. Your conferences will help writers harvest insights from taking a long look at their writing over their writing career so far. When children look across several narrative texts, you'll need to help them see commonalities. One text may be about the birth of a cousin, another about feeding a squirrel, and a third about a bully. But all three texts may be written in simple sentences, where nothing is given more emphasis than anything else, nor is anything suggested, tucked in, or alluded to. In all three texts, the characters may seem indistinguishable one from the next, and all three might have strong, interesting leads. You'll want to help writers gain some ability to see patterns in how they write, patterns that show up when texts are laid alongside each other.

MID-WORKSHOP TEACHING   Using Prepositional Phrases to Communicate Complexity

"Writers, I want to interrupt you for a moment to point out ways writers use special phrases—called *prepositional phrases*—to help communicate complicated situations in writing. Have you ever tried to explain a situation and had trouble because there were so many things to explain at the same time? That's where prepositional phrases are useful.

"There are words, called *prepositions*, that describe locations, in either time or place. Little tiny words like *after*, *at*, *above*, *before*, *by*, *from*, *in*, *on*, *out*, *through*, and *under*. There are tons more, but I think you would agree with me that these are words we use all the time. The thing is that when we use these words alongside a noun, adjective, or adverb we create something called a *prepositional phrase*. These are phrases that allow us to include more information about where or when things are happening in that sentence.

"Let's take a look at how Julie Brinckloe uses prepositional phrases in *Fireflies!* to help us know everything that is going on, even if there's a lot going on in one sentence. Remember the first line in *Fireflies!*? It starts with a prepositional phrase: 'On a summer evening I looked up from dinner, through the open window to the backyard.' By including the prepositional phrase 'on a summer evening' we get more information about when the story takes place in the same sentence that we find out that the character is eating dinner. Sure, Julie Brinckloe could have written, 'It was a summer evening. I looked up from dinner.' But the sentence wouldn't hold nearly the same amount of information and wouldn't be as complex. Later in the story after the fireflies have been caught, she uses another two prepositional phrases in one sentence when she writes, 'In the dark I watched the fireflies from my

(continues)

bed.' 'In the dark' is telling us where the narrator is when he is watching the fireflies and 'from my bed' gives us even more information about the narrator's location. She could have written 'It was dark. I was in my bed. I watched the fireflies.' But it doesn't exactly capture the smoothness, the all-at-once feeling that using prepositional phrases allows writers to achieve.

"Do you see how using prepositional phrases can be useful in your writing? It can help with complexity or add a sense of a few important details needing to be described at once. Look over your writing quickly, and see if you can mark a place where a prepositional phrase could help you describe more about what is going on in a sentence. Writers use prepositions and prepositional phrases as thoughtfully as nouns, verbs, adjectives, and adverbs. It's easy to think that words like *at* and *in* are too simple or boring, even when they are combined with other words to make phrases. But writers know that even apparently dry words can contribute to their writing in powerful ways."

Revising with a Checklist

Make a big deal out of the work students accomplished with their revisions today.

"Writers, I want to congratulate you on all your amazing work today. You transformed your desks into individual writing sheds and used those new spaces to breathe new life into your revisions. That is very mature work to be doing as fourth-graders!"

The complete Narrative Writing Checklist, Grades 4 and 5, can be found on the CD-ROM.

Share a short anecdote that involves making a To-Do list and connect this to using a checklist toward the end of this project.

"Now, I would like us to do one more thing before we pack up our things from writing today. I know that when I have a busy day, the next day, I like to lay out all my clothes and pack my school bag before I go to bed so I have everything I need and know exactly what my plans are for the next day and can sleep soundly knowing everything is in place. Writers do something like that too as they move closer to the end of a project. Except instead of laying out their clothes, they take a good hard look at their writing and make a To-Do list of what still needs to be done. One way to help you decide what needs to be included on your writing To-Do list is to return to our Narrative Writing Checklist.

Remind them of what the checklist covered and point out any highlights that you want the students to pay special attention to.

I placed the checklist up on the document camera. I read through each point, stopping occasionally to say, "And this we just finished studying, so that should be

Narrative Writing Checklist

	Grade 4	NOT YET	STARTING TO	YES!	Grade 5	NOT YET	STARTING TO	YES!
	Structure				**Structure**			
Overall	I wrote the important part of an event bit by bit and took out unimportant parts.	☐	☐	☐	I wrote a story of an important moment. It read like a story, even though it might be a true account.	☐	☐	☐
Lead	I wrote a beginning in which I showed what was happening and where, getting readers into the world of the story.	☐	☐	☐	I wrote a beginning in which I not only showed what was happening and where, but also gave some clues to what would later become a problem for the main character.	☐	☐	☐
Transitions	I showed how much time went by with words and phrases that mark time such as *just then* and *suddenly* (to show when things happened quickly) or *after a while* and *a little later* (to show when a little time passed).	☐	☐	☐	I used transitional phrases to show passage of time in complicated ways, perhaps by showing things happening at the same time (*meanwhile, at the same time*) or flashback and flash-forward (*early that morning, three hours later*).	☐	☐	☐
Ending	I wrote an ending that connected to the beginning or the middle of the story.	☐	☐	☐	I wrote an ending that connected to the main part of the story. The character said, did, or realized something at the end that came from what happened in the story.	☐	☐	☐
	I used action, dialogue, or feeling to bring my story to a close.	☐	☐	☐	I gave readers a sense of closure.	☐	☐	☐
Organization	I used paragraphs to separate the different parts or times of the story or to show when a new character was speaking.	☐	☐	☐	I used paragraphs to separate different parts or times of the story and to show when a new character was speaking. Some parts of the story were longer and more developed than others.	☐	☐	☐

fresh in your minds," or "We will be looking more closely at this one in a day or two, so if you don't have it yet, know it's coming."

Ask students to use the checklist to assess themselves as to what they have already done, and to make plans for what they still need to do.

"When we first looked at this checklist, you didn't know half of what you know now. But you have become so much stronger and smarter in just a few days! Can you go back to your checklist right now, and look at it as a to-do list? Can you look for the things you have done and check them off and the things you have yet to do and add them to your To-Do list for the next couple of days?"

Using Mentor Texts to Flesh Out Characters

J UST AS I HOPE that over time my students learn that essays, stories, and other written genres each have a "way they usually go," so, too, do I hope that you, my colleagues, will come to sense that genre-based units of study also have a familiar pattern. Early in a unit, we help students live the kind of life that writers of this genre are apt to live, collecting the sorts of entries helpful to this kind of writing. While living the life of this sort of writer, students also read texts that resemble those they aspire to write so that a bit later in the unit, they can begin to sketch or chart or outline a plan for their own first draft. Eventually, the emphasis of our teaching and our students' work shifts toward revising texts. Now students will revisit the texts they immersed themselves in earlier, only this time they'll admire and study them, asking, "What has this mentor author done that I could try?"

When I was a little girl, I often pretended to be a character from one of the novels or short stories my parents or grandparents had read out loud to me. I explored the backs of the wardrobes in my grandparents' house, hoping to find another Narnia inside them, just like in *The Lion, the Witch and the Wardrobe* by C. S. Lewis (1994). For a while, I acted just like Pippi Longstocking, producing a great deal more bravado than I actually felt inside, but I was trying her character on for size—yearning to live a life as full of adventure as Pippi's.

Characters are the heart and soul of fiction. Without strong characters, fiction falls apart. It becomes merely a reporting of events. Readers don't care what happens in the story unless we care about the character, and what makes us care is being able to see a flesh-and-blood character who shares thoughts and emotions similar to our own.

This final revision session, then, aims to help children flesh out their characters by making reading-writing connections. The session could invite students to consider any one of a zillion different aspects of character development in particular and well-written narratives in general, and hopefully it will serve you as a template for various other minilessons. For now, I've chosen to address an especially critical quality of character development and good writing. This session aims to help children more deeply understand the adage "show, don't tell" by applying it to character portrayal.

IN THIS SESSION, you'll remind students that writers study mentor authors to notice what other writers do that really works. One thing writers do is use actions and revealing details to show rather than tell about or explain the character.

GETTING READY

✔ Excerpt from *Pippi Goes on Board* or a text important to you that shows character through actions, copied on chart paper or transparency (see Teaching)

✔ Excerpt from your own writing or the class story you can use to demonstrate applying the mentor text

✔ Excerpt from *Fireflies!* or other familiar mentor text, to be projected or copied on chart paper (see Active Engagement)

✔ A second excerpt from *Fireflies!* to use in the Share.

COMMON CORE STATE STANDARDS: W.4.3.a,d; W.4.4, W.4.5, W.4.9.a, RL.4.1, RL.4.3, RL.4.10, SL.4.1, L.4.1, L.4.2, L.4.3.a

Using Mentor Texts to Flesh Out Characters

CONNECTION

Remind children of the lessons from the previous session and connect them to today's work. In this case, remind students that revision starts with rereading through a lens.

"Writers, you have learned in past years that revision begins with literally re-visioning, re-seeing your own text and that you do so to read through a lens, asking particular questions. You can reread your draft asking, 'What sense will a stranger make of this?' Sometimes when you do that, you realize that your story is a lot of 'he saids' and 'she saids'— that it almost seems to float, without being grounded in the specific world of the story."

Remind students that they can go to texts they love to figure out what the authors have done and then apply that to their own writing.

"Today I want to be sure you remember that there is a place that writers go to get new glasses—new lenses—with which to view their drafts. They go to stories that resemble the ones they hope to write. They let specific parts (or aspects) of a story matter to them. They feel the lump in their throat or see themselves pull in close at a favorite part or sense themselves getting hooked by the story."

❖ **Name the teaching point.**

"So today I want to remind you that you can read these stories and then ask, 'What did this author do that seems to work so well?' And you can reread your own draft, asking, 'Are there places in my draft where I could use that same technique?' And then, re-seeing can lead to rewriting."

TEACHING

Explain that all writers read first to be open to the power of the story and later to learn how writing is made. Demonstrate this with a text that is important to you.

"Most writers—writers like Walter Dean Myers and Eve Bunting and Eloise Greenfield—don't have a daily schedule with time in each day set aside for instruction in writing. But authors know that they can make their own writing

Notice that I've emphasized the importance of studying texts written by other authors to develop our own repertoire of techniques several times throughout this unit. If I hope this unit will truly lead children to learn to rely on mentor texts, I need to do a lot more than merely mentioning the value of mentor texts!

workshop, and to do so they read. 'I learned how to write from writers,' Cynthia Rylant says. 'I didn't know any personally, but I read.'

"If we want to learn from another writer, we first need to open ourselves to that author's story. Then, once we let a story get through to us, we stop and say, 'Why am I crying?' or 'Why is my heart ready to burst?' and we ask, 'What has the author done that makes this part of the story so powerful for me?'

"I've been rereading *Pippi Goes on Board*, a book that was incredibly important to me as a child; I've been remembering that Pippi was a hero to me. She had such bravado, such strength. Now, rereading this book, I find myself gasping at the power of even seemingly ordinary sections. For example, last night I read about how Pippi walked to town. That was it. Nothing great happened in the story. But for some reason, this section of the story really got to me. So I reread it, asking, 'What has Astrid Lindgren done in her story that makes it so powerful?' Listen to it and see what *you* think."

> *A few minutes later they were marching down the road to town—Tommy, Annika, and Pippi with Mr. Nilsson on her shoulder. The sun was shining so gloriously, the sky was so blue, and the children were so happy! And in the gutter along the roadside the water flowed merrily by. It was a very deep gutter with a great deal of water in it.*
>
> *"I love gutters," said Pippi and, without giving much thought to the matter, stepped into the water. It reached way over her knees, and as she skipped along briskly it splattered Tommy and Annika.*
>
> *"I'm making believe I'm a boat," she said, plowing through the water. Just as she spoke she stumbled and went down under.*
>
> *"Or, to be more exact, a submarine," she continued calmly when she got her nose in the air again.*
>
> *"Oh, Pippi, you're absolutely soaked," said Annika anxiously.*
>
> *"And what's wrong with that?" asked Pippi. "Is there a law that children should always be dry? I've heard it said that cold showers are very good for the health." (1977)*

"I realized that Astrid Lindgren didn't just *say* what Pippi did—that Pippi walked down the street en route to town. She *showed* Pippi doing this, and did so in a way that put a Pippi-like imprint on the experience. Pippi didn't walk to town in the same way that you and I might. She walked in her own uniquely adventurous way."

Demonstrate applying the technique you've noted from the mentor text to your own writing. Debrief.

"So, class, after I notice something that an author I admire has done, I think to myself, 'Are there places in my draft where I could use the same technique?' So let me reread our Luz story and see if I can not only tell what Luz does, but show how she does that thing—and in so doing, convey what she's like as a person."

I quickly reread the story and circled a section that described Luz trying to fall asleep at the slumber party. "I think I could write this in more detail, and this time really show Luz's fears—and show her, too," I said. I wrote:

Notice that we do not approach a text looking for examples of literary devices. We read with receptivity, letting ourselves be blown away by the story. Only later, after weeping, gasping, laughing, do we pause to think, "What did the author do to create such an effect?"

My apprenticeship in this instance is very open-ended, and you may decide to be much more explicit about the way in which a writer can emulate another text. For example, you may decide to teach children to copy sentences they love from the mentor text, to name what specifically they love about a particular sentence, and then to emulate that quality.

I pulled my sleeping bag as high as it would go without covering my nose. I heard a strange noise by the window and imagined big hairy beasts slamming though the front door, grabbing us up in our sleeping bags and carrying us away. I squeezed my eyes shut, so tightly I could see stars. "Don't think about those things," I said to myself.

"Do you see how I used some actions by Luz to show more about what she's like? That's what Astrid did with her character, Pippi, and so that's what I tried to do."

ACTIVE ENGAGEMENT

Ask children to use a mentor text, studying an excerpt for what they might try. Ask them to discuss with their partner ways to apply what they discover to the class story.

"Now let's try to do this whole process together. We've talked about how you love this section of *Fireflies!* when the narrator traipses off to bed, his jar of fireflies in hand. Tell your partner what Brinckloe has done here that works so well that you could, conceivably, try doing in your writing."

> *Daddy called from the hallway,*
>
> *"See you later, alligator."*
>
> *"After a while, crocodile," I called back.*
>
> *"I caught hundreds of fireflies—"*

I listened as children talked to teach other, and then convened the class.

Henry said, "The author uses the real words that kids say, so the story sounds true." "So let's look back at this section of our Luz story, and could you and your partner think together about whether *Fireflies!* gives you ideas for how you could revise our story?"

> The doorbell rang. "Welcome, come in," Luz said. Soon the room was filled with girls.

Before long, this section had been revised.

> The doorbell rang. "Hey!" Luz said, jumping aside in a gesture that said, "Come in!" Then Luz added, "Pizzas comin', lots of them."

If you feel it's likely your students can't yet follow this process easily, you might lengthen the active engagement section of this minilesson to include charting together the steps writers need to take to learn from mentor authors. The chart could go something like this:

Studying Mentor Texts for Our Own Writing

- Select a part of the story that works for you.
- Name specifically what the author did on the page.
- Suppose why the author did this particular thing.
- Look at your own writing and find places where it would help the text to try something similar.
- Try it!

LINK

Remind the children of all their options for revision today and any time they revise. Remind them they can always turn to mentor texts to discover ways to revise.

"So, writers, you already know that for the next few days you'll shift between writing scenes of your story and revising scenes. If you want to revise, you can definitely reread with the lens of 'Does my story make sense?' You may notice, as we discussed yesterday, that some scenes seem to float—in which case be sure to detail who is talking, where the person is, and what the person does. And you may decide to find another lens for re-visioning your draft. You can learn ways to re-see your draft if you find a text you admire, notice a section of the text that seems to work especially well, and then ask yourself, 'What did this author do that I could try?'"

Helping Struggling Readers

WHEN YOU CONFER TODAY, you'll probably check in with your struggling readers first to be sure that each one has a mentor text in hand that he or she can read. You're asking children to reread and examine the wording an author has used, and this is challenging enough when they can read the text. There are enough things for a struggling student to contend with when writing. Reading should not be one of them.

Once you've made sure that each of your strugglers has a mentor text he or she can read, you'll want to coach the child to notice something admirable in the mentor text. Help the child do so by taking any paragraph at all and then asking together, "What do I like in this passage?" It doesn't help to scan the whole text, over and over, looking for a noteworthy feature. Zooming in early on makes it more likely the child will notice craftsmanship. Help the child to talk about what the author has done. Then show the child that he or she could take that same technique and apply it to his or her own writing. You'll probably want to demonstrate this, saying, "I could imagine your story might go like this . . . " You may want to give two or three examples of the way the child could use that one technique in a variety of ways.

Of course, you'll also want to confer with your stronger writers. Resist the urge to only go to the students who need you the most and leave the more sophisticated writers alone, rationalizing that they know about writing. The truth is, even professional writers rely on the advice and suggestions of their editors to help them develop their work. It is crucial that you offer your strong writers opportunities to develop their skills as individuals.

You can offset the concern that you'll have nothing to teach your skilled writers by taking time to plan some possible teaching points.

I pulled up a seat next to Hannah, curious to know how she was doing with her character who was only five years old—the same age as Hannah's little brother.

MID-WORKSHOP TEACHING   Naming an Author's Techniques

"Writers, today we reminded ourselves that we can take courses from any writer, living or dead, as long as we are willing to really study what that author has done. We studied the way the father and son in *Fireflies!* said good night to each other—'See you later, alligator. After a while, crocodile.' But we didn't say, 'We liked the way Brinckloe's characters said good night to each other,' and we didn't have Luz turn off the light and say to her friends, 'See you later, alligator.' Instead, we named our observations, saying, 'The author uses words that people actually say to make the story sound true.'

"But some of you have been telling me that you didn't really get how to do this. Let me try to help you. First, I explain to myself what an author has done. Let's use Brinckloe's description of the dying fireflies in the jar."

And the light grew dimmer, green, like moonlight under water.

"Then I try to talk about what I notice she actually did. (I don't say how it worked: 'I can picture it.') I say what she has done.

"She wrote one sentence that has three parts to it. The first part tells what the light did (it grew dimmer), then the next phrase describes it (green), and the final phrase compares it to something else (like moonlight under water).

"Then, I try to figure out why she wrote like that. I think Brinckloe probably wanted to tell what happened, then to show how it happened. Now, having spelled out what the author did, I can try it in my own draft. So right now, reread a mentor text that matters to you, and follow these same steps. For me, I'd tell what something did, then I'd describe it, then I'd compare it to something else. Do this with your own text now, with your partner's help."

Hannah explained that she had changed the character to a little girl, "Angelina," so her story would be fiction. "Now I won't be tempted to copy my little brother," she said.

"Hannah, it's brave of you to choose a character who is five years old, and I'm glad you are drawing on what you know from your brother. And that you are taking the risk of writing about a character who is a bit different from you. Good writers are risk takers—but then, you knew that, right?"

Hannah nodded, clearly pleased by her teacher's support.

"I want to let you in on something. Lots of fiction writers say that every character in a story contains a bit of the writer. Even though I'm not like Luz, because I'm grown up and I'm not having slumber parties anymore, I still know what it's like to want to fit in with other people. And I also know what it's like to be afraid. I can take those parts of myself and let them help me as I work on my character, so that she becomes even more believable—more real—because she has bits of me inside her. Do you think there's a way you can do some of that work?"

Hannah's whole face lit up. "Well, yeah. I'm already thinking of my brother to get ideas of what a five-year-old does and thinks. And my brother is kind of a part of me. But I can also think about what *I* was like when I was five. Like, I loved art and sometimes I would get in trouble for getting into things I shouldn't have gotten into, and I could never figure out what the big deal was. I could make Angelina a little like that too." Hannah started to jot some things down right away.

Turning to a Text to Help Show Character Emotion

Share examples of actions revealing emotions. Remind writers they can do this in their own writing.

"Writers, this morning, as I was waiting for you to line up in the yard, I took a few minutes to watch the kindergartners lining up. I noticed they line up differently than you. First of all, most of them weren't talking. Yet I could still sort of tell how they were feeling. One little girl fell on the ground, then started rubbing her knee. At first she didn't cry, but then all of a sudden her lip started to tremble and a big fat tear rolled down her cheek. I could tell she was kind of surprised that her knee hurt. Then I noticed a little boy who was clutching a teddy bear to his chest. He couldn't stand still. He kept smiling and hopping up and down. I could tell he was really excited. I didn't need to hear their words to guess how they were feeling. Just by watching their actions and gestures, I could tell their feelings.

"I'm telling you this because it is really important, when you write, to use actions to show your character's feelings. Let me share with you some smart work I saw Leo do today. He studied *Fireflies!* and he noticed this section of it."

> *I tried to swallow,*
> *but something in my throat would not go down.*
> *I shut my eyes tight and put the pillow over my head.*
> *They were* my *fireflies.*

"He decided that Brinckloe used actions to show feelings: the character tried to swallow, he put a pillow over his head. So, Leo made a little tiny scene at the start of his own story and had his character do an action that showed her feeling of loneliness. You can do this too! Listen." (See Figure 13–1.)

> Alicia was a nobody. She had no friends and always sat in the corner. She was always seen walking home from school alone. None of the kids in her fourth grade class cared if she was there or not.
>
> Each night Alicia thought about friends. She dreamed about them too. One night Alicia looked out the window and saw a beautiful starry sky. She had been thinking about Tatiana, Alicia's dream friend. Alicia looked up and saw a star shoot across the night sky.
>
> Alicia made a wish, "I wish I had a friend."

Alicia was a nobody. She had no friends and always sat in the corner. She was always seen walking home from school alone. None of the kids in her fourth grade class cared if she was there or not.

Each night Alicia thought about friends. She dreamed about them too. One night Alicia looked out the window and saw a beautiful starry sky. She had been thinking about Tatiana, Alicia's dream friend. Alicia looked up and saw a star shoot across the night sky.

Alicia made a wish, "I wish I had a friend."

FIG. 13–1   Leo's notebook entry

NAMING OUR STORIES

Writers, have you ever named someone? A brother or a sister? A pet? It's an amazing responsibility. Tonight is a good time for you to consider names for your story. List ten titles, considering the significance of each. Your title, like *Charlotte's Web*, might well have a double meaning. *Charlotte's Web* is a book about a spider who weaves a web, but we know that webs are also seen as things that are very craftily made—the way that Charlotte craftily saves Wilbur's life. And *Because of Winn-Dixie* has one of the main character's names in it, but it also tells us something about the book. Things happen to Opal because Winn-Dixie is in her life.

Tonight, I want you to spend some time thinking about your favorite titles for books, and then try to figure out why you think authors chose them. After you've done that, don't just slap the first title that comes to mind on your story. Jot down a list of titles and then choose the one that truly connects to some big ideas you have in your story, one that will really catch a reader's interest.

Editing with Various Lenses

IN THIS SESSION, you'll teach students that just as fiction writers revise with "lenses," they edit with them as well, rereading their writing several times for several reasons, making edits as they go.

GETTING READY

✔ Passage from a class story, either the text you have used for demonstrations, or an excerpt from a student volunteer, you can use to demonstrate rethinking word choice, with copies for each student (see Teaching)

✔ Post-its, to mark misspelled words in student's draft (see Teaching)

✔ A chart listing conventions, spelling, and mechanics skills learned so far this year optional)

COMMON CORE STATE STANDARDS: W.4.3, W.4.4, W.4.5, W.4.6, W.4.10, RFS.4.3, RFS.4.4, SL.4.1, SL.4.4, L.4.1, L.4.2, L.4.3.b

I N THIS SESSION, as in other editing sessions, you will remind your children of all the editing skills you have already taught, including paragraphing, use of end punctuation and capital letters, use of quotation marks, use of tenses, use of high-frequency words, use of common irregular verbs, and so forth. Now you will add onto that list, with the new skills joining the others on a cumulative editing chart that remains posted in your classroom year-round. As the list grows, so do your children's abilities to effectively and independently edit their work.

Fiction stories pose special editing challenges. The stories tend to be long, which means that editing and recopying will take more than a day. The children will be chomping at the bit to share these stories, and the fact that their author celebration can't occur until they've edited and recopied will frustrate some of them. For you, the trick will be to show children that just as you earlier taught them revision is a way to honor their best efforts, so, too, editing is also a way to celebrate a text.

The second major challenge that children usually face when editing these stories is that the excitement of writing fiction will have inspired them to use more sophisticated vocabulary than they might normally use, and their stories will be chock-full of invented spellings. Fixing every misspelled word can feel like an impossible task. You will need to remind students of all the resources they already have in their "spelling toolboxes," as well as teaching them some strategies they can use to figure out correct spellings on their own. You might have already taught your class some of these strategies in your word study curriculum. If this is the case, all the better!

You will also want to keep in mind the Common Core Standards for Language in fourth grade. Are there certain standards that your students are close to achieving that you might want to highlight and push toward mastery of? Are there other standards that feel too sophisticated for this early in the year that you'll put on the back burner until later? Are there standards from the lower grades that feel important to address for students who struggle with mechanics and conventions, or standards from older grades that some students are ready to tackle now? These are a few things you will likely want to consider as you plan today's work session and possible conferences and small-group work.

In this session, you will teach students how to edit their work by rereading with great care and thinking about everything they know about grammar and punctuation. You will ask them to think especially carefully about spelling, and you will teach them how to use the wealth of strategies and resources available to them.

"In this session, you will teach students how to edit their work by rereading with great care and thinking about everything they know about grammar and punctuation."

Editing with Various Lenses

CONNECTION

Remind children that editing involves bringing all that the writer knows and is able to do to the draft. Tell students they will be rereading carefully, and relying on class editing lists, on resources such as word processors, and on each other as they seek to correct and clean up their drafts.

"You've all worked hard and should be so proud of yourselves. I know you are as excited as I am to share your stories with the rest of our community. But, before we do that, there is important work ahead. We still need to edit these stories so that not only the ideas and craft of the stories but also the spelling, punctuation, and grammar of them will all reflect the best that you can do.

"Remember, as you prepare to edit your stories, that a writer calls to mind everything that he or she knows about spelling, punctuation, and grammar. You can recall those tools and mentally lay them out for yourself even before you reread, like a carpenter lays out the necessary tools as a way to prepare for his work. Keep these tools in mind as you reread your story. While you reread, be especially on the lookout for misspelled words, because I know that many of you pushed yourselves to reach for the precisely right word as you wrote and that this led you to write with words you haven't tackled before. You were inventive spellers in this unit of study, and that's been great to see, but you will want to be sure you spell conventionally before you bring your stories to the world.

"Remember that when we want to fix up our spelling, we rely not only on the strategies we have for effective spelling, but also on resources that are outside ourselves to be sure our spellings are accurate. In particular, we rely on distant teachers—the authors of written materials—and on nearby teachers—the writers in our community—to help us go beyond what we can do on our own."

❖ **Name the teaching point.**

"Today I am going to teach you (actually, I will be reminding rather than teaching you) that before or after you edit your draft for other concerns—paragraphing, punctuation, and so forth—you will want to read your draft, checking on your spellings. Usually this means eyeing each word and thinking, 'Does this look right?' It also means rereading the letters in each word to double-check that those letters actually do spell the word you have in mind. When writers are uncertain whether a word is correctly spelled, they generally mark that word (in this class, circle it) and then they try spelling the

As you teach this minilesson, you might want to have a cumulative chart of all that the class has learned about mechanics and conventions thus far in the year close by you as you teach. That chart can contain skills you have taught during word study time as well as the writing workshop, and of course it will be a very different chart for more inexperienced writers than for children who have grown up in a writing workshop.

It would have been very easy to simply say, "Today I will teach you how to edit your draft." The reason that this teaching point is long and clunky is that I try to do more than name the subject of the minilesson. I try to actually tell children the answer to the question—in this case, I try to tell them how to edit their drafts— so that this section of the minilesson crystallizes the most important message of the session.

word again and again, drawing on all they know and on all the help they can locate to assist them with those spellings. I will show you how to go through this progression of work."

TEACHING

Referring to the good work one child has just done, emphasize that writers reread a draft many times, checking for one sort of editing concern, then another. Include in your summary of the work one child has already done an overview of how you hope children go about checking for punctuation and tense and consistency.

"Deveonna finished drafting and revising her story yesterday, and without my saying anything to her at all, she began editing it. She did something really smart that I want to remind all of you to do. She reread her draft, looking first for one kind of thing, and then she reread it, looking for another kind of thing. Each writer will proceed in a different sequence, but none of us can simply reread our draft once, fixing everything we want to fix! We all need to do as Deveonna did, and reread it multiple times.

"Deveonna read her draft first for punctuation and capital letters. She read it aloud to herself, adding in any periods that she'd missed. Like the rest of you, she didn't have a lot of trouble with end punctuation. She mostly adds periods when she drafts. But because Deveonna had tried to write this story in a way that built up tension and created suspense, she'd written with some sentences that required pretty complicated punctuation, so in this draft she included ellipses, parentheses, and lots of sentences that used commas in complicated ways. If Deveonna *had* noticed that she hadn't used a variety of punctuation, she might have regarded that as a clue that she could use editing as a time to really listen to her sentences, combining some or tweaking others so they built up the drama of the story.

"After Deveonna checked for punctuation and capital letters, she decided to reread using a different lens. This time she paid attention to her tenses. And again, she found that especially in the sections of her story where she really reached to write beautifully and well, she'd sometimes written in ways that shifted between past tense and present tense. Deveonna thought to herself, 'I better be clear. Am I writing about something that is happening now or about something that happened a while ago, like last year?' She decided she wanted the story to be in past tense, so watch and join me as I show you how she double-checked for tense consistency. Let's look at this section of her story. It tells that the protagonist, Elexa, hides behind a tree with her best friend, Lexi, hoping to hide from her stalker." (See Figure 14–1.)

When I reach her, she puts her hand on her face, and shakes her head, then points behind me. I turn, and there was the most unwanted person ever . . . "Sir Stalker Max." On the inside, I could have made my head expload. I hide behind Lexie, as if I were a baby and she was mom that has to protect me.

"Deveonna reread the first sentence. 'This sounds like it is happening now: "When I reach her, she puts . . . " That is now. If I want this to be past tense, I better change it.'"

When teaching a minilesson, we need to think of the entire sequence of work that we want to support and then we, too, can decide which part of that sequence of work will have happened offstage and which part of it will be emphasized because it actually unfolds on stage in the minilesson. In this minilesson, I summarize what Deveonna has already done, hoping as I do so to lightly support children in doing similar work. The "story" actually begins with me demonstrating how Deveonna does the one thing I want to highlight now, which is checking for tenses and misspellings.

It is crucial for you to notice that I don't go through this student's entire draft. Why do so? I can make my point much more succinctly by focusing on just a tiny chunk of the text. Notice this is not the lead of the story: the lead didn't pose as many editing issues as did this excerpt. Notice also that in the summary of how Deveonna dealt with tenses, I taught briskly and incompletely. I can't go back and teach an entire hour-long session in which I define tenses, go through the fact that action words can be called verbs, show children that verbs change in past and present and future tenses, and so forth. To write, children need to orchestrate a vast number of skills and strategies. There is absolutely no way to teach any one of those in enormous detail at one time in a minilesson. To maintain the full orchestration that comprises writing, we often teach incompletely, oversimplifying. Even if we decided to teach a subject fully and completely, children can only learn one or two increments at a time, so I think it is wise to resign oneself to the fact that we will revisit all that we teach over and over, month after month and certainly year after year, and each time our teaching can become a bit more complex.

When I reached her, Lexi put her hand on her face, and shakes her head . . .

"Hmm, that sounds wrong," Deveonna thought to herself. "Did I just switch back out of past tense? Let me look. I did. I can fix that."

When I reached her, Lexi put her hand on my face and shook her head, then pointed behind me . . . "Sir Stalker Max."

Describe and then demonstrate how the child reread, checking spellings. Highlight the fact that the writer tried the word in question several times, seeking outside resources after she'd drawn on her own resources.

"After rereading first for punctuation, then for tenses (checking that the action was either consistently in the past or consistently in the present tense), Deveonna paid special attention to spelling. She inched her way through the text, checking each and every word. When she came across a misspelled word that she knew, that was easy! She simply corrected it right then and there." I nodded toward Deveonna, "Am I describing this correctly so far?" Deveonna nodded. I returned to addressing the whole class.

"But since Deveonna is the kind of writer who pushes herself to use sophisticated language in her work, she also found words that she was not sure how to spell. For example, in this paragraph, she used some very specific, colorful words—*explode* and *protect*—and she wasn't sure how to spell those. This is what she did. Watch," I said and then circled those words. Then I showed that Deveonna pulled out a sticky note and put one beside each of the troublesome words. I retold how before having a second go, with *protet*, Deveonna reread her first try at the word, thinking aloud to herself, "Is *part* of this right?" She copied the first syllable as she'd written it. Then I reenacted her saying the word again, hearing the sound she'd deleted (the *c* sound) and adding that into her new version of the word. "Does this look right now?" Deveonna asked herself, and when she thought yes, she copied the new spelling into her draft.

"After going through a similar sequence with the word *explode*, Deveonna was still not able to correct her misspelled version: *exploded*. At that point, Deveonna asked herself whether she might be able to find that word written somewhere close at hand: perhaps on a chart in the classroom, a word list, in a story in her writing folder, or a reference book such as an atlas. Deveonna decided that she would be better off in this case asking her writing partner, who she knew was a strong speller, to help her fix up her spelling. With the help of her partner, she picked the version of the word that looked correct and made the change in her story."

Debrief, highlighting the replicable process one child demonstrated that you hope others follow.

"Did you see that first Deveonna reread for punctuation, then for keeping the action in her story consistently in the past tense or in the present tense. Then she reread for spelling and marked words that looked wrong, trying them again on the side. To try them again, she examined her initial spelling to ask, 'Is part of this right?' and copied that part. Then she tried the puzzling part first by listening again to be sure she'd represented all the sounds, then by asking herself if there were class resources that could easily help her, and finally by recruiting her partner to help. This is the sort of work each of you will want to do today and whenever you edit your writing."

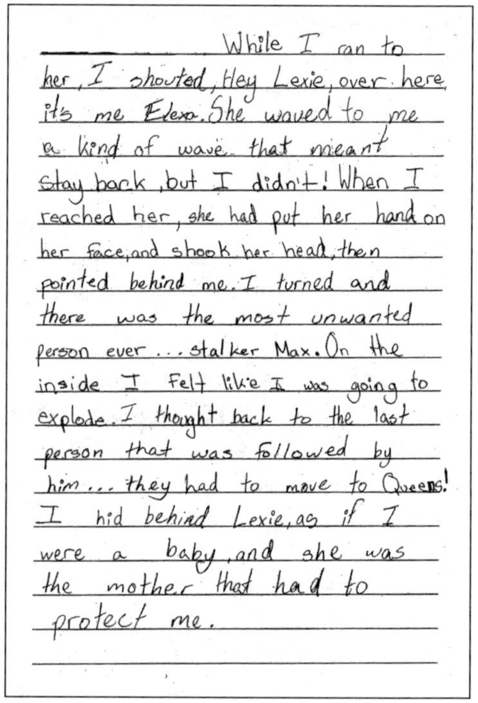

While I ran to her, I shouted, Hey Lexie, over here it's me Eleva. She waved to me a kind of wave, that meant stay back, but I didn't! When I reached her, she had put her hand on her face, and shook her head, then pointed behind me. I turned and there was the most unwanted person ever . . . stalker Max. On the inside I felt like I was going to explode. I thought back to the last person that was followed by him . . . they had to move to Queens! I hid behind Lexie, as if I were a baby, and she was the mother that had to protect me.

FIG. 14–1 Deveonna edited her tenses in the midst of her draft.

You may decide to ask your children to pull out their drafts and reread the first paragraph to check for punctuation, perhaps talking with each other about what they notice. Then they can reread for tenses, and again they could (or could not) talk about what they notice. You'd need to decide how to work your time so this process doesn't extend the length of the mini-lesson. Sometimes when teachers ask children to get started on the work of the day while they are still sitting in the meeting area, the teachers decide to bypass the link and to simply gesture to one child, then another, to move to his or her seat, continuing the work in that place.

ACTIVE ENGAGEMENT

Set students up to follow the model you have given them, editing the next paragraph of the child's story.

"Now you're going to assume the role of editor. With your partner, could you read the next section of Deveonna's story?" I said, passing out copies of just the next paragraph. "Read it once, checking for and fixing punctuation. Then read it again, checking for and fixing tenses, then put on your 'check-for-spelling' lenses. If you find a misspelled word that you can't fix immediately, have a go on the side of the page, spelling the word several possible ways. Remember that you can use resources outside yourselves, such as other writers in our community."

> He comes even closer. Lexie whispers "Oh, no." then I shout "RUN!" That's when we heard the bell, "dinnnnggg." We tried to run as fast as we can, but being so populur we don't run a lot but we try. We rush for the door, trying to slip into class without being noticed by a hall monitor or a teacher.

"Writers, as I talked to some of you about your editing work on this section, I heard many of you say that you had found places where you could fix punctuation and grammar, such as changing the verbs to past tense and capitalizing the *t* in *then*. Many of you are also thinking especially hard about spelling."

LINK

Recall what you have taught and send children off to edit their own work.

"Writers, as you edit your fiction stories or any other piece of writing, remember that all of us, as writers, take editing very seriously. We generally reread our writing once, twice, three times, and often we make a decision, saying, 'This time I will read with this lens,' or 'This time I will reread with that lens.' I have emphasized rereading for punctuation, tenses, and spelling, but you may know that you need to reread and think about characters or about being sure your draft makes sense. Remember to use the tools we have in this classroom to help you do this work: charts, checklists, grammar guides, and writing partners. You are in charge of your own writing, and the real goal is to make sure that every word, every dot, is the best that it can be."

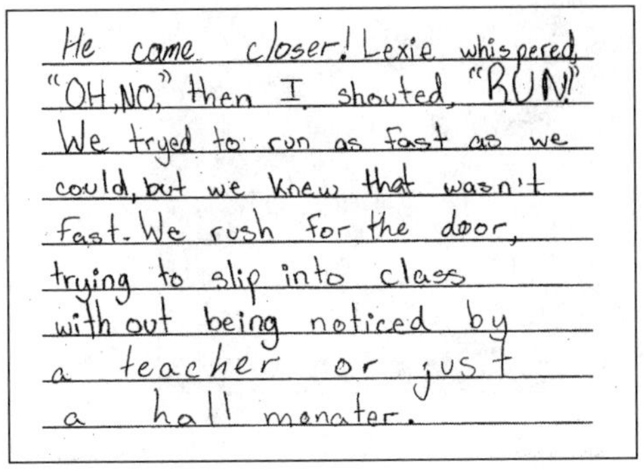
He came closer! Lexie whispered, "OH, NO," then I shouted, "RUN!" We tryed to run as fast as we could, but we knew that wasn't fast. We rush for the door, trying to slip into class with out being noticed by a teacher or just a hall monater.

FIG. 14–2 Deveonna edited her story based on input from her peers.

Making Editing Choices

"WRITERS, I GATHERED THIS GROUP because I think that as you reread your story, you will find that you are not using a variety of punctuation marks. If almost every sentence ends with a period and if you do not use parentheses, ellipses, colons, or semicolons, these are signs that your sentences plod along a bit. This is also a sign that there is one fairly easy thing you can do to make your writing a whole lot better! Right now, I can show you how you can become writers who use a variety of punctuation marks, and the important thing about this is that writers who use a variety of punctuation marks are also writers with a more elastic sense for how sentences and paragraphs of print can create mood, tone, rhythm, and feelings. I know that many of you studied this in third grade, but now that you're in fourth grade you can bring a new level of sophistication to this work as you think more deeply about the meaning behind your punctuation.

"So take just a minute and make a list of the punctuation you have already used in your story. See if I'm right when I said that I think that you've used mostly two or three forms of punctuation." The children did this and concurred. "This means your writing can get better really easily. Writing with only a few kinds of punctuation is a bit like writing with half the alphabet!

"Try revising your sentences—not toward the goal of using more punctuation, because I don't think any writer on earth has ever sat down with the goal of writing with three semicolons and an ellipsis! But try revising your sentences so that when people read your sentences they'll be swept along in the feelings you want them to experience." Then, to demonstrate what I meant by this sort of sentence, I deliberately used one, gesturing with my hand at the places in my very long oral sentence where the commas might go. "Try writing with a more elastic sense for how sentences can go, so that some of your sentences are long ones, with parts that pile up, one on top of the next, phrase after phrase, as you hear in this sentence of mine."

At this point my voice abruptly switched so I could demonstrate the opposite kind of sentences. "Try the opposite. Try making curt, brief points. Say what you mean. Be

---

MID-WORKSHOP TEACHING   Editing with Attentiveness

"Writers, can I stop you? I really, really need your attention. All eyes up here. All minds up here."

I waited an extra-long time. "Writers, right now, I have your attention. You are listening keenly, attentively, with your minds turned onto high. What I want to tell you is this: this is the sort of keen attentiveness you need to bring to the job of editing. I know this will sound unbelievable to you, but I have actually seen some people leaning back in their chairs, editing like this," I said, and role-played a lackadaisical, sloppy editor. "The word *editing* should bring to mind a person who is sitting up, pencil sharpened, with extra-keen eyesight, eager to catch each and every little item.

"To edit well, then, you need to have checklists at your side to remind you of details that deserve your attention. But you need your own personalized checklist for the ways of acting that can help you shift from playing the part of writer to playing the part of editor. Usually people use a special pen to edit. Usually people sit at a desk to edit. Often people read aloud (either actually, or in their minds) to edit. This can force you to really see and register each and every word. You need to devise your own personalized checklist for what you need to do to remake yourself from the passionate writer who writes with great fervor to the meticulous, attentive editor who doesn't let anything go by unchecked."

---

blunt. But then turn a corner in your thinking, and suddenly let your sentences be large rambling ones once again, with ideas that link together, building off each other, expanding on earlier bits.

"Just to practice writing with sentences that convey your mood, would you right now imagine that you are running, running, through the school? Partner 2, say a long, rambling sentence to your partner, showing what you pass by as you run, how your body is feeling as you get more tired. Start, 'I ran out the door . . . ' and then keep going.

"Now, just to practice writing in abrupt sentences. Partner 1, would you be the principal who catches the runner? Tell the runner to stop. Order the runner to do one thing. Then order the runner to do another thing. Show your anger. But do so in very short, abrupt sentences. Partner 1, start by saying, 'Stop.'"

After the writers did that, I said, "Right now, would you look at your story draft and see if there is one place where the sentences should push readers to read faster and faster, in a piling up, expansive, warm (or frantic) kind of way? Mark that section with a marginal note: long sentences with commas and parenthesis. Then read your draft over and see if there is one place where the sentence structure should signal that this section is abrupt. Brief. Cold. Mark that section with a marginal note: Short sentences. Perhaps ellipses. Perhaps colons before a list.

"Once you have marked sections of your draft where you could revise your sentence structure, would you go back and write-in-the-air with your partner, each of you taking a turn writing an oral version of each person's draft? Then see if you can get a small sheet of paper, rewrite the section on it, and tape it right on top of the original draft. Make sure the flap can lift up so I can later admire this important editing work.

"If you'd like a mentor text, use a copy of this draft of Ari's. In her editing she's made use of every conceivable punctuation mark—to strong effect! Listen to this." (See Figure 14–3.)

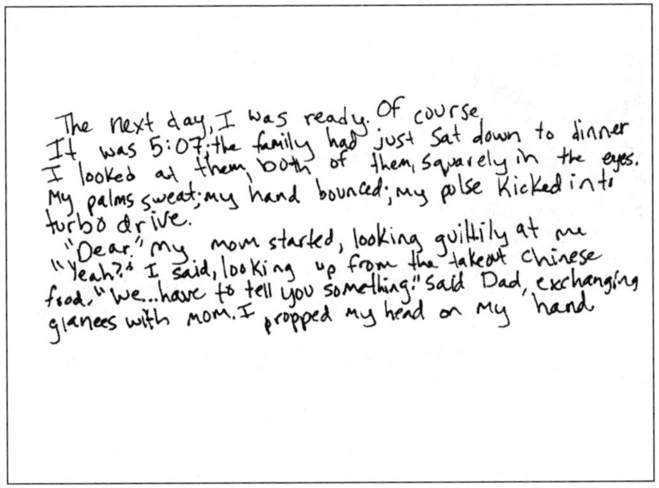
The next day, I was ready. Of course It was 5:07; the family had just Sat down to dinner I looked at them, both of them, squarely in the eyes. My palms sweat; my hand bounced; my pulse Kicked into turbo drive.
"Dear," my mom started, looking guiltily at me "Yeah?" I said, looking up from the takeout Chinese food. "We...have to tell you something," said Dad, exchanging glances with mom. I propped my head on my hand

FIG. 14–3 Ari uses a variety of punctuation to strong effect.

The next day, I was ready. Of course it was 5:07; the family had just sat down to dinner. I looked at them, both of them, squarely in the eyes. My palms sweat; my hand bounced; my pulse kicked into turbo drive.

"Dear," my mom started, looking guiltily at me.

"Yeah?" I said, looking up from the takeout Chinese food. "We . . . have to tell you something," said Dad, exchanging glances with Mom. I propped my head on my hand.

Editing with a Writing Partner

Ask children to share their work with a partner, asking for particular editing feedback, as writers do.

"Writers know that even after they've done their most careful editing, there can still be some mistakes in their stories. Sometimes they miss mistakes because they themselves don't know exactly how to spell or punctuate properly, and sometimes they miss mistakes because they just get so used to reading their own writing that they have a hard time seeing their errors. Every piece of writing needs fresh eyes. Remember that your writing partners can provide those fresh eyes for your story. In addition to helping you with accurate spelling, your partners can help you effectively edit your story for sense, punctuation, and grammar. So let your partner provide you with a fresh pair of eyes. Partner 2, will you reread and edit Partner 1's writing? As you do this, remember that the writer is the ultimate decision maker, and if someone else writes on our drafts, they do so lightly and respectfully, in pencil, not pen!"

Session 15

Publishing Anthologies
A Celebration

$\mathcal{D}$ear Teachers,

Today, rather than including a minilesson, we offer you a letter of suggestions and ideas for this mid-unit celebration. This session should be personalized to meet the needs of your students, and you should feel free to opt in or out of any of the suggestions included in this letter, knowing that what is most important is that you make this celebration work for your class. We will be doing this throughout these units of study, with the hope that this will give you a welcomed opportunity to begin writing your own minilessons, tailoring them to the particular students you teach.

When a novelist or short-story writer's book is released, it is common practice to have a book party. First, the author reads a bit of the book, and then copies of the book are available. The author autographs copies of the book. Friends and fans attend the party, and sometimes reporters come too.

Today you'll want to give your young authors a taste of what it feels like to be a famous author at a book party. The guests this time will be other children, rather than parents. The stories to be shared are longer than children's other published texts have been, and it will probably be important for the writers to have a chance to read whole stories. This means that instead of convening the entire group to hear a few shared texts before dispersing people into small reading circles, you may want to start the small circles from the start—and you may have more of these circles than usual, each containing fewer readers, to keep the pace up.

Writers always long to hear a response to their writing. One writer said that writing can feel like dropping rose petals into a well and waiting to hear the splash. So today be sure that each child has a page titled "Critics Agree" (as in advertisements for novels that feature acclaim for the text) and be sure you create time for children to write on each other's "Critics Agree" pages.

Finally, remember that although children want responses from each other, probably you will be the reader who matters most to them. How will you let each and every child know

COMMON CORE STATE STANDARDS: W.4.3, W.4.4, W.4.5, RFS.4.4, SL.4.1, SL.4.4, SL.4.5, L.4.1, L.4.2, L.4.3

that you have thought carefully about his work? I urge you, if you possibly can, to print out a poem, a story, or even to select a book that you believe in some way matches each writer in your class, and inscribe a message on it or inside the front cover. Clearly these message needn't be long if you intend to write one for every student. Instead aim for a specific detail to compliment or a piece of universal wisdom about writing.

> "Dear Author Claudia, When I read this book, Baylor's <u>I'm in Charge of Celebrations</u>, I thought of you because you have the gift of seeing and celebrating the small miracles that are everywhere in our lives. Cherish this talent of yours, because it makes you an extraordinary writer . . . and friend." Or "Dear LaKeya. I've chosen . . . "

After today, maybe not tomorrow, but sometime very soon, you will launch the final bend in this unit, where students will take on the exhilarating yet somewhat daunting task of launching their own independent fiction projects. It cannot be overstated how important it will be then for them to leave this first publication of the year, particularly one in the fiction genre, filled with confidence and a desire to do more. You will want them to view this celebration not only as a culmination of one project, but a launch into a new project.

BEFORE THE CELEBRATION

Before the appointed time arrives, you will want the room to be dressed up for the festivities. Children can work together to create carefully planned anthologies of stories and to practice reading aloud and prepare for signing autographs. On the day of the event, children can help you roll butcher paper over the tables to keep soda and crumbs from spilling everywhere, and they can decorate that paper to turn it into festive tablecloths. They can also put a carnation in a paper cup at the center of each table and drape a roll of crepe paper wherever they think best.

Ask children to perform different roles in today's celebration. Two can greet visitors at the door, four can escort visitors to their assigned small circles, one can explain how the sharing will proceed, and several can be sitting in the small groups to welcome the visitors to those groups. There are, of course, endless possibilities for ways to plan, prepare, and carry out this celebration. You will no doubt want to make sure every student has a role to play and a feeling that role is important.

When our actual appointed time arrived, I assumed my post, and the children assumed theirs. Two were at the door, ready to say, "Welcome to our fiction celebration." Others escorted the visitors to the appropriate groups, based on preplanned rosters for each group. Still other authors sat in the small groups, holding their stories, ready to welcome the newcomers to the small group.

THE CELEBRATION

You might want to bring out a large box filled with students' anthologies, and set it on the table. When I did this with my class, children craned their necks to see what was happening. I stood and, bit by bit, unwrapped the beautiful paper from the box. Finally, I opened the box, peered in, and then backed up as if to say, "Wow. You won't believe it." Reaching ever so gingerly into the box, I produced a stack of published anthologies—one for each writer and one for each visitor.

I delivered the books to each sharing circle, and one child after another read his or her story aloud. If you decide to give your writers the gift of a story or a poem, at the end of the day, as children leave to go home, you'll want to give these out. Be sure that you also send a copy of the child's publication home with an accompanying letter to parents, asking them to give the writer very specific, detailed responses.

AFTER THE CELEBRATION

You'll want to decide how to make the party a happy one for children. Do you want it to be the prelude to a special outdoor play time? Do you want the class to take a field trip after the party to the local library, which may have agreed to showcase the children's writing in a giant display case? Do you want to gather the class for some reflection about how the unit went for them and what they learned? The possibilities are endless!

Enjoy!

Lucy and Colleen

You might decide to begin the celebration with a choral reading of a poem. This can be a poem that a small group of students select to read or one that the whole class enjoys. You'll want to create an aura of significance and anticipation for the book party.

Mirror Magic by Hannah

Angelina felt as though the devil started controlling the neighborhood children and made them not want to play with her during this beautiful weather. She felt as though a gate separated her from happiness and led her to misery. She felt as though she was captured in a paper bag that led her to boredom, nothing going on in her mind except for terribly horrid thoughts about the children playing outside without her—thoughts that are too horrible to tell you. So guess what she did? She dreamt her day away.

The dream wasn't that nice either but it wasn't as bad as her thoughts. She dreamt of one day sprouting out of her small five-year-old self and blooming way up into the fluffy white clouds that tickled her nose. Then she stepped on all the children who didn't welcome her into their games. If they ran away she would reach out her longs arms and grab them, shaking them up and down, throwing them up into the air and catching them just before they hit the hard sidewalk.

FIG. 15–1   Hannah's final story

(continues)

Her dream ended when she heard her mother call from the kitchen to brush her hair. Angelina tossed and turned, moaned and groaned and finally rolled off her comfortable couch. Her knotted golden hair lay spread out on the white carpet. She felt as tired as a baby cuddled up in their mother's arms in the middle of the night, and she felt as heavy as an elephant sinking in sixty feet of deep water. So she pushed and pulled herself to roll over again and again towards the wooden stairs to get to the bathroom.

Yawning heavily, she pulled herself up the stairs. At the top she lay down and rested, practically falling asleep again until she felt a wet glob drop onto her face, which could only mean an Emimay alert! Emimay was Angelina's pet lab. She was as brown as a chocolate bar, and as friendly as when your best friend in the whole world smiles and waves at you.

Angelina quickly wiped the glob from her face away with her palm, and now with some energy she shooed Emimay off and walked into the bathroom. Her bathroom had tiled walls that were turquoise with white stripes and her bathtub had little paws to hold it up that always made her laugh when she was younger.

Angelina looked at herself in the mirror for a few seconds. She not only saw herself but the reflection of the kids that were playing outside. That was enough for her, she practically bounced off the walls. She jumped up and down again and again and then ran to the sink and banged her head on the white porcelain.

"What are you doing up there?" screamed her mother, who was confused and worried about Angelina. She lifted her face from the sink. Her head was a little red but otherwise no harm was done. "Nothing mother" she said, "I'm fine." Then she looked down to see if the sink was okay and to her surprise instead of the white porcelain, she saw something that looked like whipped cream! She dipped her finger into the soft cream and put that finger into her mouth. In that second her face turned pea green and she spit it out of her mouth onto the mirror. She looked as the slimy white cream

that had trickled down and thought that it tasted like something she had eaten before when she was younger, not knowing what it was.

"That's it!" she cried out loudly. "It tastes like my father's shaving cream, he must have left it out!" Her face looked even greener as she remembered. Staring at the cream intently, she realized the it looked like an eyeball and made another eyeball next to it.

Her grandmother was visiting and she had put all of her makeup neatly around the sink. Angelina dipped her finger into one of her tanning creams that had bumpy lumps in it and she flung it at the mirror to make a messy nose. Now she needed a mouth. She used a red makeup pencil to trace her mouth onto the mirror. This delighted Angelina so that she also traced her eyebrows with the pencil even though they weren't red. The makeup that really caught her eye was a glittering gold body spray bottle that was the exact color of her gold shimmering hair. She gripped the bottle nice and tight and sprayed all around the eyes, nose and mouth. Now all she needed was to color in the eyeballs. She found a bluish bottle that glistened on the shaving cream. The best part of it was that it smelled like blueberries.

There staring back at Angelina was her masterpiece of all masterpieces that enchanted her heart. It had changed her boring day into a fabulous day. "Angelina" she heard he mother call. "Dinnertime, hurry, the landlord will be coming soon." Angelina glanced one last time at the picture in the mirror before she needed to go down to dinner and then gleefully skipped down the stairs.

She smiled throughout dinner eating all her veggies and slowly savoring her dessert. But her smile turned around when the doorbell rang and the landlord walked in. He hated them. He thought they were slobs and didn't like their sense of humor. Angelina and her family didn't care for him either.

His tie was purple, resting on his green shirt. His thick eyebrows were neatly combed but Angelina couldn't be 100% sure because the hair on his head was resting down on them, just about covering his green as grass eyes. He had a habit of fiddling his fat fingers, which bothered Angelina.

FIG. 15–1 (continued)

"So how's my baby doing?" he said as he patted a table to his left. "Fine" said Angelina's father, Tony. "Was I talking to you?" questioned the landlord as Tony turned around and grumbled under his breath. That basically kept happening between the two as they walked throughout the first floor.

Walking up to the second floor, Angelina felt as bored as she had in the morning but then she remembered her masterpiece in the bathroom. They were all heading in that direction when she stopped and decided to wait in case she was going to be in trouble. She heard her mother gasp and the landlord exclaim, "Wonderful!" Her dad never liked anything the landlord liked, so as he was about to say "ugh" instead he said, "It is wonderful." They looked at each other, slapped each other's backs with a loud "thud" and chuckled, as they walked down the steps to have dessert together.

Angelina sat down at the table looking at her half eaten dessert of cherry pie and whipped cream listening to her father and the landlord chatter away gleefully.

"I guess my artwork brings people together," she said proudly. Then she frowned and said "Now I need to make something for my mother and the neighbors." She quickly gulped down her dessert and took out some paper, glue, string and a few markers.

Angelina's day had definitely changed.

FIG. 15–1   (continued)

①

Jane's First Sleep Over

Hannah

One spring, sunny day June and Abby's families all went for a picnic in Central Park. They played baseball, tag, duck-duck goose and other fun games. Abby's brother Jack and Jane's brother Rob thought the baseball game was the most fun because they both scored runs. Jane's sister Anna and Abby's sister Robin thought the picnic was fun and they should plan another one again soon. The parents Mary, Chriss, Mel and Kevin thought it was a great idea to have another picnic in Central Park because it was big and there were great places to play.

Later in the day when the sun was setting over the carousel and they were about to leave Abby asked, "Hey Jane do you want sleep over at my house tonight? Jane's face froze and for a second she didn't say anything then Jane said, "I can't sleep over."

"Why not?" questioned Abby. Before Jane was able to say anything Abby added, "you aren't scared are you?"

"No way, of course not!" said Jane. "I just can't." All of a sudden Robin and Anna started to chant "Jane is scared, Jane is scared."

"At least I'm smarter than you guys!" Jane said as she huffed off. But Jane thought about how Robin and Anna were right about her being scared. She felt like a baby which made her feel bad inside. Why couldn't she sleep over at Abby's house? She'd played there a million times but she'd never slept anywhere but at her own house with

②

her parents right across the hall.

Coincidentally, two weeks later Jane and Abby's families had tickets to "Typo" at the New Victory Theater. After the show Abby asked again.

"Jane, do you want to sleep over at my house?"

"Why don't you sleepover at my house?" said Jane.

"But I always sleepover at your house and you never sleep over at my house. I think Robin and Anna are right when they said you're scared to," said Abby.

"Well I'm not...it's just... I don't want to," said Jane.

"You don't want to! That hurts my feelings! Anyway, I think you're scared and you're lying to me. Maybe if you tried to sleep over at my house you might like it," said Abby.

"Fine" said Jane "I'll do it just to show you I can. See you Friday night after school."

When Jane walked away she thought I hope I won't embarrass myself and start crying like a baby for my Mom and Dad or worse wake up in the middle of the night and want to go home. Yikes! I can't believe I just said yes thought Jane. But I have to because Abby looked so excited and I did say I would.

Friday came along quickly and Jane was pretty nervous and excited at the same time to sleep over at Abby's house. At first the girls were having a blast. Jane and Abby watched their favorite movie "Elf" and said the lines they knew by heart.

③

They played Candy Land and watched the Disney Channel. They painted eachother's nails and put on make-up. They ordered chinese food and ate until their stomachs ached. Abby's Mom came in the room and told the girls it was time for bed. As Jane got into the bed next to Abby she started thinking about her Mom and Dad. She got quiet and her eyes filled with tears. Abby noticed and said, "let's play one more game in the dark with a flashlight so my parents won't see the light on." The girls played game after game of War until Jane and Abby fell asleep.

Jane woke up the next morning when she heard Abby in the bathroom brushing her teeth. As she layed in bed she smiled thinking about all the fun she had and how proud she was that she made it through the night without her parents. She couldn't wait to tell her family how much fun she had and how she wanted to do it again soon.

FIG. 15–2   Hannah's final story

Embarking on Independent
Fiction Projects

BEND IV

Launching Independent Fiction Projects

Dear Teachers,

Congratulations on completing your first publishing cycle of the year! You and your students have much to be proud of. It would be tempting to wipe off your hands, pack up all the charts, pieces, and mentor texts from this unit, and then move on to your *Boxes and Bullets: Personal and Persuasive Essays* unit. And you might still opt to do that. However, I have come to believe that when children are able to immediately put their newly learned writing skills to use in another way, they are more likely to become owned by the student, and not just set aside and forgotten.

If you choose to follow the final bend in this unit, you will start projects that might outlast this unit. In other words, in this final bend, students will learn how to apply everything they learned so far in the realistic fiction unit to develop, plan, and implement fiction of any sort for the rest of the year, in much the same way that in reading workshop you expect students to always have an independent reading book of their own choosing up and going no matter if the class is studying historical fiction or in book clubs. In fact, you might launch your essay-writing unit in writing workshop while many of your students continue to work on this last fiction piece in their spare time. One caveat: since most of your teaching is about independence and transference of skills rather than specific craft or structural moves, you might see a small drop in the quality of craft and structure of these pieces. Know that this is to be expected since this will not be your focus in the last bend. However, you will get a strong sense of what craft and structure work your students have internalized from the unit. And, as always, you can pull small groups or add minilessons as makes sense for you and your students.

To prepare for this session, you will likely want to gather all of your charts from the unit in one place, make sure your students have access to their recently published pieces (or copies of them), and gather old mentor texts as well as an example or two of mentor

Common Core State Standards: W.4.3, W.4.4, W.4.5, W.4.8, W.4.10, RL.4.1, RL.4.3, RL.4.10, SL.4.1, L.4.1, L.4.2, L.4.3

150

Grade 4: The Arc of Story

texts that are fiction, but not realistic. You will want to pick mentor texts that do a nice job balancing both fiction writing skills you have taught and new skills you'd like the students to discover. Picture books are ideal, as are stories from short story anthologies and magazines.

MINILESSON

You will want to make a big deal about how students have wrapped up their first fiction pieces. You might want to tell a story to illustrate how once people learn skills, they carry them with them from that day forward (such as spending several focused days learning to ride a bike and now being able to do it every weekend without major thought).

You might say, "Today I will teach you that writers don't just leave their writing skills in writing workshop. Instead, they carry those skills with them wherever they go, knowing that they can develop and carry out their own fiction writing projects not just now, but for the rest of their lives by recycling the things they learned. Specifically, they can remember what they learned about creating story ideas to begin new projects."

You will want to explain to students that even though they just finished a fiction piece, you know that many of them are already planning their next pieces, and that since they are newly expert fiction writers, you think it makes a lot of sense for them to try their hands at planning an independent fiction writing piece. You will let them know that just like the piece they just completed, they will want to start with story ideas and characters—that they won't just go from zero to published! They still need to work through the process.

You might decide to show them a few mentor texts, perhaps ones you have already read or know they are familiar with. You could pull down the fiction charts and theorize how this author got this or that idea or might have created characters. For example, the "How to Write a Fiction Story" chart that you worked on toward the end of the last bend would be ideal to revisit here. Some teachers find it most effective to model with their own writing, referring to prior lessons from the unit as they model coming up with a brand-new idea. You will want to show them how because they have just finished a fiction piece they can move more quickly through this one. Whatever you choose to do, you will want to teach in such a way as to make students chomp at the bit to try their hands at writing yet another fiction project.

Students will need a rehearsal for their new projects. You might find it easiest to have the students work on a class project together, having them develop possible story blurbs together. You could also use this as an opportunity for students to run their individual ideas by their partners before they return to their seats. If you choose this option, you will likely want to voice over as they are brainstorming, reminding them what they know about coming up with story ideas.

Most of the time we try to wrap up minilessons reminding students of the repertoire of strategies they already know for whatever work they are doing during independent work time. Today is no different. However, you will want to remind them that they are now the ones setting the pace and imagining how big or small their projects might be, so they will want to consider those things as they plan their work.

How to Write a Fiction Story

- Develop a strong story idea, character(s), and setting.
- Spend time planning how the plot will go, making sure there is an arc to the story, trying again and again until the plan feels just right.
- Draft the story scene by scene, only using summary when needed.
- Study other authors for ways to make the story better.
- Make sure there is trouble in the story, and write an ending that resolves that trouble.

CONFERRING AND SMALL-GROUP WORK

You can anticipate that many students will have one idea they get attached to right away and don't feel compelled to keep trying to write other story blurbs. They will likely want to race willy-nilly into drafting. This is natural, and if you remember, was exactly what they wanted to do at the beginning of their first fiction piece. To combat this, let students know that this fiction piece will move quickly, so it's important to take advantage of every opportunity to make sure the work they are doing is the best it can be. Developing several ideas and then choosing the best one is a great example of that. You will also want to tip your cards a bit and let them know that before their work time is over they will likely be creating characters.

For students who are having a hard time coming up with new story blurbs, steer them toward inspiration. This could include mentor texts, rereading old ideas, brainstorming with a partner, or revisiting charts. Show them that they have many resources to tap to garner ideas.

MID-WORKSHOP TEACHING

You'll want to gather the students together and make a note that many of them have already landed on their idea for their newest fiction story. Let them know that you are teaching the next step for people who are ready and for people who will be ready soon. Review some of the character work your class did at the beginning of the fiction unit, highlighting the areas to which you want students to pay particular attention. If you opted to create a class story, you will likely want students to try creating a class character as well.

SHARE

To reinforce the goals of this last bend, highlight the places where you saw students recycling work they did earlier in the unit. You might also decide to mention students who used their resources, reviewing notes, returning to texts and anchor charts, and so on to make sure that their fiction knowledge and their new fiction projects are woven together seamlessly.

Enjoy!

Lucy and Colleen

Planning and Drafting Stories with Agency

THERE IS LITTLE DOUBT that you have a lot on your plate right now. You might have assumed through the entire realistic fiction unit that your students were given a lot of independence and agency and that they took advantage of those opportunities. And they likely did. However, yesterday you probably also witnessed that your students were capable of even more divergent agency and independence, and you might even find yourself reeling from the sheer number of different ideas and project scopes. Rest in the knowledge that this initial energy will die down a bit and that students will soon settle into a project groove that will be much easier to manage.

That said, know that many of your students likely have independent writing projects that they have been working on since they were much younger. They have been writing fairy tales and superhero fan fiction on the backs of scrap paper at the kitchen table since they were able to hold a pencil. They can handle it. You have simply opened the door and allowed them to bring in their moonlighting fiction. As exciting as that can be for students, it is also very important that you explicitly teach them that they have learned a lot about writing fiction and that they should apply those things every time they embark on a new fiction project, inside and outside of the classroom.

This is especially important because, after this unit, most of the writing done this year will be of the opinion and informational variety. If they want to continue honing their fiction writing skills during this school year after this cycle, they will need to learn how to manage writing stories mostly on their own time, outside of the class units of study. This final bend allows you (and them) to remember and reuse what they recently learned, but this time with increased agency and independence. Nowhere is this more crucial than in the work of planning and drafting.

In this session you will teach your students that they need to learn to be their own editors, spotting when plans might be too ambitious or too flat, when drafts are too brief or ramble on for too long. You will likely want them to pull out their plans and first drafts from their most recently finished pieces so that they can see what they were capable of then and can work to match that level of work, if not exceed it.

IN THIS SESSION, you'll teach students how writers quickly apply their planning and drafting skills to new projects.

GETTING READY

✔ Chart prepared ahead of time titled, "Fiction Writers Study Their Own Best Work To . . . " (see Teaching)

✔ A copy of the demonstration story arc from the first fiction piece

✔ A demonstration draft that students have worked with before

COMMON CORE STATE STANDARDS: W.4.3, W.4.4, W.4.5, W.4.8, W.4.10, RL.4.1, RL.4.5, SL.4.1, L.4.1, L.4.2, L.4.3

Planning and Drafting Stories with Agency

CONNECTION

Tell a story that illustrates outgrowing a teacher.

"When I was getting ready to go to my first sleepover party, I remember my brother saying to my mom, 'I can't believe you're letting her go! I don't think she'll be good unless you're around telling her what to do.' My mom laughed and said, 'Well, teaching her to be good is part of my job, and the only way I'll find out if I'm doing it right is if she can be good when I'm not there to tell her what to do.'"

Let students know how proud of them you are and that you want them to begin to rely more and more on their learning.

"I started thinking about that when I began to imagine what I would teach you today. Yesterday was all about remembering what we did with coming up with story ideas and developing characters. And so many of you did so well—I was so proud! I could tell you had learned a lot. And I know a lot of you are still doing that work. But some of you are ready to move forward to plan your new stories and maybe even begin to draft them, and I was thinking about what I can teach you to help you move onto the next step of the process without me watching over you quite so much or doing what my brother called 'telling you what to do.'"

❖ **Name the teaching point.**

"Today I want to teach you that writers can be their own best editors and teachers. They do this by studying their own best work to remind themselves what they are capable of doing. They can look closely at their best plans for stories, and their first drafts, to note what they did well and resolve to do even better."

TEACHING

Mention the work you did together studying a mentor text and how that influenced their writing for the better.

"Remember how we spent a lot of time when you were writing your first fiction pieces studying mentor texts, especially *Fireflies!*? We spent a good amount of time studying how that author wrote the perfect lead or developed the

Since the students will cycle through the entire writing process again, you can expect that they do so with more independence, although they may need a few reminders. Now would be a good time to pull out all the charts you made earlier in the unit and draw students' attention to them. This can serve as a reminder for how much they have learned and that they can use everything they know to write new stories.

setting just so. You tried to walk in her footsteps, trying some of the same writing moves that she tried, knowing that by studying writers who came before you, you'd be able to learn from what they already knew and push our own writing forward."

Explain that they can also mentor themselves by studying their past writing work.

"Now, you have developed some experience writing fiction yourselves. You shouldn't start from scratch, as if you don't know anything. And while it's important that you do still study mentor authors, and we'll be talking about that in another day or two, it's also very important that all writers study their own best work. We do this for a few reasons." I pulled out a chart I'd prepared ahead of time, and read through the points.

Fiction Writers Study Their Own Best Work To . . .

- Notice what they did well and make sure that they do that again in their next projects
- Study the places where they could have done better and resolve to do so
- See ways they can ratchet up their work for next time

"So, I'm going to take out my story arc and my first draft from my Luz story and see if I can begin to do that work."

Model studying your story arc from your last fiction story to identify what you did well and want to include in your new piece, as well as what you want to do differently this time.

I pulled out my story arc and draft and taped them to the board.

- Luz looks at a calendar and starts writing lots of birthday invitations and gets worried people will find out about her fear of the dark.
- Her friends don't like her games.
- Her plan to leave the closet light on fails.
- She has to face her fear of the dark OR her fear of being embarrassed.

Then I took on the pose of serious writer, notebook and pen in hand, jotting down as I talked, looking back to the chart that laid out ways to look at my work. "So, I'm thinking that what I like about this story arc is that the story is clear. It has one main problem and a clear resolution where Luz really changes. But I'm thinking now that maybe I could just start my new story right in the action, instead of having the build-up scene, like I had in this story where Luz thinks about the party and makes the invitations. Like, maybe in my new story, about a boy named Michael who wants to ride his bike to school and his mom won't let him, I can start right in the action, and if I need to give background information I can do it with a flashback, or just by showing the character remembering, instead. Actually, that would be a way to make any good story arc even better!"

- Michael's mom gets on her bike and tells Mike to get in the kid's seat.
- Michael says no.

You will notice that I have placed a large emphasis on having students study their own writing to develop goals for making their writing stronger. Here, I once again ask the students to reflect on their writing, reinforcing the point that writers can learn from their own work.

- Michael and his mom have an argument where he stands up for himself.
- He and his mom come up with a compromise where he can ride his own bike, but his mom rides with him.

ACTIVE ENGAGEMENT

Ask the students to practice studying your draft for writing moves they think you should keep and ones they think could be improved upon.

I then turned to a page from the draft of my earlier story that the students had worked on with me before.

> I checked all my stuff at least three times. I made sure my secret night-light was pushed all the way to the bottom of my pillowcase where no one would see it. Then I walked over to the table and rearranged the napkins. Everything on the table was yellow. Yellow wasn't my favorite color, but a lot of the girls coming to the party wore yellow all the time, so I thought they'd like it. And like me.
>
> First Marta came in. Then Joy and Tish walked in together, helping each other carry all their sleeping stuff. I helped carry things to the corner of the room where my mom and I decided we would keep the stuff until it was time to go to sleep.
>
> "So what are we going to do first?" Joy asked.
>
> I looked around at all my friends. I was so excited that my party was finally happening that I almost forgot the games I had planned.

"So, could you help me continue with this work? Can you study this section of my draft with a partner and name the things you see that you think I should include in my new draft, and the things that you think I can improve upon?"

Guide the students to move beyond naming what they see in text-specific terms to naming what they see as transferable writing strategies.

The students turned and talked to their partners, finding it relatively easy to mention things they thought were worth doing again and things they thought I could do better. However, I needed to coach the students into not being only text specific ("I like how she made Luz . . . "), but instead saying something that was a writing strategy that could be applied to their own writing: "I liked how she used actions to make us understand the characters. She should do that with her new story and make sure she uses a lot of actions to tell us how Michael is feeling."

Throughout this unit and in other units, the teacher has been the one to name the transferable strategies that they want the students to notice. Here we ask that students do this work. You must have confidence in your students' ability to pull out writing strategies, especially ones you have taught in this unit. Of course, you will scaffold this work for them as needed.

LINK

Name the different work students will be doing today, tucking in suggestions of things they might want to try.

"Writers, you are going to really need to make some smart plans for your work today. Starting today, you are going to find that many of you are moving at different paces and working on different things as you become more and more independent with your fiction writing. Some of you still want to go back and spend some time on developing possible story blurbs. Or maybe you did that and are now ready to work on developing your characters. Many of you came up with the perfect story blurb and developed your characters yesterday. Today you are ready to plan out your story arc and begin drafting."

Reiterate the power of studying one's own writing and becoming one's own teacher.

"Before you do any of those things, I urge you to consider looking back at your own work to see what you knew to do before and want to be sure to include again, and what you know you can do better next time. While I will be bopping around the room to confer with you today and the next few days, I won't always be able to work with you on your fiction stories. It's important that you learn, starting today, how to be your own teacher."

Creating Active Characters to Create Strong Narratives

WHEN CONFERRING WITH STUDENTS TODAY, you will likely be on the lookout for issues and problems that showed up when your students were first developing story arcs and drafts a few weeks ago. You will also want to look for places where students are reusing the skills and strategies they learned while writing their last fiction piece. Make a point to compliment those students in big and public ways. You will want students to feel successful and driven to continue to regularly incorporate their writing skills anytime they write, regardless of whether or not you reminded them to do so.

You will also likely notice new areas that students might need guidance with. One common example is that many students will likely want to revert to creating characters to whom things happen. In other words, they create passive characters who have their homework stolen or whose parents forget to wake them up. We can and should look at these choices and see the approximation work at hand (they are making sure their plots have trouble, after all) and also know that they love their characters (who are often thinly veiled fictional versions of themselves) so it is difficult to make these characters guilty of anything. That said, we also want to guide our students toward making stronger choices for their stories. The best stories are the ones where the characters are active, particularly active in the trouble. So if a character loses his homework, it would be a more compelling story if he lost it because he was in a rush to play soccer and left it on a bench where it probably blew away, or if the character is late to school because she tells her mom she can wake herself up, then forgets to set the alarm.

You might need to go through a few different options with students who have this issue, starting with how they want the story to end, how they want the character to change, and then help them to work backward so that the student is able to design a story wherein the characters are actively involved in the events. You might also want to point to mentor texts so that students can see how most strong stories have characters who are actively involved in the events of the story and don't just have events happen to them.

MID-WORKSHOP TEACHING   Making a Pacing Calendar

"Writers, can I have your eyes up here?" I interrupted the students' writing and directed their gaze to a student's calendar. "I was just meeting with Hannah and thought I would share what she was doing to make her new fiction project go more smoothly.

"Hannah knows that we only have a couple of days left to work all together on our latest fiction projects and that most of us will need to continue to work on them in our free time after that time is up. She thought if there was no whole-class pacing to follow, it would make a lot of sense to make her own pacing. She did this by thinking about when she wanted to finish her story, keeping in mind her after school activities and other class deadlines. She then made mini-deadlines—when her revisions would be due, when her editing would be done, for example. These mini-deadlines will help keep her from rushing too fast or from lollygagging when she should be pushing ahead.

"If you would like to have a calendar for the school year to help you keep pace of not just this project, but any other independent writing projects you do this year, let me know and I'll make sure to get you one."

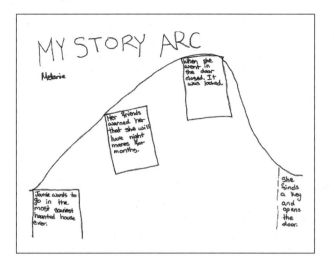

FIG. 17–1 In Melanie's story arc she just has the character accidentally find the keys.

Text in story arc diagram:

MY STORY ARC

Melanie

Jamie wants to go in the most scariest haunted house ever.

Her friends warned her that she will have night mares for months.

When she went in the door closed. It was locked.

She finds a key and opens the door.

Left draft page:

Melanie

Haunted
House
Disaster

"Hey guys lets go inside this haunted house" Jamie said. They all walked up the stairs.

"No way I'm going inside" her best friend Jazzlyn said replied.

"Trust me Jamie this haunted house is the most scariest house ever. Ive been in this haunted house. and had night mares for weeks" her another friend Layla said. Jamie walked up the last step.

"I'm not afraid to go inside" Jamie said. "Fine don't say that we didn't warn you" they both said. Jamie walked inside. I didn't look so scary she said.

The door quickley shut. She ran back to see if it would open.

"Dang it, it won't budge. I have to find another way out" Jamie said. All of a sudden Jamie gets scooped by a cart.

Middle draft page:

"Hey let my down" she screamed. She swung around in circles over and over again. Then Mummies, ghost, spiders, and witches were following her.

The cart came to a stop, but the monsters were still following her. I hope I make it out of her alive. she thought to herself. She saw a little flash-light. Thank god it still works she thought. She searched every where for help. Then she saw something in the corner. she ran to go see what it was. It was a little black box with a key in it. She took the box and ran as fast as she possibly could. She finally got to the door.

She took the key and opened the door.

"I'm so happy to see you guys, I thought I was going to die in there" Jamie said.

"What did we tell you Jamie, you need to listen more aften" Layla said.

"Remind me to never ever go in that house ever again" Jamie said in a scaried voice.

"Now that we got that out of the way, let go to Sarahs Halloween Party because I'm starving" Layla said.

Right draft page:

"He to I starving" Jazzlyn said.

"Then what are we waiting for lets go" Jamie said.

FIG. 17–2 In her draft, Melanie makes her character actively look for help.

Working on Independence through Partnerships

Point out students who have been actively working with partners during today's work time.

"Writers, I just wanted to call attention to some writers in our midst who are halfway to being expert independent writers. Writers who might put me out of a job sooner rather than later. You might be wondering what makes these writers so strong. I'll tell you. They are learning how to build relationships with other writers."

Convey to students that the most independent writers are also the most interdependent.

"I can already tell by the looks on some of your faces that you are surprised by what I just said. How can you be independent if you're working with other people all the time? Well the truth is, every writer needs to share her writing with other writers eventually. You all need to have someone to bounce your ideas off of or share a part that you are excited about, or ask for advice when the work gets hard. If you don't find other writers who are in the same boat as you are, peers, you will always be reliant on your teachers or other people with more experience to do those things for you. So, to be independent, you need to learn to build connections with other writers."

Suggest to students that they build on current partnerships and perhaps add to them so that they can create a community that will support them long after this piece is through.

"Today, whether it's right after we wrap up, during lunch, or as we pack up today, I'd like you to consider your partnerships. Do you want to invite another partnership to join you and your partner to form a club? Do you and your partner want to make regular times to meet to share your work? Maybe you and your partner want to watch another partnership have a conversation so that you can get ideas for how you can make your partnership, and thus your writing, even stronger. Whatever you decide to do, I want you to know that long after this project is done, as you go on through this school year, as you move out of fourth grade and on up the grades, it will be very important for your independent writing life to have a community of other writers you can rely on to encourage you and give you feedback and support so that you can keep setting and meeting your writing goals."

Although we strive to build independence, we also know that writers, and people in general, need to build relationships that support their growth and can propel them toward their goals. Here, I emphasize the importance of partnerships for sharing writing. This requires that you build a strong sense of community in your classroom and teach students to become effective writing partners.

MAKING OUR OWN HOMEWORK ASSIGNMENTS

For the past few days in writing workshop, you have been using all that you have learned to embark on independent fiction stories. So far, while you all started together, I see a huge variety of things you are doing, how far along in the process you might be. Some of you are still gathering story blurbs. Others of you are developing characters or story arcs. There are even a few who have confided that you are getting ready to draft tomorrow. You have been making your plans for writing workshop each day and then following through on them. You should be proud!

It doesn't make sense, then, for me to give everyone in the class the same homework assignment, since you are all at different places in your projects. You know best what you need to work on next. Right now, I'd like you to think for a minute about what is next for your project. What do you need to work on—the very next thing? How much time can you devote to that work tonight for homework? It could be that you know you have to go on a hunt for mentor texts, and you have thirty minutes to visit the library after school. Or it could be that you know that you are ready to complete your story arc, and that you could finish it up for sure when you get home. When you know what you should and can do for homework tonight, make a small box on the next blank page in your notebook. Record your homework assignment inside it. Tomorrow, when we come back together, we'll see how successful you were at completing your own homework assignment. This is exactly the kind of work you'll be doing every day if you decide to keep your independent fiction projects going throughout the school year.

Mining the Connections between Reading and Writing Fiction

IN THIS SESSION, you'll teach students that writers study the work they do as readers of fiction and graft those skills into their revisions.

GETTING READY

✔ Fiction books students are currently reading

✔ A stack of picture books and texts you can use to model choosing a mentor text

✔ Chart paper to record student discoveries about mentor texts

✔ *Fireflies!* or another mentor text that has a lot of tension and conflict (see Conferring)

✔ Chart titled "Ways Writers Support Each Other" (see Mid-Workshop Teaching)

COMMON CORE STATE STANDARDS: W.4.3, W.4.4, W.4.5, W.4.8, RL.4.1, RL.4.3, RL.4.5, RL.4.10, SL.4.1, SL.4.2, L.4.1, L.4.2, L.4.3

T HE LAST BEND IN THIS UNIT is meant to guide your students toward not only continuing and transferring their fiction writing skills, but also facilitating their independence so that they can continue to write fiction across the year. We felt it very important, in light of this, to connect their writing work not just with carefully selected mentor texts, picked because of how closely aligned they are to fourth-graders' zones of proximal development and the way they highlight the skills we most want to teach, but also to help students mine the connections between their reading and writing lives.

In this session you will ask students to review their reading experiences thus far this year. If you have a thriving reading workshop, this will require little more preparation than to ask students to bring their book baggies with them to the next writing workshop minilesson. If you are not teaching a reading workshop, then you will want to give students a day or two's warning that you will be asking them to bring current and recently read books to writing workshop. You might want to preview the books, just to make sure that most students are in fact holding books they can read and that they are at least partly fiction titles.

Once students have their books in hand, you will want to show them how every time they are reading, they can also be studying writing. You will want to teach them how to read everything with the lens of a writer, to study sentences, structures, word choices, and turns of phrases that affect them, and then to see how they might try some of the things they admire with their own writing. Of course, as part of this work, students might realize that not all the books they are reading will be ones that they will be able to, or want to, learn about writing from. They might discover, as part of their goal to become stronger writers, that they will want to step up their book choices, at least part of the time. As Francine Prose, author of *Reading Like a Writer* (2007) says, "I've always found that the better the book I'm reading, the smarter I feel, or, at least, the more able I am to imagine that I might, someday, become smarter."

You will want to build off that energy and help guide the students into a short inquiry of their reading lives, specifically, what they can be learning about writing fiction through their reading.

Mining the Connections between Reading and Writing Fiction

CONNECTION

Ask students to go through their books, talking a bit to their partners about the ones they are reading currently or have recently finished.

"Writers, I asked you to bring your independent reading books with you to the meeting area because we are in the midst of writing new fiction projects, and we know we can learn a lot from reading other writers. Can you look through your books right now and talk with your partner about the books you are currently reading or have just finished? Can you tell them a bit about the plot, characters, setting, and what you like or don't like about that book?" I listened in to the partner conversations, noticing that most of the conversations were about their experiences as readers.

Once again, I draw on mentor texts to help my students create a vision of the type of writing they can produce. I bring home the fact that writers are constantly drawing inspiration from other writers, constantly trying out strategies that professional writers use, and most importantly, constantly working toward becoming stronger writers.

Point out that most of them were talking about books like readers, but they are now experienced fiction writers and should be looking at books all the time as writers as well.

"Wow! Based on just what I was hearing you talk about, I can tell that we have some fantastic books in our midst that I just can't wait to read! So exciting, sad, funny, and moving! The characters are believable, the settings rich, the plots have you at the edge of your seats. It seems to me that we do a lot of amazing work reading our fiction. And earlier this year we began to do some really great stuff when we studied mentor texts to help us get ideas for writing fiction. But I didn't really hear anyone talk about their chapter books with a fiction writer's eye. The thing is, we not only can do that work. We should do that work."

❖ **Name the question that will guide the inquiry.**

"So, my question for you is this. What are some ways that fiction writers can read fiction so that they are not only enjoying the story, but also strengthening their fiction writing skills? In other words, what are ways we can choose and use the fiction we are reading to help us become better fiction writers?"

This session set up as an inquiry, a time for students to discover for themselves. Rather than you pulling out a specific writing strategy to teach them, you are teaching them to study texts closely and in a way that is transferrable to any text in any genre.

TEACHING AND ACTIVE ENGAGEMENT

Model looking through a stack of books to find one that feels suitable to study with a fiction writer's lens.

"I'm going to try to answer this question myself, and I'd like you to watch me as I do, thinking about how you might do the same things, or what you might do differently." I reached for a stack of chapter books and pictures books I knew were familiar to the students either through read-alouds or book talks. "So, I think before I choose a text to study, I should probably think a little bit about my story. Since my story is different now, it's all about Michael and his desire to ride his own bike to school, I think I want to think a little bit about the kinds of books I have that are sort of like my story. Like a mix between funny and serious." I looked through the stack, making it clear I was thinking through each book's similarities in tone to my own story. I finally stopped at *Joey Pigza Swallowed the Key*, by Jack Gantos (2011). "This is perfect. It's both funny and serious—just like I want my book to be."

Talk through a few things you had admired as a reader and rename them as strategies a fiction writer can use.

"Next up I want to go back to some places in the book that I really liked when I read it. Luckily, I marked some of those pages with sticky notes, but some are just places I remembered. Like one that comes right to mind is the shoofly pie incident when Joey loses control after eating shoofly pie. It was so funny! And a little bit sad. Let me go back to that section and see if I can understand how Jack Gantos made that scene *both* funny and sad."

I flipped back to the pages, making a show of rereading. I intentionally did not read aloud the section or project it because I wanted students to be paying less attention to the text and more attention to what I was doing as a reader and writer. "Oh, so one of the things that made me laugh was how over the top Joey was. Like, maybe one thing I can do in my own writing to make it funny is exaggerate things a bit, make things that happen realistic, but big." I turned another page. "And here's a sad part, when Joey realizes how wild he's been acting and feels bad, but also feels like he can't help it. I think one thing Jack Gantos does to make the reader sad is to get into the main character's head and highlight the difference between what the character wants and what actually happens."

Name what you just did as a reader and writer as if it was something you just discovered in your own inquiry.

"So let me think back to our inquiry question. What are ways we can choose and use the fiction we are reading to help us become better fiction writers? Well, just looking back at what I did just now, I noticed that when choosing a text to study, I based it on what text I thought was similar to the kind of mood I wanted for my own. And when using the text, I first looked at where I was moved as a reader and then tried to name what the author did to have that affect on me." I took a quick second to jot these things down on our class charts.

Ways Writers Choose Mentor Texts

- Look for a text that has a similar mood to the text you are working on.

Ways Writers Use Mentor Texts

- Find places where the text made you feel an emotion as a reader and name how the mentor author did that.

A bonus from the teaching you do in this session, aside from the obvious writing benefits, is that you are subtly modeling the unguilty, rich life of a reader. You are reminding children that you not only love to read, but that there are many benefits from reading as well.

Ask students to look through their current stack of books and find one they think is worth studying as writers, encouraging them to articulate to their partners the ways they determined which book to study.

"Readers and writers, you might find as you ask yourself the same question I asked myself, namely, what are ways can we choose and use the fiction we are reading to help us become better fiction writers, that you start by doing some of what I just did as a reader and writer. That's great. But I'd also like you to push yourself to go past that as well. Try to spy on yourself and see what is going through your mind. For example, if you just really like a book and want it to be your mentor, try to talk through your thinking with your partner to see if he or she can help you tease out what it could be."

The students looked through their book baggies, some flipping straight to pages that were marked with sticky notes or dog-eared. Other students seemed to be making small piles on the floor in front of them, taking in each book in turn, trying to decide which would be the one. I circulated through them as they worked, listening in as they talked to partners, coaching some who were getting stuck on the verbiage.

After it seemed that most students had chosen a text and talked about their choices with their partners, I reconvened the class. "Writers, after watching and listening to you, I have a few more things to add to our chart."

Ways Writers Choose Mentor Texts

- Look for a text that has a similar mood to the text you are working on.
- Pick a text that uses language you admire.
- Find a text that has a structure you would like to try.
- Choose a text that has a strength that is a goal for you to work on.

Guide students toward looking through their books with a writer's eye, giving them time to both read and talk with their partners.

"So, now that you all have texts that you want to study, let's take some time to think about how we can use these texts to make our writing better. Can you, right now with texts in hand, brainstorm with your partners different ways you can study and learn from your mentor texts? As you come up with ideas, be sure to try them out in the text that you have chosen to see if these ideas will really work."

Once again the students turned and talked to their partners while I circulated. I made a point of pushing the students to be as specific as possible when discussing various ways they could use their mentor texts. If students said a one-word or pat answer, I pushed them to say more. I also encouraged them to look back at the chart to see if any of the reasons they chose a mentor text in the first place might give some insights into ways to use the mentor text.

Once the students had had several minutes to talk and try, I pulled the group back together and returned to the second chart, recording the students' discoveries.

Just as I did in the last session, students are naming writing strategies, but this time ones they notice in books written by professional authors rather than in their own writing. Both are important, of course, and both serve the same purpose—for students to notice ways in which they can become more powerful writers.

Ways Writers Use Mentor Texts

- Find places where the text made you feel an emotion as a reader and name how the mentor author did that. Try it in your own piece.
- Study the sound of the text and describe how the mentor author gave the story that sound. Experiment with similar moves in your story.
- Record the mentor author's story structure, maybe using a story arc. Try placing your own story in a similar structure.
- Highlight the strongest parts in the story. Look for places you can try similar things in your own work.

LINK

Explain to students that while the work they started today will be very useful for their current independent writing projects, knowing how to choose and use a mentor text is something they can use for the rest of their writing careers.

"We were quite the inquirers today, weren't we? And you know, these charts have just begun. I feel like all year we'll keep adding to these charts as we choose new mentor authors for different reasons and discover new ways to improve our writing from studying these texts.

"I know you are all in different places with your new stories today. Some are drafting, some are revising, and some of you have returned to your notebooks. No matter what you are doing today, I do want you to know that knowing how to choose and use a mentor text is not just something for this current project. It's something you can use your entire fourth-grade year and for the rest of your writing life. As long as you're readers, you can learn ways to improve your writing in remarkable ways."

Developing Conflict and Tension

YESTERDAY YOU REMINDED STUDENTS that the best characters are the active ones. When students do that sort of character development, they often find that the conflict and tension in a story sort of builds by itself. If, however, you are noticing students who are having a hard time creating believable conflicts (or any conflict at all), or there is a conflict but very little tension, you might want to pull those students into conferences and small groups to address those issues. When fiction writers adopt a conflict- or tension-building strategy well, they can use that same strategy over and over for almost every story that they write. (Just think of James Patterson!)

While there are countless ways that writers can create conflict and build tension, you will likely want to focus on just a couple of ways. You might mention that one easy way to create conflict is to have two characters in competition for something. Another easy way is to give a character a big desire for something, as well as big obstacle. Yet another way to increase conflict is to force characters who don't get along to be together (families, classmates, people stuck in an elevator). Increasing tension often happens naturally once a conflict is developed, but it is also fairly simple to increase tension by increasing a character's motivation, imposing a time limit (think Cinderella), or raising the stakes on whatever it is the character is trying to achieve. Noah Lukeman's *The Plot Thickens* (2003), a book written for professional writers, has several easy-to-modify ideas for this work.

You would be wise to have students grab their recently chosen mentor texts and try uncovering their mentor author's strategies for developing conflict and increasing tension. You might also want to have a text in mind that you can use to show how tension and conflict can be ratcheted up. *Fireflies!* is a great example, but so are lots of other short picture books such as Gary Soto's *Too Many Tamales* and *"Let's Get a Pup" Said Kate* by Bob Graham.

See Aliya's revision to her story arc shown in Figure 18–1 on the following page.

MID-WORKSHOP TEACHING
Learning to Support Other Writers

"Writers, can I have you put your pencils down for just a few minutes?" I asked and waited until all eyes were on me before continuing. "Yesterday we talked about how important it is for writers to have an ongoing writing community. How even though we write alone, to be independent we need to have other people's support and feedback. I noticed that many of you firmed up those relationships yesterday and today. I know that we know a few things we can do to support our partners, so I thought I would add those to a chart, along with a few other ways we can support our partners":

Ways Writers Support Each Other

- Be a sounding board by listening to each other's ideas and giving feedback on those ideas.
- Give each other specific compliments.
- Make suggestions for mentor texts or other resources that might help.
- Remind each other of deadlines.
- Make suggestions, when asked, to help make the writing better.

"Can you look over this chart right now and see which, if any, of these things you've done with your writing partner? Can you make a plan to try to do something you haven't done yet? And in the future, if you find you are running out of ways to support your partner, or your work together is just getting stale, please look back at this chart to remind yourself of some of the possibilities."

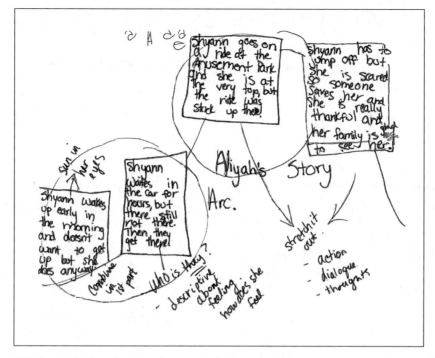

FIG. 18–1   Aliyah revised her story arc to increase tension.

Gearing Writing Toward a Particular Audience

Explain to students that while it's important that they are writing something they want to read, it's also important that they have a particular audience in mind.

"Writers, one of the ways that independent fiction projects, or any independent writing projects at all, are different than other pieces is that these new stories are ones you are mostly writing for yourselves. Sure, we're talking about the writing now and I'm teaching you some lessons now, but the time will come for us to move on to our next unit, and many of you will either still be working on these pieces or you will be starting new ones. This is a bit different because we won't necessarily be having a whole-class celebration for these pieces every time you publish one. That means that many of you are writing for yourselves.

"However, I also want to plant another idea in your head. When authors write, yes, they write for themselves. But they also write with a particular audience in mind. Maybe it's a special person or a particular group of people. But they all think of this audience all the time as they write. This gives you another lens you can use to help you develop and draft and revise. If my audience is my mom, I might not include as many silly moments in the story because she doesn't have much of a sense of humor. But, if my audience is you, I know this class loves to laugh, so I'll definitely want to include the occasional silliness.

"Can you right now tell your partner who your audience is? And how writing with that audience in mind will affect how you work on your story going forward?"

Although I want my students to write for themselves and work toward personal goals, I also want them to understand that many professional writers write to appeal to others—to move them or make them laugh. Even if your students do not desire public attention on their writing, you will still want them to know how to angle their writing with a particular audience in mind, teaching them to shift their writing depending on the intended reader.

Focusing the Reader's Gaze

IN THIS SESSION, you'll teach students how writers can learn from visual artists and help readers visualize from different angles to make a variety of points.

GETTING READY

✔ A short video clip of a film or television show that shows a variety of camera angles, or a prepared storyboard of a film or television show that shows a variety of camera angles (see Teaching)

✔ A prewritten excerpt of a demonstration draft to model revising with an eye toward camera angles (see Active Engagement)

✔ An additional excerpt of a demonstration draft for student practice

✔ Copies of the Narrative Writing Checklist, Grades 4 and 5 (see Share)

I N THIS FINAL BEND, much of the teaching has been focused on teaching students' transference and independent application of their recently honed fiction writing skills. While you almost always offered choice in previous bends, there was still a very clear road map that most students were apt to follow. However, in this bend you have cracked those choices wide open, and students have no choice but to chart their own course. These are high-level tasks that you are asking your students to undertake, very much aligned with Webb's depth of knowledge level 4 and the highest instructional levels suggested by Danielson's Framework for Teaching.

This session will continue to ask students for that transference from their study of fiction, as well as integrating new strategies gleaned from other disciplines, in this case, the visual arts. You will take a fresh approach to teaching students different ways to revise and be specific. Virtually all of your students have watched a movie or television show, or at the very least have seen photographs or paintings. Many of them are more familiar with television watching and movie viewing and the terms and concepts of those forms than the literary terms around reading books. Today's session will show them how to connect the deep and powerful literary work you have and will be doing all year with their primary cultural experiences.

Ahead of today's session you will want to rent or download a movie or television show popular with your students and appropriate for school. You will want to vet it ahead of time, teasing out the perfect clips to show students the differences in effect between wide, medium, and close-up shots. If that won't work for you because you don't have access to the technology to show the clips, you could always "storyboard" or sketch to illustrate the difference between the different shots.

COMMON CORE STATE STANDARDS: W.4.3, W.4.4, W.4.5, W.4.8, RL.4.3, SL.4.1, L.4.1, L.4.2, L.4.3.a, L.4.5.c

Focusing the Reader's Gaze

CONNECTION

Tell students you had an epiphany yesterday while watching a movie.

"Last night I was rewatching that movie *Toy Story 3*. You know, the one that came out a couple of years ago that's all about those toys who get sent to a horrible day care center when their original owner, Andy, grows up and gets ready to go to college. There was a part where the camera pans over the boy Andy's bedroom, and you get a sense of this place where they've all been living, how the boy has changed and grown. Then, just a little while later there's another shot where most of the toys are all lined up, and you get a sense of all the main characters—who they are as individuals and what their relationships are like with each other, like how Mr. and Mrs. Potato Head are exchanging glances the way old married couples do. Then there's a close-up of just Woody's face. And you can tell by the look on his face that he's really concerned. I'm sure the other characters were concerned as well, but the filmmakers wanted us to really focus on Woody and how he was feeling, so his face fills up the whole screen.

"That's when it came to me that what they do in movies and television shows, moving from showing the whole setting (a wide shot) to showing a few things or characters a little bit closer (a medium shot) to going in on just a character's face (close-up) is exactly the kind of work we should be doing as writers."

You will want to choose a movie that you know most, if not all, your students have seen so they can engage with your story and understand how it connects to today's teaching.

❖ **Name the teaching point.**

"Today I want to teach you that fiction writers can get inspired to ratchet up their writing from unexpected places, including other kinds of art like movies and television. Specifically, you can learn from the way a camera focuses on settings, actions, and characters, deciding how much to show or not show and with what amount of detail. You can look back through your drafts and decide if there are places where you should cover more ground or places where you should show greater detail."

TEACHING

Introduce a video clip, recruiting writers to notice close-ups, medium shots, and wide shots.

"I thought what we could do today is view a clip of a video, where you'll notice when the camera is showing a wide shot, medium shot, or close-up. I want you to be paying attention to what's happening in the scene when each of those things is happening." I played about one minute of a scene, calling out as they came up, "Close-up," "Medium shot," and "Wide shot."

Rewatch the video, this time with students assigned to different angles to focus on, looking to understand why the filmmaker made those choices.

"Now, I'm going to have us watch it again, but this time I'm going to divide us up a bit. This section of the room," I pointed to the left-hand side of the rug, "will be looking for times the scene is in wide shot." I then pointed to the group of students seated in the middle of the room. "You will be looking for any medium shots." I then gestured toward the students sitting on the right. "You will be keeping your eyes peeled for any close-ups.

"But here's the thing. I don't want you to just look for those shots. I want you to pay attention to what is happening in the scene and to see if you and your partner can decide why the filmmakers decided to focus the camera in that way. What is it doing for the story? How is it helping you as a viewer?"

After the students watched the clip a second time, they were full of things to say. "I noticed that when a character was having a strong emotion, they did a close-up," said one. "I noticed when there was a big action, or they needed to let us know where the story was taking place they went for a wide shot," said another. "I thought there were more medium shots than anything else. Like, those are the shots that just moved the story along."

Connect the film shots back to fiction writing. Explain to students that writers also describe some aspects of their stories with more encompassing detail and some with the tiniest detail, depending on the purpose.

"Writers, so many of you noticed that filmmakers choose to focus in different ways depending on what they are trying to show in their story. How does the character feel? Probably a close-up of the character's face, maybe her hands because she is making a fist. How do these people feel about each other? They might want to opt for a medium shot so you can see the people close enough to notice how they interact with each other, but not so close that you can't see what else is going on. And if there's a need to understand the setting or to notice large actions, such as travel, a wide shot is used.

"You might be wondering if I forgot that we're writing stories here, not making films! But the truth is, a lot of fiction writers who write short stories and novels pay a lot of attention to how close or how far they want to bring the characters to the action. They decide when they should zoom in on something and give people a bigger sense of other things."

Model revising with an eye toward the angle of the camera.

"So you all know that my new story is about a boy who doesn't want to ride on the back of his mother's bike anymore. He wants to ride his own bike to school. So he confronts his mother, and in the end she lets him ride his bike, but she

In this session, we once again use a mentor for students to pull techniques from, but this time we decided to use a different medium—video. This can help your students see that they can learn from many different sources, studying them the way they would a book or their own writing. This is also especially helpful for students who may not necessarily love to read books because you can engage them in the skills they would use to study a book as they study the video.

rides with him. If I go back and look at my story arc, I want to revisit the part of the story where he decides to stand up to his mom. This is how it goes right now."

Michael put on his helmet and turned to head over to the bike where his mom was waiting. "Jump on," she said. Michael suddenly couldn't imagine riding on the back of this bike one more day to school. He was in fourth grade, after all.

"So, if I want to imagine this like a movie or television show, I want to think about how the camera angles would go and then revise in the places where the camera angles are different than what they are now. I would say most of my writing seems to be medium shots. Which is okay for some places, but not for others. For example, I could do a close-up of Michael during the part where he decides he's not going to ride on the back of the bike. Let me try that."

Michael's face burned and his eyes got blurry. He was crying, but they weren't sad tears, they were embarrassed tears. He felt as if he was a big piece of metal and the sidewalk was a giant magnet. He knew he couldn't get on that bike.

"Now, I feel like right after that I could go for a wide shot, since he's thinking about fourth grade and the rest of the world, so I could show the setting around him."

There were kids all up and down the block, grabbing their backpacks and heading off to school. He saw some on scooters, their parents walking along beside them. Others were walking with friends, sneakers on sidewalk, laughing and waving to other kids they knew. Most of them were his age or older. They all looked very happy, and very grown-up.

"Oh, I like that much better. I think the reader now gets a sense of really what Michael was thinking and feeling and what the street looked like. They get a much better perspective because I am switching my writing camera around."

ACTIVE ENGAGEMENT

Enlist students to help revise your draft with camera angles in mind.

"I'd like you to help me out a bit with revising my story with the camera angles in mind. Can you look at the next paragraph in my story, and with your partner think about any camera angles we can try that would make it easier for my readers to really picture what's happening?"

"No. I want to ride my own bike," Michael blurted. His mom shook her head. "I'm not getting on that bike. I'll walk to school instead." He took off his helmet. He didn't care that everyone on his block could hear him shouting.

Some students will likely find this work difficult. You may then decide to ask more questions or provide more prompts to focus this work a bit more. You might break down the work by saying, "Let's try writing the beginning of my story from this angle. What would it sound like if I were to really zoom out here to show the whole neighborhood?"

The students turned and talked to their partners. "I think that Mom is sort of left out of this scene. I think a close-up of her face would be helpful," Hannah said. She then wrote-in-the-air, "His mom shook her head slowly, almost as if she couldn't believe what she was hearing. Her eyes squinted and she bit her bottom lip. She looked like she wanted to say something, but she couldn't think of anything."

LINK

Reiterate that writers can revise by reconsidering the angle they are writing from. Remind the students that they know a lot about writing and revising, not just from writing class, but from lots of different areas in their lives.

"What a fun session today! I feel like I learned so much with you. In particular, I learned that I tend to write at the same angle all the time, and many of us do. We can do some really great revision work by thinking through the angles we are writing from, being inspired by film and television to see that different angles help to tell different aspects of a story.

"That makes me think that we can probably get ideas for ways to improve our writing from everywhere, not just writing workshop. We can pay close attention in math class or soccer practice or even while grocery shopping. Ideas for how we can make our great writing even better are hiding everywhere if we just keep our minds open to look for them."

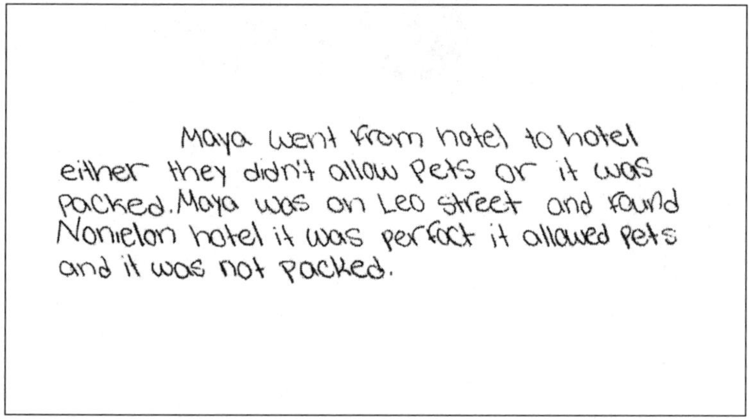

Maya went from hotel to hotel either they didn't allow pets or it was packed. Maya was on Leo street and found Nonielon hotel it was perfect it allowed pets and it was not packed.

FIG. 19–1 Janelly tries a wide shot.

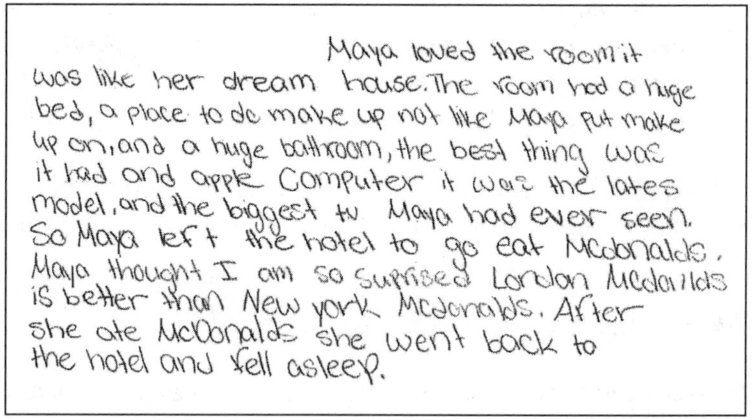

Maya loved the room it was like her dream house. The room had a huge bed, a place to do make up not like Maya put make up on, and a huge bathroom, the best thing was it had and apple computer it was the lates model, and the biggest tv Maya had ever seen. So Maya left the hotel to go eat Mcdonalds. Maya thought I am so surprised London Mcdonalds is better than New york Mcdonalds. After she ate Mcdonalds she went back to the hotel and fell asleep.

FIG. 19–2 Janelly tries a medium shot.

The Power of the Perfect Word

❝ WRITERS, I GATHERED THE GROUP OF YOU HERE TODAY because you are all doing such hard work on picking great words to use in your stories. You are using fancy, must-look-up-in-the-dictionary words and words that are hard to spell but are fun to say. You have bowled me over with the amount of care and time you've spent on thinking of these words." The students nodded.

"I wanted to let you in on a little secret about picking the perfect words. Fiction writers want to be like professional baseball players who catch a pop fly. We want to make it look very natural, like we haven't spent hours practicing. And sometimes when every word we use is extra sparkly, it makes it look like we're either working too hard or showing off a bit. Neither is a good thing. One of the best ways to do that work is to look carefully at your nouns and verbs. Make sure they are as precise as possible. When you use the perfect noun or verb, you can often get rid of some of the extra words that go with it. So for example, in my story, I originally had a sentence that looked like this."

> Michael got slowly onto the shiny, crimson bicycle with colorful reflectors and a small mesh basket on the back for his school books so they wouldn't get bent or get in the way of his riding.

"It's a fine sentence, but it's a little bit clunky and extra-wordy. Let me try again with strong nouns and verbs."

> Michael climbed onto his red bike to check out all the safety features.

"Writers, my second try used more precise words. It didn't get all bogged down in tons of extra-fancy words. When I did that, the fact that Michael *climbed* on his *red* bike really popped. Often fewer, carefully chosen words are better than a bucket of words added everywhere."

MID-WORKSHOP TEACHING **Creating Leads that Move Quickly into the Action and Don't Just Give Background Information**

"Writers, can I stop you for just a second?" Once all eyes were on me I continued, "When you were writing your first fiction pieces, you learned how writers don't start far, far away from the action of the story. They start their stories right at the action. Well, we need to continue to do that work in these new fiction pieces as well as any ones we might write in the future. We start our stories by placing the reader right in the thick of the action.

"Sometimes the reason we include all these little details that introduce our characters and tell about what they look like, where they live, and who's in their family is because we wrote all these details out and we don't want to waste them. They represent a lot of work, after all! But when we do that, when we write things like, 'Hi, my name is Michael and I live with my mom in a two-bedroom apartment with a pet dog and a goldfish named Goldy,' our readers' attention starts to fade.

"So what can you do instead, if you want to make sure your readers know those things, but you don't want to bore them? Well, you already know how to balance your story by weaving together details about setting, thinking, dialogue, and actions. In just the same way, you are going to weave in details about your main character. Writers don't write everything they know about their characters all at once. Instead, they need to carefully balance their stories by weaving in a bit of detail about character here and there, along with all the other kinds of details. Imagine that your story is on a stage, and you are raising the curtain ever so slowly, so the audience sees just a tiny bit at a time. Doing this creates suspense and drama in your stories."

Returning to the Narrative Checklist with Increasing Independence

Have students revisit the Narrative Writing Checklist to check in and move forward.

"Writers, you might have noticed that while you were working I placed a copy of our Narrative Writing Checklist on each of your tables. Can you put your pens down and turn your attention to the checklist and me for a few minutes?" Once the students had shifted their focus, I continued, "You'll remember this checklist from a week or so ago. You might have thought that now that we are working on independent fiction projects we weren't going to look at this checklist again. However, it is so important that you return to this checklist, not just today, but for the rest of the year.

"There's a book for grown-ups called *The Checklist Manifesto* by Atul Gawande. It talks about how powerful it is for people, particularly experts, to have a checklist whenever they do important things. So surgeons have a checklist every time they do surgery, pilots for whenever they fly a plane, and architects for when they plan buildings. I would argue that every time we create a piece of writing we are also doing something important. And even though we have become quite expert, there are still times when we might forget to do something that we know how to do.

"Today I want you to think about using this checklist not just as a way to assess yourself and see how you're doing, but also as a checklist to see what you still need to do and set goals for yourself. You can and should look at it today. And since I won't always be teaching fiction, but you might very well be writing it in your spare time, I also think it would be a good idea to look at it whenever you are working on a new independent fiction project, all year long."

The complete Narrative Writing Checklist, Grades 4 and 5 can be found on the CD-ROM.

Narrative Writing Checklist

	Grade 4	NOT YET	STARTING TO	YES!	Grade 5	NOT YET	STARTING TO	YES!
	Structure				**Structure**			
Overall	I wrote the important part of an event bit by bit and took out unimportant parts.	☐	☐	☐	I wrote a story of an important moment. It read like a story, even though it might be a true account.	☐	☐	☐
Lead	I wrote a beginning in which I showed what was happening and where, getting readers into the world of the story.	☐	☐	☐	I wrote a beginning in which I not only showed what was happening and where, but also gave some clues to what would later become a problem for the main character.	☐	☐	☐
Transitions	I showed how much time went by with words and phrases that mark time such as *just then* and *suddenly* (to show when things happened quickly) or *after a while* and *a little later* (to show when a little time passed).	☐	☐	☐	I used transitional phrases to show passage of time in complicated ways, perhaps by showing things happening at the same time (*meanwhile, at the same time*) or flashback and flash-forward (*early that morning, three hours later*).	☐	☐	☐
Ending	I wrote an ending that connected to the beginning or the middle of the story.	☐	☐	☐	I wrote an ending that connected to the main part of the story. The character said, did, or realized something at the end that came from what happened in the story.	☐	☐	☐
	I used action, dialogue, or feeling to bring my story to a close.	☐	☐	☐	I gave readers a sense of closure.	☐	☐	☐
Organization	I used paragraphs to separate the different parts or times of the story or to show when a new character was speaking.	☐	☐	☐	I used paragraphs to separate different parts or times of the story and to show when a new character was speaking. Some parts of the story were longer and more developed than others.	☐	☐	☐

Choosing Punctuation for Effect

W HEN PRIMARY-GRADE STUDENTS first learn about punctuation, they put exclamation points and questions marks everywhere. They can make the reader read in any way they want! The power is dizzying. Somewhere on the way to fourth grade, the glamour of punctuation wears off. It has as much excitement as tying one's shoes (another thrilling activity when you're six years old). Instead, fourth-graders often come to us viewing punctuation as something that has to be done, and done correctly, much like brushing your teeth. It is necessary and sometimes tiresome.

Today's session is aligned with Common Core Language Standard 3b, which asks students to "choose punctuation for effect." This is something your students also studied in third grade, but on a different level, building on third-graders' newfound command of conventions. This session is designed to freshen up your fourth-graders perception of punctuation and fill them with a feeling of power and control over punctuation. You will want to approach this session with as much enthusiasm and energy as you can muster. Additionally, you will want to set aside emphasizing punctuation for "correctness," even though there is very much a time and place for that. Students will be much more likely to be concerned with the conventional use of punctuation once they feel an affinity for the power of it. So instead, angle your teaching toward playfulness and a spirit of exploration while they draft and revise with punctuation in mind. You will be richly rewarded when you soon see that your students would not dare forget an endpoint again!

IN THIS SESSION, you'll remind students that writers use punctuation to make sentences easier to understand, as well as to have an effect on how their readers engage with the text.

GETTING READY

✔ Two previously used excerpts from your demonstration text that will benefit from punctuation revision, one for demonstration and one for student practice

✔ Chart with endpoint punctuation students already know (optional)

✔ "How to Write a Fiction Story" anchor chart (see Share)

COMMON CORE STATE STANDARDS: W.4.3, W.4.4, W.4.5, W.4.8, W.4.10, RFS.4.4, SL.4.1, L.4.1.f, L.4.2, L.4.3.b

Choosing Punctuation for Effect

CONNECTION

Tell a story about a time you or someone else had a good time controlling a situation.

"Yesterday I watched some kids playing Simon Says in the gym. I was particularly interested in the kid who was Simon. She looked like she was having a blast telling people what to do. And when people did something she didn't say 'Simon says' in front of, she seemed very happy to catch people. That got me thinking about being a writer and how as writers we are sort of playing a game of Simon Says with our readers. We're the ones who tell them what words to read and how to read those words."

Name the teaching point.

"Today I want to teach you that fiction writers don't just choose to use certain punctuation because it's the correct way to use it. Writers also use punctuation to affect their readers—to control how readers read and understand the stories that the writer writes."

TEACHING

Name a few familiar pieces of punctuation students are sure to know and what these are used for.

"You know that different forms of punctuation have different jobs. You know that question marks help writers to ask questions, exclamation points show excitement (good or bad), ellipses (dot-dot-dots) can help build tension, and dashes can chop a sentence up. You probably know lots and lots more. Thumbs up if you are thinking of a few other types of punctuation I haven't mentioned yet." Most students raised their thumbs.

Demonstrate returning to a draft with an eye toward revising with punctuation in mind. Show how writers can consider using punctuation for clarity and effect.

"I'm going to go back and look at a piece of my draft we worked with a few days ago. I want to see if there's a way I can use punctuation to affect the reader. I want to be Simon for my readers and tell them exactly how to read the sentences in my story, how to understand them, and in the process make my piece even better. To do that I need to ask

◆ COACHING

By now, your students have had plenty of time for writing narratives and have noticed elements of strong narrative writing. You mainly focused on craft in this unit and getting students to write with clear and focused storylines and complex characters. Today you and your students will shift your attention to another way to make their writing stronger—punctuation. It may be helpful to make a chart with the different types of punctuation you expect your students to use.

You will want to look through your students' writing to notice what types of punctuation they use often, and those that they do not use at all. You may decide to demonstrate how to use the types of punctuation that your students are not using to show them different possibilities.

myself what is supposed to be happening in my story. What are my characters thinking and feeling? Is there a way I can use punctuation to make that more clear?

"Let's take a look at this piece." I read aloud the following excerpt.

> Michael put on his helmet and turned to head over to the bike where his mom was waiting. "Jump on," she said. Michael suddenly couldn't imagine riding on the back of this bike one more day to school. He was in fourth grade, after all.

"Hmm, I think the first sentence is fine as it is. A period just makes a sentence matter of fact. I'm just describing what happens. But looking at the next sentence, I'm thinking the mom was more enthusiastic than saying 'jump on' so plainly. She's excited to ride the bike with her son. She has no idea that he's feeling like a baby. So if I change the ending of her sentence to an exclamation point, it shows how she's feeling and also how it's different from what Michael is feeling. So I'll write,"

> "Jump on!" she said.

"I think the next sentence is also fine. It's just a plain thought. And I think it really pops at how plain it is now because it's next to his mom's exclamation. But the last sentence feels a little like he's hesitating. Like he's thinking a bit. And I know right after this he's going to decide to fight to not ride the bike. So a period doesn't really cover all that. Maybe I can use an ellipsis to signal to the reader that he's lingering, that he's thinking."

> He was in fourth grade, after all . . .

"Oh, I really like this! Just a little change, and yet it makes everything so much clearer and better."

Debrief about the strategies you used when considering punctuation use.

"Did you see how I carefully reread thinking about what was really happening in my story, and also how I wanted my readers to read it? I was making sure I was being really clear as Simon. How much fun is that?"

ACTIVE ENGAGEMENT

Invite students to help revise another section of your draft with an eye toward using punctuation for effect.

"Can you help me with another part of my story? It happens just a little bit later when Michael finally decides to speak up for himself. Can you work with your partner to see if there are any ways I can revise my punctuation to make it stronger? Here's the section."

Note that I am not focused on what is correct or incorrect in this session. Rather, I want students to buy in to the idea that punctuation is more than that; it can have a power that writers can wield over their readers. If this idea inspires them to write with more standard conventions usage, so much the better!

"No. I want to ride my own bike," Michael blurted. His mom shook her head. "I'm not getting on that bike. I'll walk to school instead." He took off his helmet. He didn't care that everyone on his block could hear him shouting.

Students launched into excited conversations, imagining all the different ways they could punctuate the paragraph. After giving them a chance to imagine several possibilities I pulled them back together.

"Writers, I just got a ton of great ideas. You also noticed something I hadn't noticed before. If Michael is supposed to be shouting, he definitely needs exclamation points. Such good eyes you have!"

LINK

Remind students of their own goals for today's writing that they should continue to follow through with, and reiterate today's teaching point.

"I know many of you have long lists of things to work on today with your pieces. I know some of you are drafting. Some of you are doing major revisions. Others of you are returning to mentor texts. Many of you will find that if you really put your minds to it you will accomplish several things during today's workshop. But, before you head off, I want you to also hold onto what you learned about today. I think it's super exciting to think about all of the power we have over exactly how our stories are read by our readers! I hope that you remember this for today and for always, that punctuation is powerful stuff."

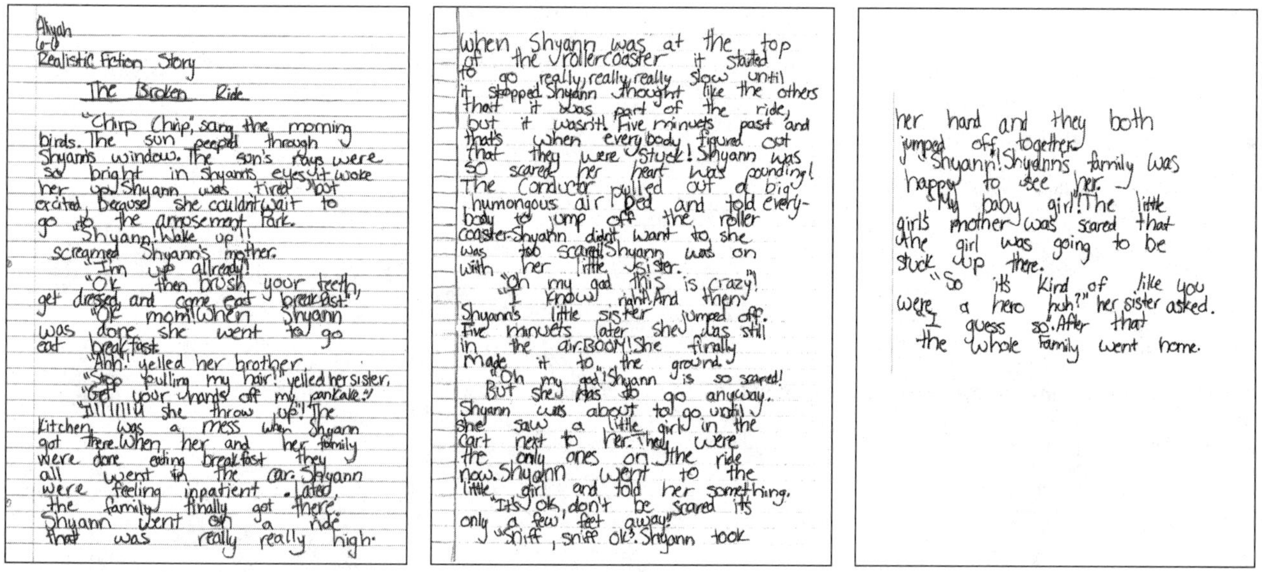

Aliyah
6-6
Realistic Fiction Story

The Broken Ride

"Chirp Chirp", sang the morning birds. The sun peeped through Shyann's window. The son's rays were so bright in Shyann's eyes it woke her up. Shyann was tired but excited, because she couldn't wait to go to the amosement Park.

"Shyann! Wake up"!! screamed Shyann's mother.

"Im up allready!"

"Ok then brush your teeth, get dressed, and come eat breakfast!"

"Ok mom! When Shyann was done she went to go eat breakfast.

"Ahh!" yelled her brother,

"Stop pulling my hair!" yelled her sister,

"Get your hands off my pankake!"

"Illlllllll" she throw up"! The kitchen was a mess when Shyann got there. When her and her family were done eating breakfast they all went in the car. Shyann were feeling inpatient. Later, the family finally got there. Shyann went on a ride that was really really high.

When Shyann was at the top of the rollercoaster it started to go really, really, really slow until it stopped. Shyann thought like the others that it was part of the ride, but it wasn't! Five minuets past and that's when everybody figured out that they were stuck! Shyann was so scared her heart was pounding! The Conductor pulled out a big humongous air bed and told everybody to jump off the roller coaster. Shyann didn't want to, she was too scared! Shyann was on with her little sister.

"Oh my god this is crazy"!

"I know right! And then Shyann's little sister jumped off. Five minuets later she was still in the air. BOOM! She finally made it to the ground.

"Oh my god"! Shyann is so scared! But she has to go anyway. Shyann was about to go until she saw a little girl in the cart next to her. They were the only ones on the ride now. Shyann went to the little girl and told her something.

"It's ok, don't be scared it's only a few feet away!"

"Sniff, sniff ok". Shyann took her hand and they both jumped off together.

"Shyann! Shyann's family was happy to see her.

"My baby girl"! The little girl's mother was scared that the girl was going to be stuck up there.

"So it's kind of like you were a hero huh?" her sister asked.

"I guess so". After that the whole family went home.

FIG. 20–1 Aliyah revises to make her punctuation more powerful.

Setting Students Up for Independent Success by Pulling Groups with Similar Needs and Placing Them on a Similar Path

ONE OF THE MOST IMPORTANT TOOLS you can give your students on their path to independence is an understanding of the value of interdependence. They need to learn how to rely on people (other than their teacher) to support them, give them feedback and even to learn from others. Just a few sessions ago you were teaching your whole class ways to better support their partners. Today's small-group work builds on that teaching while zeroing in on students who are ready for more. While it might seem early in the year to do this kind of work, you no doubt already have students in your class who are very much ready to build a network of writing support for themselves. They just might not have realized that this was a possibility for them. While the students will still be meeting in the classroom, during times that you have set aside, it will be up to the students to instigate and plan these sessions.

You might take one of these last fiction sessions to play interdependence matchmaker. Look for possible partnerships and groups of students who have something in common and seem ready to work fairly autonomously with other students. Perhaps you can gather that group of kids who are aiming to write funny stories. Or maybe that group of students who are enamored with a particular mentor author or type of fiction. You can gather those students and explain to them that you think they have a lot in common with each other. Name those similarities for them. "When I think of funny stories, I think of you four," you might say, or "You are the word lovers of the class. I know that if anyone in this class is going to be playing with fancy language it will be you three." You can suggest that they make a point to meet regularly to share their writing, to problem solve, to share tips.

You will likely want give them some pointers for ways to share their writing with each other, how to refer to class charts and mentor texts for possible feedback ideas, and also tell them when it might make sense to get a teacher's help.

MID-WORKSHOP TEACHING   Fixing Run-On Sentences

"Writers, can you all find a good stopping place and join me on the rug for a few minutes?" Once students had gathered on the rug I said, "As I was walking around working with you, I was noticing that many of you were wrestling with those little boogers of the sentence world—the run-on sentence. Some of you were getting frustrated because you knew something wasn't right, but you didn't know how to fix it. That's what I want to teach you right now—a few ways you might fix some run-on sentences.

"I want to let you in on a little secret that one of my writing teachers once told me. When people start to have more complicated thoughts and ideas, they begin to write more run-on sentences. As you know, a run-on sentence isn't just a long sentence. It's a sentence that is longer, is usually made up of more than one idea, but is also missing something. Sort of like when you're building a puzzle and there's one part left that still sticks out. It doesn't attach to anything else so it doesn't have a smooth edge. Here's an example of one from my fiction story."

Michael felt the hot tears running down his face, he was so embarrassed he wanted to run and hide under his bed where no one would see him.

"Do you see how this sentence has more than one sentence inside it? How it's only separated by a comma? There are lots of different ways to make sure you have smooth edges. You can separate a sentence with more than one subject and predicate into two parts with a conjunction (*and, or, but*) linking the two different parts. I could do that with my sentence."

(continues)

Michael felt the hot tears running down his face AND he was so embarrassed he wanted to run and hide under his bed where no one would see him.

"You can also break a sentence with more than one subject and predicate into two new sentences with new end points for the new ends of the sentences. Let me try that now."

Michael felt the hot tears running down his face. He was so embarrassed he wanted to run and hide under his bed where no one would see him.

"Looking at these two options for this run-on, I like breaking it up into two sentences better. But sometimes you might find that you like using a conjunction even better. Later on this year we'll study other ways to fix run-on sentences. These two strategies are a great start though!"

Preparing Tools for Independent Fiction Success

Explain that tomorrow will be the last day set aside to work on their independent fiction projects, so they need to spend some time thinking about and gathering tools to help them work on those projects independently.

"Writers, I am so impressed with your commitment to your projects. You are treating them with such care and making sure everything is just so. Tomorrow will be our last day to work on these independent fiction projects as a class. After tomorrow, we'll be moving on to other new and exciting units. But many of you, in fact, likely most of you, will still be working on your independent fiction pieces in your free time. It is so important then that you make sure to think about what tools you might want to have on hand to help you finish this project and maybe even start new fiction projects in the future.

As you near the end of this unit, take some time to compliment your writers and allow them to gather their thoughts so they are prepared to publish their fiction pieces. By reflecting on the tools that they need and find helpful, they are also reflecting on what they have learned about themselves as writers. Although the content of their writing is important, the tools they use to write are just as, if not more, important, and you want to acknowledge this.

FIG. 20–2   Mark circles words he wants to replace for better spelling and vocabulary. He decides he needs a dictionary as a tool.

"Think for a minute. What are the things that you used on a regular basis to help you with your fiction writing that you know you will likely want to have on hand after tomorrow? Are there charts that you referred to all the time? You might want to copy them down in your notebook or ask me if I can get a copy for you such as our 'How to Write a Fiction Story' chart. Is there a mentor text you found particularly helpful? You might want to check it out of the classroom library or maybe start a sign-up sheet so that other students who want to use it can take turns. Are there spelling and editing tools you found useful? You might consider making a personal word wall or personalized editing checklist. Calendars, special paper, whatever those tools might be, when you have a sense of what you might want, make a list of those things in your notebook, and today and over the next couple of days make a point of gathering those things."

How to Write a Fiction Story

- Develop a strong story idea, character(s), and setting.
- Spend time planning how the plot will go, making sure there is an arc to the story, trying again and again until the plan feels just right.
- Draft the story scene by scene, only using summary when needed.
- Study other authors for ways to make the story better.
- Make sure there is trouble in the story, and write an ending that resolves that trouble.

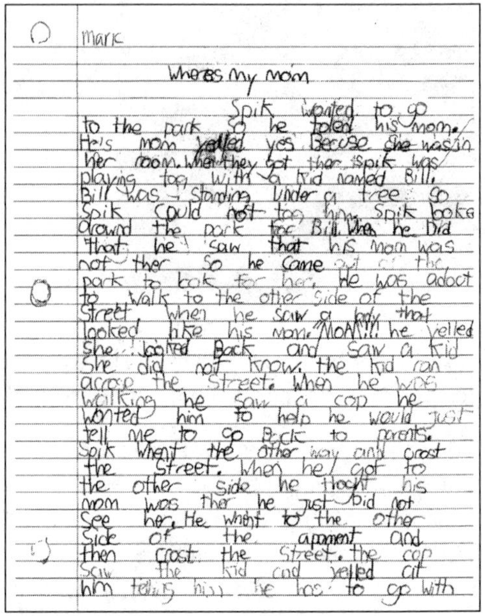

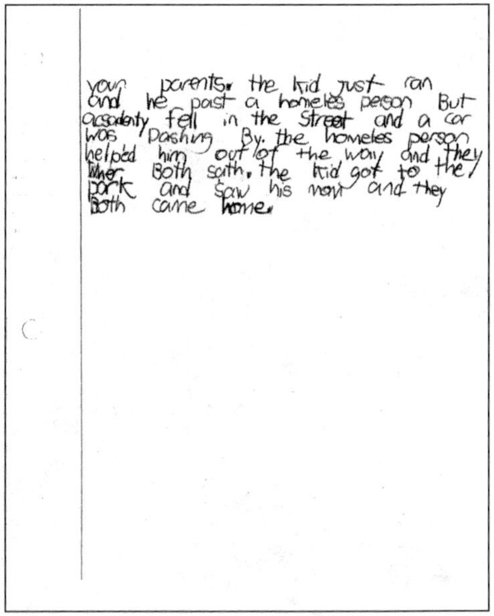

FIG. 20–3   With dictionary in hand, Mark is able to make his changes independently.

STUDYING A MENTOR TEXT FOR PUNCTUATION

Writers, as we near the end of this unit, and we get ready to move on from fiction to other genres, I want to remind you that no matter what we are studying in class, or even after you leave me and work with other writing teachers, that you always have a teacher available, whenever you need help for something. You already know these teachers as "mentor authors." We've talked a lot about them during this unit—how you can turn to mentor authors for inspiration, for ideas for structures, to study beginnings and endings. But did you know that we can also look to mentor authors for more technical things, like punctuation?

Tonight, when you go home, I want you to pull out a mentor fiction story, ideally one you know very well, such as *Fireflies!* This time, I'd like you to study it for punctuation. How does this author use quotation marks with dialogue? How does she use commas? Paragraphs? Choose a few lenses to look through; focus on things you know you need to pay more attention to in your own writing. Then go back to your story and apply some of what you learned from your mentor author to your draft.

Surveying Your Work and Planning for the Future

$\mathcal{D}$ear Teachers,

This letter marks the end of this unit. Congratulations! As we have done elsewhere in this book, this session will be written in letter form to both streamline the unit and to offer a few different options for tailoring the work of this session to the needs of your students.

BEFORE THE CELEBRATION

Today you will want to give your students another opportunity to work on their independent fiction projects, this time with the angle of surveying what they have already accomplished, as well as planning for how these, and possibly future projects, might go. You might begin today's session by having the students pull out their current drafts and lay them alongside the Narrative Writing Checklist, and guiding them to note which things on the checklist they have accomplished, which they are starting to work on, and which they still need to tackle. Or you might have them take their first published piece of the year and lay that beside their latest draft and look across both pieces to see what are some new good things they are doing and what are some things they did in their first piece that they want to bring into their latest.

You might then encourage them to take a few minutes to reflect on what they noticed and either talk through their observations with their partners or write a paragraph or two with their goals and plans for this project. If these reflections are written down, students will be able to look back at them as the year progresses to monitor when the goals from the beginning of the year have been reached or if they might want to reevaluate their goals.

You will also want to let students know that you will be moving on from fiction to personal and persuasive essays after today. Share how impressed you are with how far they have come with their independent projects and that you have every hope and expectation that they will make time on their own when they are between projects, or simply have some spare time to write, to return to these projects to finish them. In fact, you wouldn't

COMMON CORE STATE STANDARDS: W.4.3, W.4.4, W.4.5, W.4.8, W.4.10, RL.4.10, SL.4.1, L.4.1, L.4.2, L.4.3

be surprised to hear that some even start new fiction projects after their current ones are complete. Project the belief that they have learned so many important skills that it is hard to imagine them being anything but successful as they embark on their independent projects. That said, you might in fact have students for whom the idea of keeping an independent writing project up and going past the time where there is explicit, unit-based support seems impossible. While you do not need to push them toward keeping these projects going, neither should you share any doubts you might have about their capabilities. It has been my experience that when it comes to students working on independent projects, it is often the students we least expect who are the most diligent. If you and your students opt to continue to nurture independent fiction projects throughout the year, the reflecting they do today will become even more important.

You will want to spend a good portion of your conferring time today meeting with as many students as you can. You'll want to assess the current state of their pieces and their plans for finishing these pieces and offer any supports (such as mentor texts or access to helpful charts) that will help students maintain their momentum. Additionally, you might want to spend some time meeting with partnerships and encouraging them to be each other's biggest cheerleaders and task masters.

CELEBRATION

During the share time, you will likely want to have a mini-celebration of sorts, whether it's a quick share of working titles for projects or a chance for students to fill in this (or another reflective) sentence: "I used to think _____ about fiction, but now I think _____." Perhaps students will leave their projects in their current states of development on their tables and write a quick description on an idea card that describes where they are in the process. They can then leave that card next to their work. Students can go on a gallery walk of each other's current works in progress, oohing and ahhing at how far everyone has already come.

You will also surely want to return to the Narrative Writing Checklist with your students. This could be something done on the day after you wrap up your unit, as a whole-class experience, or else on a student-by-student, group-by-group basis as students and their projects are ready for that self-assessment.

AFTER THE CELEBRATION

Finally, after this unit is wrapped up and you have moved on to essay writing and the units that follow, you might be wondering if it's likely or even possible for students to continue their independent fiction projects and for you to support them in that endeavor. While it is true that not every student will keep up their independent fiction writing, it is important that students have that as a viable option, partly because it is important for students to have work of their own where they are regularly and actively transferring writing skills. It is also important because fiction is the only narrative unit currently in this series, so if students who thrived on fiction cannot carve out their own niche, they might not get another opportunity to work on it this year.

If you decide to pursue this work, here are a few tips to help you and your students carry on their independent fiction projects past the beginning of the year. You might want to post a calendar where students who are working on projects can record their deadlines. That way you can easily check in with students when you see self-set deadlines approaching. You might also want to create a special basket or bulletin board where students can place their independently published projects. This is both to celebrate the students who are still committed as well as to give inspiration to students who might want to join them. Teachers who have independent projects successfully going in their classrooms are sure to give students time regularly (once a month, during choice time, when there's a substitute teacher) to work on their projects. This time does not displace time for students' regular curricular work but is additional time carved out in the schedule. If you are interested in learning more about independent writing projects, you can refer to *Independent Writing* by Colleen Cruz (2003).

No matter if you manage to keep independent fiction writing projects going throughout the school year or let them fizzle out after this unit, you can rest assured that students will reap huge advantages from learning how to design their own projects and recycle their hard-won fiction writing skills.

Best,

Lucy and Colleen

The complete Narrative Writing Checklist, Grades 4 and 5, can be found on the CD-ROM.

Narrative Writing Checklist

	Grade 4	NOT YET	STARTING TO	YES!	Grade 5	NOT YET	STARTING TO	YES!
	Structure				**Structure**			
Overall	I wrote the important part of an event bit by bit and took out unimportant parts.	☐	☐	☐	I wrote a story of an important moment. It read like a story, even though it might be a true account.	☐	☐	☐
Lead	I wrote a beginning in which I showed what was happening and where, getting readers into the world of the story.	☐	☐	☐	I wrote a beginning in which I not only showed what was happening and where, but also gave some clues to what would later become a problem for the main character.	☐	☐	☐
Transitions	I showed how much time went by with words and phrases that mark time such as *just then* and *suddenly* (to show when things happened quickly) or *after a while* and *a little later* (to show when a little time passed).	☐	☐	☐	I used transitional phrases to show passage of time in complicated ways, perhaps by showing things happening at the same time (*meanwhile, at the same time*) or flashback and flash-forward (*early that morning, three hours later*).	☐	☐	☐
Ending	I wrote an ending that connected to the beginning or the middle of the story.	☐	☐	☐	I wrote an ending that connected to the main part of the story. The character said, did, or realized something at the end that came from what happened in the story.	☐	☐	☐
	I used action, dialogue, or feeling to bring my story to a close.	☐	☐	☐	I gave readers a sense of closure.	☐	☐	☐
Organization	I used paragraphs to separate the different parts or times of the story or to show when a new character was speaking.	☐	☐	☐	I used paragraphs to separate different parts or times of the story and to show when a new character was speaking. Some parts of the story were longer and more developed than others.	☐	☐	☐

Superficial

Niki and Chloe walked into school. Kids were slamming lockers and papers were thrown everywhere. Suddenly, there was a smell so great it could make the flowers pop up. The smell traveled through the halls, past the lockers and over the garbage that was everywhere. It was fruity passion Herbal Essence. Niki looked. Soft blonde hair was swaying in the distance. There was only one thing it could be . . . Samantha Stillman.

Niki pulled on Chloe's arm. "C'mon, Chloe." They moved behind the lockers.

"What?" Chloe asked, still looking down the hall at Samantha.

"I don't want her to see me. She's probably going to make fun of my clothes again." Niki lifted her backpack shaking with fear. "I hate her!" Niki glared.

"She's not that—" Chloe stopped herself midsentence and looked at Niki.

"Don't tell me you were going to say that she's not that bad. She's terrible!" Niki wanted to scream out, but she didn't want anyone to see her behind the lockers.

"Hey!" a voice said. Niki's heart beat out of her chest. She looked up to see Samantha Stillman standing in front of her.

Niki opened her eyes wide and looked straight up at Samantha. "What do you want?" she asked shaking. It seemed like the walls were closing in on her. She wanted to walk behind the lockers, turn and run the other way, but she didn't.

"I just wanted to see your new, I mean, your clothes from the back of the closet," Samantha said laughing. Niki stared at her hard. Chloe looked at the floor. "C'mon, Chloe. We have class," Niki said. But Chloe just stood there. Niki wanted pull Chloe away and run down the hall. But she did nothing.

"I have a question for you, Chloe," Samantha said gritting her teeth at Niki. "Why are you friends with her?" Samantha motioned with her chin in Niki's direction.

"Because," Chloe said proudly. Niki gave her a nudge. Samantha stared. Chloe's face turned red. "She, um, well, I don't know. I mean—" Niki wanted to crawl away.

"I mean, like she has the worst taste in clothes, right?" Samantha said cutting Chloe off.

"Yes. I mean no. I mean I don't know!" Chloe whined. Niki turned away. She didn't get it. She and Chloe had made a pact-Best Friends Forever.

"Sorry, Niki," Chloe whispered.

"Chloe," Niki said, turning around and wiping the tears from her face. But it was too late.

"Let's go," Samantha said. They all stood in the hallway looking at each other. Doors were opening and closing as kids went to class. Samantha pulled Chloe by the shirt and together they followed the rush of other kids.

The doors shut behind them as they walked off to class. Niki stood alone and wondered if it was worth being class president. I should have known after beating her last year in the election. If you mess with Samantha Stillman, she'll mess with you.

Niki started to walk to class, not sure which way to turn now that she was all alone.

FIG. 21–1   Beccah's final story

Spencer Bellhorn Is Not a Wimp by Caleb

Fifteen minutes had passed and I was tired of watching the charcoalblack squirrel run up and down the big oak tree that shaded Kolben St. from the bright morning sun.

Where was Sarah? Had she forgotten? No, Kolben St. had been our meeting spot for the past three years. She's probably sick, I reassured myself. "Yeah," I mumbled, "sick," and set off to school.

"How's it going?" yelled Mr. Crabapple from his porch.

"Great!" I lied.

Then Mr. C smiled a smile I wish I could smile. But I couldn't. I could only manage a frail grin; like the one you see from a sick grandmother. I bit my lip until I couldn't feel it anymore. My eyes twitched side to side like a nervous squirrel. I closed my eyes and repetitively muttered, "Sarah's with me, Sarah's with me, Sarah's with me," trying to convince myself she really was. I walked past every house like in it was a man with a knife.

That day the elm trees leading to the playground of the Mario Gabinetto School seemed bigger, but then again so did everything.

"Auggghhh!" screamed a voice as something collided with my chest. Then all I felt was the hard playground concrete against my cheek.

"Sorry." I apologized as I stood up and brushed myself off.

"Watch where you're goin'!" growled a voice that I thought I had heard before. All at once I realized I what I had bumped into. It was Humphrey Dugbill, the meanest bully in the history of Butts, Missouri.

I absentmindedly tried to walk away so that the oversized predator wouldn't prey on me. My puny frame is no match for his bulging one. I wanted to shrink and shrink till he couldn't see me anymore. "Well, well, well, if it isn't Spencer Bellhorn! About to get beat up and without your girlfriend to protect you!" he emphasized the word girl a lot.

"Any last words?" he asked smugly. What was I going to do? Where was Sarah when I needed her?

Right on time, the "Bading-A-Dinga-Ding" of the 9:00 bell filled the air. "Saved by the bell, Bellhorn—I'll see you after school!" Humphrey yelled over the crowd of screaming kids.

I couldn't pay attention to Mr. Jimenz in math class because I was thinking of a plan, a plan to defend myself against Humphrey. Could I run away like all the other kids had done? No, I would have to stick up to him. Then a thought crossed my mind. Humphrey had never actually punched someone, he had just threatened to! So why should I be afraid? It was a risk, But also, it was the only way.

I stood in the playground of the Mario Gabinetto School to await my fate. If my plan worked, I would never need Sarah to defend me again. If it didn't, I would.

"Spencer?!!" growled a voice behind me, "I thought you would run away like all the other wimps. Oh, well, all the better for me!" I didn't have to turn around to know who it was.

"Whatever, Humphrey," I said calmly. Kids of all shapes and sizes gathered to watch. I could hear a "Yeah Humphrey" chant starting in the crowd.

Humphrey braced himself. With his fist up and the grimace on his face he looked like a heavyweight boxer. I didn't pose like him. I just stood there, arms folded, and a grin on my face. He picked up his fist and pointed his elbow towards the clouds behind him.

Sarah's definitely not my girlfriend!!!!!!!!

"This is gonna work!" I thought and grinned.

His fist shot forward. The grin faded from my face.

I felt like Roger Clemens had thrown a fastball at my face. My head hit the ground. I lowered my hand to my upper lip. I lifted it back up. I saw red.

Humphrey and the other kids smirked. Their smirk turned into a giggle and they started to walk away like I wasn't really there. I needed help; couldn't they see that. They just left me in the dirt, like I wasn't there.

I wanted to cry, I really did.

Then I remembered Humphrey's words; "I thought you would run away like all the other wimps" I didn't run away! I wasn't a wimp. Even though I was standing there with a bloody nose, I felt like I had won. It was then that I realized that everyone at one point in his or her lives needs to be protected. Even the mighty Roger Clemens has bodyguards, and he isn't a wimp, I'm not a wimp.

Spencer Bellhorn is not a wimp.

FIG. 21–2   Caleb's final story